THE JOHNSON TREATMENT

How Lyndon B. Johnson Took Over
the Presidency and Made It His Own

THE JOHNSON

TREATMENT

How Lyndon B. Johnson Took Over
the Presidency and Made It His Own

by JACK BELL

HARPER & ROW, PUBLISHERS

NEW YORK, EVANSTON, AND LONDON

*A salute to the Americans who man the difficult
and often dangerous outposts of freedom,
specifically including our own beloved Morey and Marian*

Contents

THE JOHNSON TREATMENT

*How Lyndon B. Johnson Took Over
the Presidency and Made It His Own*

1 A Man of Action Takes Over

THE TALL, BAREHEADED MAN who would be President within five hours lounged relaxed against a pillar. He was all but unnoticed in a Fort Worth, Texas, hotel lobby jammed with excited Texans waiting for a glimpse of, a smile from and possibly a touch of the hand by John F. Kennedy.

Lyndon Baines Johnson was patiently fulfilling the secondary role to which he had resigned himself even in his native Texas on this fateful morning of November 22nd. He, too, was waiting for "The Boss" to make his appearance so that they could walk together, with Johnson a step behind, across the street to a parking lot where the youthful President would greet a crowd which had been gathering in a drizzle since dawn.

Police had cordoned off a path through the lobby for Kennedy to follow from the elevator. On the opposite side from the noisy, milling crowd Johnson stood with only a Secret Service man beside him.

As I hurried down the corridor toward the door, a familiar voice said softly, "Hey, there, Jack."

Turning quickly, I replied, "Why, hello, Lyndon, I didn't see you there." This was the last time that I was ever to call him

Lyndon in his presence. Henceforth, it would always be "Mr. President."

The Vice President and I chatted briefly about the political situation. The presidential team of Jack and Jacqueline Kennedy had scored a smash hit in supposedly politically hostile Texas.

"We've got this civil rights thing whipped," Lyndon said. "They've quit blaming Kennedy for it. They think it's inevitable. I think we're going to be all right in Texas in November."

The crowds in San Antonio and Houston and on their arrival in Fort Worth the previous day had been enthusiastic. South Texas had been tested and found favorable, now Dallas lay ahead. Johnson was as confident as a man sitting at ease under the apple tree in his own back yard that the welcome for the presidential pair in Dallas would be exuberant.

The Vice President had worked hard with friendly Texans to make this political show one of the biggest. It was to demonstrate that the people of Texas really liked President Kennedy and what he stood for.

Through it all Johnson had taken a back seat except when the President had insisted that he come forward and share the plaudits of the crowds. It was a measure of restraint in the man that the once flamboyant Democratic leader of the United States Senate could stand in the shadow of a back-row youngster without a syllable or a gesture of complaint or without any outward sign of regret.

This did not mean, of course, that Johnson had permitted himself to become a political eunuch. Quite the contrary. Throughout the administration he had placed key men in key jobs, with the generous consent of Kennedy. Johnson had insisted also in tight-rein control of Texas patronage to help hold together his personal political organization in his home state.

Knowledgeable about such things, Kennedy was a willing contributor toward the Vice President's effort to maintain the Johnson prestige despite the latter's handicap of a secondary office in which he could only carry out and not initiate policies. Among many other lesser appointments, Kennedy had cheerfully named handsome, gray-haired, soft-spoken John Connally as his Secretary of the Navy. From this job Connally had plunged into the Texas maelstrom and, with Johnson's help, had emerged with the governorship.

Senator Ralph Yarborough, a voluble liberal, had long been at political odds with Johnson and Connally. The Senator had the firm idea that the Vice President and the Governor were grooming Representative Joseph M. Kilgore, Democratic House member, to oppose him for renomination in 1964. Johnson was, of course.

Because of this Kennedy was deeply, albeit diplomatically, involved in his tragic Texas trip with trying to restore political peace between his Vice President, the Governor and the Senator. When there were published reports that Connally was trying to freeze Yarborough out of some of the functions attendant to the President's visit, Kennedy promptly invited the Senator to ride with him to Texas on the presidential plane, *Air Force One*.

In flight Kennedy performed the customary political ritual of emerging from the executive quarters to chat with Yarborough and five Texas Congressmen who were aboard. Mrs. Kennedy, whose aversion for political forays had been put aside for this trip, came out of the private quarters looking stunning in a white wool bouclé dress.

This was the first political trip Mrs. Kennedy had made since the tragic death of her prematurely-born son, Patrick Bouvier Kennedy, on August 9th. She had not liked political campaigning and had felt her place was at home. She once remarked, "I was reading Carlyle, and he said you should do the duty that lies nearest to you. And the thing that lies nearest to me is the children." But Kennedy had persuaded her to come along on what was, for practical purposes, the first significant foray into the hinterlands in the second-term race.

But all of this attention did not mollify Yarborough. Before the plane touched down at San Antonio International Airport he had told newsmen he wanted his friends to take no offense at the slights he said had been pressed upon him by Connally. Then he added, "Governor Connally is so uneducated governmentally, how could you expect anything else?"

When the plane landed, Yarborough had been assigned to a car near the front of the motorcade which also was to be occupied by Johnson. This obviously was done at Kennedy's direction to force these two squabbling individuals into close quarters where they might decide that it was better to compromise than to fight. In a huff, Yarborough declined the assignment to ride with the Vice President and hitched passage in a car further back in the procession. Johnson gave no outward sign he minded this rearrangement. But word of how his two supporters were acting was relayed to Kennedy.

When he walked out of the Fort Worth hotel lobby the next morning, Kennedy overtook Yarborough on his way to the presidential car in the motorcade that was about to depart for the airport.

Striding up to the Senator, the President said in a low but commanding voice: "Ralph, you get in that car with Lyndon. Now get in." Kennedy walked off, having performed the last personal political chore of his life. Yarborough got in the car. The motorcade rolled through packed streets to the airport, where *Air Force One* took off on a brief flight to Dallas's Love Field.

So it was that Lyndon Johnson and Ralph Yarborough, sitting as far apart as possible with Lady Bird Johnson between them in the roomy rear seat, were riding in the third car of the motorcade when those murderous three shots rang out on a Dallas street.

"Except that the Lord keep the city, the watchman waketh but in vain."

These words, which John F. Kennedy intended to utter at a

luncheon at the Dallas Merchandise Trade Mart about 1 P.M. local time, were prophetic. Thirteen minutes after that hour came the first authentic word that he was dead.

The Lord was not keeping the city of Dallas that day. Its citizens had smiles, applause and cheers for the young, vigorous President and his wife. The watchmen of the Secret Service, working within their physical limitations, had striven in vain to protect the world's most important individual.

There was gaiety in the crowd and on the face of the President a look of genuine enjoyment he always seemed to experience in campaigning as he debarked from *Air Force One* when it landed at Love Field on the crisp, golden morning of November 22.

The President and his wife shook hands with the usual welcoming committee and he headed like a homing rocket for the fence behind which the cheering crowd was contained.

There he stuck out both arms to shake as many hands as possible. Only a step behind him was Jacqueline Kennedy, wearing a fuchsia-colored suit and carrying a bouquet of red roses. Never before had Mrs. Kennedy joined so actively in the political handshaking.

When the President and his wife got into the open White House limousine which was to take them on their fateful ride, Governor and Mrs. Connally joined them, sitting on the jump seats ahead. The motorcade pulled out with the "Queen Mary," the Secret Service car bearing heavily armed agents, following the President's car. Johnson, Mrs. Johnson and Yarborough were in the third automobile.

The Secret Service had opposed this motorcade. It had plugged for a quick, well-guarded trip from the airport to the Merchandise Mart. The Secret Service argument was simple: It could not protect a President who moved slowly in an open car through streets lined by high buildings from which a rifleman with a telescopic sight could fire from a window at any vantage point. This exposure of the President it was assigned to protect was the living nightmare of the service. It could not guard any President against what it regarded as the Chief Executive's own folly.

Standard operating procedure obtained on that day. The Secret Service was overruled by a Chief Executive who had mentioned casually to a friend that morning how easily a President could be killed. It was important to Kennedy, to Johnson and to the Democrats of Texas that the President expose himself in person to the crowds that had gathered in Dallas.

Only a few days earlier Kennedy had told the Secret Service he no longer wanted its men to ride the rear steps on each side of the presidential limousine. The President felt this was an unneeded display of security measures. It was left to history to decide whether, if there had been guards that close at hand, the second and fatal shot would have reached its mark. But all Presidents felt they must be nonchalant in the presence of potential danger. It was regarded as the manly thing to do.

If this was political commercialism, no President who desired to retain his high office could resist it. Kennedy, who ordinarily was diffident toward any exhibition of personal enthusiasm directed toward him, nevertheless could drink and enjoy the wine of crowd adulation.

There was a great deal of adulation in Dallas that day for a President whom a majority of the voters had not supported at the polls a year earlier. And it was in Dallas that Lyndon and his wife had been roughed up and spit upon in 1960. Dallas had a guilt complex about its lunatic fringe of ultraconservatives which it tried to throw off with a warm-hearted, outgoing reception of the President and his charming lady. Here and there there were homemade Goldwater signs. But even these were considerably less than caustic, as if their bearers were carrying out a prescribed ritual to which they had not really pledged their hearts.

The welcoming crowds on Dallas's Main Street had been colorful with brightly dressed women and men in sports attire.

A Negro on a bicycle had paced the presidential car through the throng until a uniformed policeman skidded his rear wheel with a kick and the bicycle rider came down with a belly-whopper. Another youth had sprinted wildly down the edge of the crowd in bare feet until another policeman deftly sent him sprawling into a knot of squealing spectators.

But suddenly the cheering din was over. The motorcade turned off the main street, progressed at a measured pace one block to the right and turned left in front of a building which bore the curious name, "Texas School Book Depository." We in the press pool car joked that perhaps this was where Texas political campaign funds were collected and deposited.

Incongruously at that moment a giant firecracker went off somewhere nearby. These Texans, some of us thought, are going a little too far by firing off some cherry bombs in celebration of the President's visit.

Then there was another explosive crack. This time the sound was ominous. It had the authority of a rifle shot. Then there was the awful, unmistakable third crack of a big-game rifle in action. Hardly more than fifteen seconds had elapsed between the first shot and the last.

Malcolm Kilduff, White House assistant press secretary, who was seated ahead of me in the pool car, screamed, "My God, they're shooting at the President!" Instinctively we reporters started to surge out of our car, the fourth in line in the motorcade, to rush toward the President's limousine.

The President's car had seemed to halt, but at that moment it spurted forward through an underpass and we scrambled back to our seats with shouts to our driver, "Keep up with him."

People on the grass nearby were diving to the ground. Atop a small knoll a man pushed a woman to the ground and leaped protectively over her.

As we careened crazily down a freeway in pursuit of the White House car each of us reviewed swiftly in our minds what had happened. There could be no doubt that the shots had been fired at the motorcade.

Had someone been hit or was the Secret Service only rushing the President out of a danger zone? Everybody was down in the President's open car, but this was standard procedure in an emergency. The only man visible besides the driver in the "Queen Mary," which was keeping pace with the White House limousine, was an agent. He thrust a submachine gun menacingly in the air but did not fire it.

While we roared down the freeway the hope recurred that no one had been wounded but that this was only an escape from a danger zone. There was the thought that perhaps one of the doughty men guarding the President had been hit. It was impossible at the moment even to entertain the idea that the President or Mrs. Kennedy had been shot.

But the horrible truth came home to us when the speeding cars swirled into a drive and slammed to a stop at the ambulance entrance to Parkland Memorial Hospital. We newsmen sprinted up to the White House car, there to find the President of the United States sprawled face down in the back seat—to all appearances dead.

Mrs. Kennedy had just been helped from the car. Governor Connally, blood all over his shirt front, was being placed on a litter, his wife supporting his head.

To a Secret Service man posted by the presidential car, I asked, pointing to the President, "Is he dead?"

"I don't think so, but I don't know," he replied.

There was barely time to glance toward the ashen-faced Johnson, being escorted from his car, his right hand gripping his left arm, as we ran for telephones.

Only then could our minds accept the fact of assassination. Most of us were too busy in the hours that followed to give much conscious thought to it. But our hearts were hung with leaden shame that senseless slaughter such as this could take place in the United States.

Was the veneer of our civilized democracy so thin that assassination had become a political weapon? This was for unstable populations where men shot down others to attain power. Were we, the American people, to blame for permitting a madman to pick off a President because we demanded that the man who held the office pass among us and press our hand in order to reassure us that he was in tune with our thinking? Was any such satisfaction of our individual egos as voters worth the price we paid for it this day? It did not seem so.

The torment of guilt and shame took a long time to abate. But eventually the answer came that while the life of an individual might be taken wantonly, government went on with a continuity of purpose without respect to the person who filled the President's chair.

In a cubicle to which he had been escorted by Secret Service agent Rufus Youngblood, near the hospital emergency room, where doctors were working frantically in the futile effort to revive the dead President, sat the man into whose hands already had been thrust the baton of power.

Johnson hadn't known clearly what was happening in the motorcade. But Youngblood had recognized the sound of the first shot for what it was. He shoved Johnson down on the floor of the car in which they were riding and leaped over him to shelter the Vice President with his own body.

Startled, Johnson asked what was happening. Youngblood replied that it appeared someone in the White House limousine, possibly the President himself, had been hit. There was not much time for conversation on the thundering ride. But when his car pulled up a few feet from Kennedy's at the hospital entrance, Johnson knew the President had been dangerously, if not mortally, wounded.

As he sat, awaiting word on the outcome of the surgeons' efforts, Johnson's mind was busy. It occurred to him that perhaps there was an international plot to kill all of America's leaders. His inquiries about Kennedy's condition brought no reassurances. He was forced to think, against his will, what must be done, and quickly, if the awful responsibility descended upon him. He was described as shaken but calm throughout the brief ordeal.

Outside the cubicle, milling White House aides, members of Congress and others showed the profound shock that was to reverberate around the world in a few minutes. We were almost certain that the President was dead, but no one—including a Roman Catholic priest who had given the Chief Executive the last rites—was absolutely certain that all life had departed.

From the outside world, to which I was linked by the telephone line to the Dallas Associated Press bureau, the rumors rolled in. First there was one that Johnson had had a heart attack. Then there was another on its heels that the Vice President had been wounded. Neither could be verified until I saw Mrs. Johnson approaching down the corridor, flanked by Secret Service men. Jumping in front of her, I said, "Is Lyndon all right?"

"Yes," she replied.

Knowing that she had just visited the emergency room, and noting the tears in her eyes, I asked, "Is the President dead?"

She made no reply when a Secret Service man expertly gave me his elbow and sent me staggering back to my phone as the door to the cubicle closed behind them.

Secret Service agent Emory P. Roberts came into Johnson's cubicle at 1:13 P.M., Dallas time, to tell the Vice President that the President had been critically wounded and that he was not expected to live. Johnson asked about Connally and was told that the Governor had been seriously wounded but probably would live. Roberts urged that Johnson make plans to return immediately to Washington.

Mrs. Johnson, who was with the Vice President, asked if she and her husband could see Mrs. Kennedy. (Mrs. Johnson said the Vice President first suggested this.) Youngblood, a forceful agent who knew his business, ruled that Johnson could not leave the room, in which the shades had been drawn and to which none but White House staffers and members of Congress were being admitted.

Mrs. Johnson went out to find Mrs. Kennedy and do what she could while the Vice President stood and sat disconsolately, greeting in low tones Representatives Jack Brooks and Homer Thornberry and Clifton Carter, who gained access to the room.

At 1:20 P.M. Kenneth O'Donnell came into the room to announce in a low voice, "He's gone." Then, raising it, he said, "The President is dead, Mr. President."

O'Donnell said the new President must return to Washington and urged Johnson to leave immediately to board *Air Force One* for that purpose. The President asked, "What about Mrs. Kennedy?" O'Donnell replied that she would not leave without her husband's body.

"Neither will we," Johnson replied firmly. He added that he was not going to fly away to Washington and leave Mrs. Kennedy behind to attend to the arrangements for transporting the body of the dead President back to the capital.

O'Donnell, who claimed in his testimony before the Warren Commission to have seen the impact of the shot that hit Kennedy and killed him, said the new President must get out of the hospital to a safer place. Johnson agreed to go to the presidential plane, as soon as it could be arranged. But he stipulated it would not take off until Mrs. Kennedy and the body of the late President were aboard.

Johnson subsequently said in a statement to the Warren Commission that while he was in the hospital cubicle he was so stunned by the "magnitude of our personal loss of this great man and good friend" that the only outlet for his and Mrs. Johnson's grief was "our sharp, painful and bitter concern and solicitude for Mrs. Kennedy."

Malcolm Kilduff, encountering O'Donnell as he came out of

the cubicle, said the news of the death had to be released and suggested this be done quickly.

"Well," O'Donnell replied, "you are going to have to make the announcement. Go ahead. But you better check with Mr. Johnson."

Kilduff said that when he walked into the cubicle to tell Johnson, "very frankly I didn't know what to call him and I just blurted out 'Mr. . . . Mr. President,' and he turned around and I will never forget the look on his face . . ."

When Kilduff suggested an immediate announcement, Johnson replied, "No, Mac, I think we had better wait for a few minutes.

"I think I had better get out of here and get back to the plane before you announce it," Johnson continued. "We don't know whether there is a world-wide conspiracy, whether they are after me as well as they were after President Kennedy, or whether they are after Speaker McCormack or Senator Hayden. We just don't know." Speaker John W. McCormack had become the next in line for the presidency. Senator Carl Hayden, as presiding officer of the Senate, would have been in line at any time a President died if there were at that point no Speaker.

While this was happening, Jacqueline Kennedy was saying goodbye to her dead husband with a farewell kiss and slipping her wedding band on his lifeless finger.

As quietly as possible the Secret Service arranged to use the unmarked car of Dallas Police Chief Jesse E. Curry to whisk the new President to the airport, where *Air Force One* stood in readiness. While he was waiting for Mrs. Kennedy and the coffin bearing the dead President's body, Johnson called Attorney General Robert F. Kennedy at the latter's Virginia home to offer his condolences and to ask if Kennedy had any objections to his taking the oath immediately. Kennedy said he had none.

Awaiting the arrival of Federal District Judge Sarah T.

Hughes, Johnson summoned O'Donnell and Lawrence F. O'Brien, two of his predecessor's aides, to the card table where he sat—apart from the big chair that had been reserved for Kennedy—to tell them what he was to tell others of the staff, Cabinet and department heads, that he needed them more than Kennedy had.

"There's no law that says you've got to stay with me," he told the two aides. "I need your help badly. And not just now but from now on in." They said they would stay.

At 2:38 P.M. Dallas time, Johnson stood in the crowded plane, placed his left hand on the Bible, raised his right hand and repeated the presidential oath read to him by Judge Hughes, first woman to swear in a Chief Executive.

Mrs. Johnson, clad in beige and wearing a string of pearls, stood at his right. At his left was Mrs. Kennedy, still in the fuchsia-colored suit, splattered with her husband's blood.

When he had completed the oath, Johnson turned to kiss the dead President's wife, whispering to her, "You're so brave to do this and I'll ever be grateful to you." He kissed his wife and turned to embrace Mrs. Evelyn Lincoln, Kennedy's personal secretary.

Then the thirty-sixth President of the United States said, characteristically, "Okay, let's get this plane back to Washington."

A new era had begun in America.

Extraordinarily calm and composed, Johnson acted swiftly. While Mrs. Kennedy grieved alone in the presidential compartment where the casket had been placed, Johnson put in a phone call from the jet plane to Mrs. Rose Kennedy, mother of the slain President, at Hyannis Port, Massachusetts.

"I wish to God there was something I could do," he told her. Mrs. Johnson got on the phone to add, "We feel like the heart has been cut out of us. Our love and prayers are with you."

In rapid-fire order the new President placed calls to arrange meetings with Cabinet members so that he could ask them to stay on and to congressional leaders to meet with him on his return. To each of these groups his appeal would be: "I'm the only President you have. I need your help. Please help me."

The President also called Mrs. John Connally, wife of the Governor of Texas. He had been seriously wounded by the fire directed at the presidential car in which he and she were riding.

When his plane landed at Andrews Air Force base, near Washington, two hours and twenty-one minutes later, the solemn-faced President walked mournfully to a cluster of microphones to declare:

"I will do my best. That is all that I can do. I ask your help—and God's."

When he landed on the White House lawn by helicopter a few minutes later, Johnson was met by Secretary of Defense Robert S. McNamara and McGeorge Bundy, presidential assistant for national security. Tucking his wife's arm in his own, Johnson walked through the rose garden, conferring with them. At the French doors of the Oval Room presidential office, the new Executive paused momentarily. Then, pushing open a door, he walked alone across the threshold to the massive responsibilities that lay before him.

But he did not stay. Instead, he sent Mrs. Johnson home to their Northwest Washington residence, and strode across the street to the garish Executive Office Building, where he had maintained a sumptuous office suite. Kennedy, knowing his Vice President well, had arranged to make available these executive offices to him. Other Vice Presidents had had to get along in less ornate quarters provided in the Senate Office Building and the Capitol.

Sitting down at his ornate desk, the new President wrote in longhand letters to Caroline Kennedy and to John, Jr., W. Averell Harriman, the Undersecretary of State, and Senator J. William Fulbright of Arkansas, chairman of the Senate Foreign Relations Committee. Typically, Johnson was on the phone much of the time. He received a call from Harry Truman, put one in to Dwight D. Eisenhower and then called Sargent Shriver, head of the Peace Corps and Kennedy's brother-in-law.

When the congressional leaders came in at 7:40 P.M., Johnson urged them to forget party differences for a while. The nation must present a united front, he said.

The subsequent flurry of telephone calls included one to Herbert Hoover, who had gone to bed and could not be awakened; to Senator Richard B. Russell of Georgia, his old mentor; to Speaker McCormack; to Supreme Court Justice Arthur Goldberg and to Edward M. (Ted) Kennedy, brother of the dead President. There was also a reassurance call to Keith Funston, president of the New York Stock Exchange, which had closed shortly after the news of Kennedy's death was broadcast.

When Johnson went home around 9 P.M., it was to a discussion with old and trusted friends of what the future might bring. He had snacked at the Executive office and was in no mood for the chicken dinner that Lady Bird thoughtfully had whipped up with the assistance of Mrs. Elizabeth Carpenter, her woman-of-all-work press aide.

On hand were Jack Valenti, Houston advertising man, Clifton Carter, an aide, Bill Moyers, the assistant director of the Peace Corps, Mr. and Mrs. Horace Busby and Dr. Willis Hurst, Emory University heart specialist who had looked out for Johnson since his 1955 heart attack.

The talk went on until after midnight, when all retired to bed. But shortly thereafter Johnson called in Valenti, Moyers and Carter, who were spending the night, to come to his room to talk some more. This discussion ended at 3:30 A.M., when the yawning participants went off to bed again. Those who worked for Johnson devoted their days to him and often did not own their nights.

At 8:55 A.M. on the Saturday after the fateful Friday Johnson drove up to the White House Executive Wing and strode inside. He talked to Bundy in a basement "situation room." A stupefied outpouring of grief, shock and anger had been the world's response to Kennedy's assassination. There were some misgivings registered around the world about what Johnson's ascension to power might mean in the way of altered American policies. Johnson felt that these must be answered quickly with reassurances that the attempt of Kennedy to improve East-West relations would be continued. He told Bundy he wanted to pick up the Kennedy-Khrushchev private correspondence and asked the aide to be ready with some suggestions on that score.

Thirty-five minutes later, when he walked across the street to the familiar surroundings of his old vice-presidential office, Johnson felt that he was beginning to get a grip on the very personal administration which Kennedy had conducted. His predecessor had imposed his own strong views on domestic and foreign policies on all those who worked under him.

Kennedy had been particularly adept at operating in the international field, with only assists from Secretary of State Dean Rusk and Bundy. He had a storehouse of knowledge, a sharp wit and an indefinable grace that his successor readily recognized he did not possess. But what Johnson did own—and perhaps Kennedy did not—was a doggedness which would overcome many obstacles that would have appeared to a man of fainter heart to be insurmountable.

Johnson would bend his prodigious energy to the tasks at hand. He would be no caretaker of the Kennedy administration. He would be as scornful of the title of "acting President" as John Tyler, of whom John Quincy Adams had written in his diary on April 16, 1841: "I paid a visit this morning to Mr. Tyler, who styles himself President of the United States, and not Vice President, acting as President, which would be the correct style. It is a construction in direct violation both of the grammar and context of the Constitution, which confers upon the Vice President, on the decease of the President, not the office, but the powers and duties of the said office."

Johnson would not follow the example of Tyler, who fired all of predecessor William Henry Harrison's Cabinet except Secretary of State Daniel Webster, but he would be just as obdurate that he was President, and not a Vice President acting as such.

While Johnson was laboring to pull together an administration which had been shattered to the core, Mrs. Kennedy was beginning the task of packing the Kennedy belongings for removal from the White House. The Johnsons had felt that they must not intrude upon the household until the bereaved widow had had time to decide what she wished to do with the family belongings and could move elsewhere in comparative comfort.

Because she had solicited and obtained so many American antiques as permanent possessions of the White House, Mrs. Kennedy personally had to sort out what were hers and the late President's personal belongings. No crew of professional packers could do the work. But by noon on November 24 the late President's office was bare except for a new red rug which just had been put down and the historic desk which Mrs. Kennedy had found in the White House basement and refurbished for her husband's use. This, too, would go when Johnson took over and ordered a new decor for the Oval Room.

The obligations of the presidency closed in tighter on Johnson in his first meeting on the morning of November 23 with Secretary of State Rusk. Rusk was a Johnson favorite because he personally had insisted that, as Vice President, the Texan be briefed daily and fully on international developments. Then McNamara came in for a fifty-minute conference on the world military situation.

In touching all bases, Johnson had asked former President Eisenhower to call on him and the General arrived at 11:00 A.M., wearing a broad black band on his left arm, to head the list of dignitaries who joined the President and Mrs. Johnson in paying their respects to the slain President in the East Room of the White House.

During the funeral ceremonies, viewed on television by most

Americans, Johnson stayed discreetly in the background. Only once did he permit his own feelings to intrude into the Lincolnesque rites.

When the Secret Service asked him to ride and not to walk to the Roman Catholic church where the final service was to be held because it could not guarantee protection in the streets, Johnson replied unemotionally, "I would rather be dead than be afraid to die."

He walked.

The presence of General Charles de Gaulle, striding militarily up Connecticut Avenue, with King Baudouin of Belgium and Queen Frederika of Greece pacing him in splendid array, upheld Johnson's decision to be among the pedestrians.

The conclusion had to be that when the chips were down in either the ceremonial or political aspects of the presidency, this man Johnson almost always made the correct decision.

Johnson recognized and confronted immediately the problem of maintaining his predecessor's organization and his policies. The country would come to realize only gradually that the administration of Kennedy, the erudite Harvard scholar and intellectual kinsman of the Adamses of Massachusetts, had become the administration of Johnson, the country boy who taught school as Lincoln did and who was in the modern tradition of Jackson, the man of action.

Backstage, Johnson carried on a political operation that, had he been alive to see it, Kennedy could have saluted as worthy of any he had attempted.

On his first Sunday in office, November 24, 1963, Johnson came to grips with what was to be the most worrisome foreign problem of his first year in the White House—Vietnam.

The Johnsons started the day by attending St. Mark's Episcopal Church on Capitol Hill. There they joined in the mourning and the prayers for Kennedy. Attending an after-service coffee hour, the new President shook hands with members of the congregation before he and Mrs. Johnson were driven back to the White House to join in the procession when Kennedy's body was taken to the Capitol to lie in state in the Rotunda. There the President and the First Lady stood during the memorial services.

Back in his office in the Executive Building across the street from the White House by mid-afternoon, Johnson canvassed the situation in South Vietnam with Ambassador Henry Cabot Lodge, who had been called home by Kennedy for a report. Afterward the President endorsed Kennedy's pledge to "persevere to victory" in the fight against the Communist guerrillas. He said also he was standing by Kennedy's timetable of withdrawing one thousand American troops from Vietnam by the end of 1963 and withdrawing the remaining fourteen thousand by the end of 1965.

After his conference with Lodge, Johnson found time to meet with an Illinois delegation to the Kennedy funeral. It was headed by Governor Otto Kerner and Mayor Richard Daley of Chicago. The President also received the Attorney General and the Speaker of the House of Texas. Shortly after Johnson left the Executive Building for his Northwest Washington residence at 7 P.M., Robert Anderson, former Secretary of the Treasury in the Eisenhower administration came down the stairs. The presidential consultation with old and trusted Texas friends was beginning.

First the new President had to reassure Kennedy's personal lieutenants they were urgently needed in the new administration. There must not be any suggestion that the changeover signaled any abrupt break away from the established order. One by one, he called in Kennedy's closest advisers, humbly pleading for their help and convincing most of them that not only he but the nation needed them.

He was especially kind to Bob Kennedy, a young man of whom he had not been particularly fond, but one the new President felt needed sympathy and consideration more than any other at this point.

When a columnist went off the deep end to suggest that Johnson and Secretary McNamara couldn't get along, the President picked up the phone on Thanksgiving Day to tell the Secretary to pay no attention to these rumors, that his high standing with the White House would be undiminished in the new regime.

He again urged Rusk to stay on. Johnson's instructions to Rusk had been to clear matters with him by telephone instead of by the memos that Kennedy preferred. This marked the first of many changes the new President was to make in the methods of operation in the highest office.

Bundy was assured that none of these changes meant that he would be by-passed in his task of interpreting international actions or giving advice on them. It simply meant that, where Kennedy had seemed to want access to every detail of every situation, Johnson preferred to know only what the core of the problem was and to have advice from all available sources before deciding how to attempt to solve it.

There had been a period during Johnson's vice-presidential days when he looked upon Bundy and McNamara as a team inclined to disregard the Joint Chiefs of Staff in making their decisions. He had had an almost reverent respect for the opinions of high military men as a Senator and he carried this over into the vice presidency. But being President was different, as he learned quickly.

The breath-taking course of the new presidency went on relentlessly. After Kennedy's burial on November 25, Johnson met with world leaders at a reception in the State Department. He had become acquainted with most of these world figures because Kennedy had thought the Vice President ought to do more than merely preside over the Senate and consequently had dispatched Johnson as his personal representative on world excursions.

Imperious French President Charles de Gaulle got quite a hand when he walked into the reception. Johnson had met De

Gaulle on a visit to France in 1961. When he walked into the General's vast Paris office, he had been greeted with, "What did you come to learn?"

"Why, General, anything you wish to inform us about," Johnson shot back.

Two more different men than De Gaulle and Johnson hardly could be imagined. As one small example, De Gaulle had no telephone in his office while Johnson often kept three or four hot at the same time. Nevertheless, Johnson was not particularly perturbed about De Gaulle's methods or his manners. As the President told associates at the time, "When the chips are down, we've been able to count on him."

The day following the funeral was a busy one for the President. He took on other world leaders at twenty-minute intervals. Among these was grim-visaged Anastas I. Mikoyan, First Deputy Premier of the Soviet Union. The two men had met before, but this time the Russian was on hand to size up Johnson, the President, and to communicate his assessment of the new administration to the Kremlin.

What came through clearly in these two days of meetings was that the new Chief Executive would not be overawed by any foreign potentate. What was also clear to his visitors was that while the new President might not possess the brilliance of his predecessor, he was no whit less determined about where he stood.

The diplomats who met him in those two days either came around to Johnson's practical Texas level when they talked or they went home wondering where they had missed connections with the new American Chief Executive.

2 A Master Plan Unfolds

ALMOST FROM THE MOMENT he took the presidential oath, Johnson had been unfolding a master plan designed to win the presidency in his own right and—in the course of the nine years of service that might be accorded him—to carve for himself a favorable place in history.

He must enlist in his cause the followers of Kennedy, the intellectuals, the unionists, the Negroes, the unemployed, and the poor. He must placate some of Kennedy's enemies, such as the businessmen, and war on others, such as the hate-mongers. But, most important of all, he must get Congress off the dead center, where it had stalled under Kennedy. In Congress lay his greatest hope for domestic achievement. But it also offered a constant threat to his course in foreign affairs.

While he was meeting with the world leaders, Johnson had to take the time to put out a fire in the Senate. He knew exactly the right men to call and the right thing to say—that this was no time to be kicking a new President in the shins and stirring up trouble with the Russians. He got his way. After an official letter giving his views in diplomatic terms had arrived, the Senate rejected a restriction on the sale of wheat to the Soviet Union.

Johnson had determined that when a decent interval had elapsed after the Kennedy funeral, he would make a personal appeal to Congress for its cooperation and for action on the Kennedy program. He had given this a great deal of thought, discussing all aspects of his proposed address with his aides and advisers.

The new President turned to an old Kennedy hand, Theodore C. Sorensen, for help. The tall, pleasant-faced Sorensen, a liberal from Nebraska, had handled most of Kennedy's hot ones. He had helped draft legislation, had tackled administrative problems and had advised Kennedy on everything from politics to foreign affairs.

Sorensen wrote in Kennedy style, a distinct handicap as far as Johnson was concerned. The new President's forte did not lie in the turning of pungent or witty phrases, as had Kennedy's. Johnson enjoyed talking with small groups where there was a play of personalities and ideas were tossed about freely. But a formal speech was another matter.

Kennedy put his squiggles on almost every page of any manuscript prepared for him, editing and re-editing it. Many times I had seen him sit at a speakers' table and pencil in changes in phraseology—or even insert some idea that just came to him—while he was waiting to be introduced. Like Adlai E. Stevenson, Kennedy was a last-minute polisher of phrases. This was not a habit Johnson shared. He preferred to speak from a clean copy, though he didn't always stick to the text. He was at his best when he rambled on in a folksy way, but this wasn't always possible.

Two days after he became President, Johnson put Sorensen to work on a basic draft of the speech. He also commissioned Professor John Kenneth Galbraith of Harvard, who had served Kennedy as Ambassador to India, to write a competing draft. A third version was whipped into shape by Horace Busby, former Texas newspaperman and business news writer. Busby, who was associated with Johnson when the latter ran the Senate

Preparedness Subcommittee, later joined the White House staff.

Sorensen's draft was adopted as the basic document because it said what Johnson wanted to say. But it was primarily in the language of Kennedy and not his successor.

Enter at this point an old friend of Johnson's of the early New Deal days, Abe Fortas. An ex-Yale Law School egghead, Fortas had skillfully managed Johnson's case in the courts when the Texan won election to the Senate in 1948 by a margin of 87 votes out of 988,295 and his opponent charged fraud. Fortas took the Sorensen text and converted it into Johnsonese.

So when he went to Capitol Hill on November 27, just five days after the assassination, the new President was expertly prepared for a dramatic and emotional effort to unify the Congress and the American people behind him and to assure the Free World that America would hold firm as its anchor.

Standing in the rostrum in the well of the House of Representatives, where the legendary Franklin Roosevelt had locked his leg braces and gripped the podium to remain erect, Johnson waited for the applause to die down as he spread his text before him, donned his spectacles and prepared to speak.

Behind him sat the two old men of Congress who had moved up the line of succession to the presidency. House Speaker John W. McCormack, at seventy-two, had served in Congress since his election in Massachusetts as a Democrat in 1928. The gray, bespectacled Speaker was a man of Congress, with no executive experience. Beside him, his hearing aid adjusted to catch Johnson's words, was eighty-six-year-old Senator Carl Hayden, President pro-tempore of the Senate. Hayden had been elected to Congress when his state of Arizona was admitted to the Union in 1912. He moved to the Senate on March 4, 1927.

Johnson began speaking in a modulated voice in the hushed chamber, crowded with members of both houses, the Supreme Court and the diplomatic corps. In the jammed galleries facing him, television cameras carried his message to an audience of millions.

With a humility that had not always marked his rough-and-tumble political career, Johnson said in the beginning, "All that I have I would gladly give not to be standing here today."

He went on to say that "the greatest leader of our time has been struck down by the foulest deed of our time." He described the Kennedy dream of equality at home and peace in the world.

"This nation will keep its commitments from South Vietnam to West Berlin," he declared firmly. "We will be unceasing in the search for peace, resourceful in our pursuit of areas of agreement even with those with whom we differ, and generous and loyal to those who join with us in common cause."

As a politician who had said early in 1960 when he was disclaiming any intention of contending for his party's top nomination that "I don't think any Texan will be elected President in my time," Johnson took pains to alleviate any suspicion that he would be a sectional Chief Executive.

"We will serve all the nation, not one section or one sector, or one group, but all Americans," he said. "These are the United States—a united people with a united purpose."

Recalling that for thirty-two years Capitol Hill had been his home, Johnson gave the lawmakers a lift with a pledge to respect "the independence and integrity of the legislative branch." In the light of this, they did not mind so much his prodding of them "to act wisely, to act vigorously, to act speedily when the need arises." They hadn't acted that way for Kennedy. But the brutal murder of the young President had placed upon them a new impellent for support of the Kennedy programs.

The members of Congress applauded loudly when the new President said that no memorial oration could more eloquently honor Kennedy's memory than prompt passage of the civil rights.

"We have talked long enough in this country about equal rights," he said. "We have talked for one hundred years or more. It is time now to write the next chapter—and to write it in books of law.

"I urge you again, as I did in 1957 and again in 1960, to enact a civil rights law so that we can move forward to eliminate from this nation every trace of discrimination and oppression that is based upon race or color. There could be no greater source of strength to this nation both at home and abroad." Democrats and Northern Republicans applauded vigorously.

Johnson told the lawmakers that "no act of ours could more fittingly continue the work of President Kennedy than the early passage of the tax bill for which he fought all this long year."

The longest outburst of applause came when Johnson urged Americans to end the preaching and the exercise of hate and violence.

"Let us turn away," he said, "from the fanatics of the far left and the far right, from the apostles of bitterness and bigotry, from those defiant of law, and those who pour venom into our nation's bloodstream."

With characteristic caution, Johnson avoided at the outset any specifics which would have boxed him in on the terms of the civil rights and tax bills. The new President's success as a member of Congress had lain in his ability to compromise and to persuade men to go along when they were reluctant to do so. His presidency would bear the same trademark.

Johnson had passed his first vital test in the presidency with the approval of the nation and the world. His "let us continue" struck a popular note. His call for action—and he used that word or a variation of it fifteen times in his brief address—touched the mood of a citizenry wondering what it could do to help make amends for the frightful happenings in Dallas.

At the outset Johnson had clothed his presidency in dignity. If he was later to blur this image by his personal exuberance, there was no flaw in this solemn hour. Congress in return had laid aside its customary partisanship and members had interrupted his speech thirty-two times with applause. When he had ended, members and visitors in the galleries gave him a prolonged standing ovation.

True, the Southern Democrats had sat on their hands when he spoke of civil rights. But they made up a minority that had to be ground down in the master plan for election to the office he was filling. In his address, Johnson had stripped away reservations that civil rights leaders had about him. In his televised address, he had committed himself to the Negro masses. An impressive response of approval came from the Leadership Conference on Civil Rights, representing seventy national religious, civic, labor, fraternal and civil rights organizations, from the National Association for the Advancement of Colored People, the National Urban League and the Southern Christian Leadership Conference.

Dick Gregory, Negro comic who participated frequently in civil rights demonstrations, quipped after hearing Johnson, "Twenty million of us unpacked our bags."

One essential requirement of the master plan had been met—the civil rights supporters of Kennedy had been recruited to the Johnson colors. They would not be permitted to stray if the new President could prevent it. He was confident that he could.

The editorial reaction was favorable, ranging from comment that Johnson displayed "the firm hand of a strong man with steady purpose and a brave spirit," to assertions that "he turned despair into hope" and "rose to the occasion superbly."

Unusual precautions had been taken in transporting the President from the White House to Capitol Hill. He was heavily guarded as he was driven through streets from which traffic had been cleared. But he was cheered along the way by friendly crowds confined to the sidewalks and building entrances.

As an indication of how heavily he was leaning on Kennedy's staff in this period, Johnson brought along with him three aides of the former President. They were Sorensen, Lawrence F. O'Brien, special assistant for congressional relations, and White House press secretary Pierre Salinger. Of these only O'Brien would remain after the exodus of Kennedy men that began shortly.

After he had finished his speech and been congratulated by McCormack and Hayden, there was a brief, poignant moment in which Johnson, on his way out of the chamber, paused to clasp the hand of Attorney General Robert F. Kennedy. Johnson was sad-faced as he spoke a few low-voiced words. The stunned brother of the dead President, who would serve his successor diligently for nine months despite their differences in viewpoint, somehow managed a smile.

Because of the solemnity of the hour, Johnson resisted the impulse, to which he was to yield on several later occasions, to sit down to lunch with his old colleagues. Instead, he and Mrs. Johnson were driven back to the White House, where they lunched with their two daughters at the President's desk.

The changeover in the White House command staff began on that day. Bill D. Moyers, Deputy Director of the Peace Corps, moved into the office of Kenneth O'Donnell, who had been Kennedy's appointments secretary and his knowledgeable link with the Democratic party organization. O'Donnell would return to serve Johnson as a political troubleshooter.

Moyers, an ordained Baptist minister, contributed some high-level intellectual attainments to the Johnson staff. Otherwise it was not notably studded with them. A graduate of the University of Texas, Moyers had spent a year at the University of Edinburgh in Scotland on an international fellowship. He had attended Southwest Baptist Theological Seminary in Fort Worth, Texas. He had signed up to teach ethics at Baylor University, Waco, Texas, when Johnson called him in to help in the 1960 election campaign.

Moyers, who was twenty-nine years old when he joined the White House staff, had first met Johnson in 1954 as a political interne in the Senator's office. Within a couple of months he had moved into the Johnson home in Washington. As the top man on the political team working for Johnson's election as Vice President, the youthful Texan had the full confidence of his boss.

With his quiet, calm, simple manner, Moyers furnished a sharp contrast to his principal's explosive energy and earthy, hot-tempered personality. As could almost no one else, Moyers could say "no" to Johnson and get away with it. He was one of the few assistants—as the staff saying went—that Johnson had never "read out of the human race."

The President was noted for his impatience with his aides. When he wanted something, he wanted it instantly and was likely to bellow if he didn't get it. Staff members had to be available on the double all the time. They weren't supposed to be out to lunch if he needed them. They couldn't count on going home to dinner with their families nor could they assume that Sunday might provide them with at least one day of rest during the week.

In the period in which he was preparing his State of the Union message to Congress, Johnson called in a prominent Senator to go over it with him. His visitor suggested that it might be wise to provide Democratic members of both houses advance excerpts, with quotes on specific subjects so they could flood the news media with favorable statements on the address as soon as it was made.

The President thought this a splendid idea. He picked up a phone to call Jack Valenti. The aide's secretary answered. No, she said, Mr. Valenti wasn't there at the moment. She thought he had stepped across the hall to another office.

"Find him and get him in here," the President snapped.

When Valenti arrived in a few minutes, Johnson blazed, "I don't want you to get more than ten feet away from that desk of yours at any time unless somebody knows where to find you. When I want you, I want you."

For Johnson it was difficult to apologize after such blowups. But staff members who were raked over the coals often found themselves summoned in the presidential presence the next day to be asked for advice on an important matter. This was Johnson's way of indicating, without saying so, he was sorry he had exploded.

If he was demanding in his dealings with his employees, Johnson was soft-hearted about their welfare. An aide who mentioned casually that he didn't feel too well was likely to find himself bustled off to undergo an examination by a corps of doctors who would be paid by Johnson.

The President remembered birthdays and anniversaries. He was a quick man with the flowers and a cheery note if any friend went to the hospital or encountered some other misfortune. More than one newsman, overtaken by a serious and costly illness, got a discreet and personal offer from Johnson of financial assistance.

While he was Vice President, Johnson learned one day that an attractive young Texas girl who had been working on his staff as a stenographer planned to quit to be married. Congratulating her, he asked where the ceremony would take place. It came out that her parents (her father was a filling station attendant) could not afford to come out to Washington for the wedding.

Johnson made up his mind quickly. The wedding would be followed by a reception for the bride and groom at the Vice President's Washington home. Out of his own pocket Johnson provided round-trip transportation funds so the bride's parents could see their daughter suitably launched in matrimony.

Marriage also had tightened Jack Valenti's ties to Johnson. The Houston advertising man's firm had handled the Texas advertising for the 1960 campaign. He had met Johnson at a coffee hour in 1958. What was more important, he had met

Johnson's pretty secretary, Mary Margaret Wiley, and had courted her on frequent trips to Washington. Johnson thought he couldn't get along without her. But he changed his mind and gave the bride away at a gala wedding in Houston.

Mrs. Valenti, who had put in long hours in Johnson's inner office for nine years, conceded that the President was a difficult man to work for. But she said that, as with anything else difficult or exacting, the individual employee reaped benefits accordingly.

"Mrs. Johnson has often said that her husband stretches her," Mrs. Valenti remarked with a smile. "He does this with his staff and pulls out the best they have." Her estimate of her former boss: "A warm and compassionate person."

Valenti, whom Johnson called to his side before he was even sworn in as President, did about everything the Chief Executive wanted done in a hurry. Short, dark, dapper and energetic, he was on hand to have breakfast with the President when the latter awoke at 6:30 A.M. He was at his elbow throughout the day. No one saw more of his chief than Valenti.

But it was soft-spoken Walter Jenkins, who had worked for Johnson for nineteen years, on whom the major staff administrative burdens fell. A gentle, dark-haired, bespectacled Texan, Jenkins had the tremendous capacity for work that the President demanded from all of his employees. He was privy to all of Johnson's affairs, having served as treasurer of the Austin, Texas, radio-television company the Johnsons owned until he went to work in the White House. There was no question that Jenkins had the total confidence of the President, but he was not the all-around utility man Sorensen had been to Kennedy.

Johnson's relations with his staff differed greatly from Kennedy's. With Kennedy a half-dozen aides shared a working relationship with the President that was extremely close. But when he knocked off his office chores early in the evening, Kennedy virtually walked out of their lives until the next morning, except for possible emergency telephone calls. He felt he needed relaxation and he preferred talking with close friends who seldom mentioned presidential problems, or reading or listening to music.

Johnson just plainly never really relaxed except briefly on social occasions. He took his burdens with him into the swimming pool and into the residential area of the White House. An aide or a friend invited to have a swim with him usually found himself plied with presidential questions. He didn't need it at the White House, but in the pool at his Texas ranch Johnson had a specially grounded phone floating on the water so that he could reach anybody he suddenly might decide to call.

Johnson might invite aides to have a social drink or even to stay for dinner. Or, he and Mrs. Johnson might drop by an assistant's home to chat. But his associates learned from experience that the talk would revolve around the President's problems.

Kennedy had been an omnivorous reader of reports and state papers at night. But he paced his physical exertions deliberately to cope with the continual pain in his injured back and to be certain that he would be fit for the day ahead. Johnson seemed to thrive on a fantastic amount of activity, despite the massive heart attack he had sustained on July 2, 1955.

After watching Johnson in action for several months, then Secretary of Commerce Luther H. Hodges voiced the opinion that the new President worked much harder than his predecessor. "The pace is faster, much faster," Hodges said. He added that Kennedy "stopped at dinner time." Johnson, he said, "seemed to work at it right on through the evening." Because of this, it was Hodges' opinion that Johnson was "closer to the individual problems that affect every department."

Because Johnson himself needed so little sleep, it never seemed to occur to him that others might require more than he. Often on his vice-presidential trips abroad when he thought the day had gone well, the boss would keep his staff up until 4:30 A.M. telling the individuals how good they were. If things went wrong, it might be the same hour before he rounded up each one's idea of why the effort had gone sour. In either event, he was ready to go again at 8 A.M. "It wasn't that he wasn't considerate of other people's comfort," an associate explained. "It just never occurred to him that some people need more sleep than that."

While he solicited advice from his staff, Cabinet members and others, when Johnson made up his mind his aides knew there was no room left for further argument. Secretary of Agriculture Orville L. Freeman, who had agreed with all the other Kennedy Cabinet members to stay on, pointed this up one day when he was asked what suggestions he had received from the White House about a pending farm bill. "The President is not in the habit of giving suggestions," Freeman replied. "He just issues orders."

However, the Johnson staff, with its complement of Kennedy holdovers, needed time to mesh its gears. In the last week of November, 1963, it was not quite up to the task of producing two major speeches for the new President. Accordingly, Johnson's "fireside chat" to the nation via television and radio on Thanksgiving Day was regarded as something of a flop both in content and in its televised presentation. His theme was similar to that of the appearance before Congress. He urged his listeners to "banish rancor from our words and malice from our hearts." He called for an end to "injustice or intolerance or oppression to any of our fellow Americans . . . whatever the color of their skins."

While he was fulfilling his ceremonial and political obligations in public the new President already had brought into action what was widely known during his leadership days in the Senate as "the Johnson treatment." He had resolved that he would name the highest level commission possible to make a full inquiry into the assassination, to quiet the rumors that were going around the world that a conspiracy had been responsible for his predecessor's death.

Johnson wanted Chief Justice Earl Warren to head this commission and Warren didn't want to do it. The Chief Justice felt that Court members should not engage in such outside activities but should confine themselves to judicial matters.

The white-haired Chief Justice, who had united the Court in the historic school desegregation decision of 1954, was a determined and stubborn man. When he went to the White House to discuss the matter with the new President, he had decided—irrevocably he thought—that he would say "no" to Johnson's request.

The President listened quietly while Warren outlined his objections. Then he made a deeply emotional plea to the Chief Justice to serve his country in whatever capacity might be asked of him. Johnson was so persuasive that Warren found himself unable to say he would not undertake the task. When he left, Johnson had his agreement that he would serve.

This was only one facet of "the Johnson treatment." Another showed when the President called his old friend Senator Richard B. Russell at Winder, Georgia, to tell him he was appointing him a member of the commission. Russell protested that he was loaded down with work as chairman of the Senate Armed Services Committee and as top-ranking member of the Senate Appropriations Committee. He just couldn't take on another assignment, he said.

"Well, Dick," the President said, "this is going to be mighty embarrassing for me. We've already given the press an advance statement naming the members of the commission and you're on it. I hope you won't let me down."

Grumbling that of course he wouldn't, Russell assented.

These were among the more subtle aspects of the Johnson treatment.

While he served as the Senate's Democratic leader, the Texan had maintained a furious pace. Operating from his front-row desk he was always prodding everyone in sight to get along with the business in hand. He was forever fidgeting, twisting, bobbing up and down. He busied himself collaring colleagues, thrusting his face up within inches of his victim's as he argued and cajoled. He was then the Senate's man in motion, as he later was to become the nation's man in motion.

There was no gainsaying the record. Johnson was effective in the Senate. What Lyndon wanted, Lyndon nearly always got. As one frankly jealous colleague of those days assessed the situation: "Lyndon has been riding the merry-go-round for a long, long time and he hasn't missed a brass ring yet."

Johnson's accomplishments did not come easy in the Senate, as they would not in coping with the nation's problems. The Senate is not by nature a cohesive body. It is made up of individuals who have as much right as any colleague to assert themselves, and most of them not inclined to submit to any discipline. There is a minimum of party loyalty on which to rely. An individual Senator's political needs come first. If they do not clash with the party's, well and good. But if there is such a collision, party leaders trying to write the administration's record usually have to look elsewhere for the votes they need.

It was in such situations that Johnson exhibited a keen insight into human nature and an ability not only to judge men but to juggle them. He blended badgering with persuasion, flattery with threats. He offered future favors and reminded recalcitrants of help given in the past. He promised campaign assistance, financial or otherwise, or hinted that it would be withheld.

Throughout, however, there was a delicate balance in his maneuvering. He never—or almost never—threatened the wrong man or attempted to twist an arm stronger than his own. He always checked with Russell and the late Senator Robert S. Kerr of Oklahoma on general policies, but never tried retaliation against them when they did not go along with him.

Johnson always said that his method of operation involved his favorite quotation from Isaiah, "Come now, and let us reason together." If the result of such consultation produced a compromise, it would be measured by whether it was prudent legislation or action for the nation.

If, as Harry Truman once said, the biggest task of the presidency is to persuade people to do something they ought to be doing anyhow, Johnson seemed expertly qualified on that score.

When he was dealing with members of Congress, Johnson was on home ground. These were men primarily of action and not of contemplation. He knew intimately the orderly processes of their lives, how they managed their existence and coped with their problems. He knew how they reacted to given situations and how hungry they were for national recognition. Where he could, he gave it to them.

For Kennedy, the lawmakers had been pleasant people with whom he conducted necessary business. He was uncomfortable with individuals who spoke either in platitudes or clichés or who talked nothing but politics, as most of them did.

Johnson, on the other hand, had sought these people out as social equals. These were his friends and companions of years, and the new President could not resist, in his early days in the White House, returning to them. At every opportunity, just as Truman had done before him, Johnson took a brief respite with his old cronies. He dashed unannounced to Texas delegation luncheons. If there was a cocktail party honoring a senatorial friend, he would be there.

No Congress had ever known a Chief Executive as well as the Eighty-eighth's members knew Lyndon Johnson. In the eight years of the Eisenhower administration he had become the second most powerful man in government. Working closely with the late Speaker Sam Rayburn, he had shown his skill as a compromiser who picked and chose among the Eisenhower programs. He pushed through those he favored and he shelved those he opposed.

There were those who remained in Congress who said that

as a Democratic leader Johnson had been bombastic, overbearing, boastful, vain and corny. But in the same breath they acknowledged that this extraordinary man was shrewd, forceful, knowledgeable and competently able to dominate them despite the resentment they sometimes felt at what they characterized as his high-handed methods.

As President, Johnson knew well the value of personal contact with the legislators. Tirelessly he got on the phone to every member, Democratic and Republican, he thought might be persuaded to go his way.

From his own experience, the President was aware that the way to woo legislative support from any Senator or Representative was to make him feel important. A telephone call to some lawmaker congratulating him on a speech he had made or asking for his advice on an important policy matter enhanced the recipient's prestige. It was a rare member who could resist the subsequent temptation to say, "When the President asked me about that, I told him . . ."

If this inflated the members, nothing pleased their wives more than to feel they had finally arrived at the inner circle of Washington social life. Many of these ladies, who had read enviously in the society pages of the White House gaiety during the Kennedy administration, suddenly found themselves, and what they wore, discussed on the same pages. This was insidious, heady wine that seldom wore off by breakfast time and was remembered long thereafter. One freshman member of Congress explained it succinctly. He said that when he and his wife went home during the Kennedy regime the women were always asking what Jackie Kennedy was really like.

"My wife was embarrassed," he said. "She really couldn't say what Jackie Kennedy was like because she had never been to the White House and she hadn't met Mrs. Kennedy.

"You know how folks at home are. If you live in Washington they think you go to the White House every night. It just doesn't work out that way if you are a first-year Congressman.

"Well, when Lyndon got in, we got an invitation in the next couple of weeks to come to dinner at the White House. My wife went out and bought a new dress we couldn't afford, but I said, what the hell, it probably only comes once in a lifetime.

"It was quite a party. My wife danced with the President and Mrs. Johnson took her and a lot of other wives upstairs to look at the living quarters.

"When we went home to our district the next time, my wife could quote the First Lady on a lot of things. She was quite a social success.

"Maybe you think I ought to ignore all of this stuff when it comes to voting on something Lyndon wants. Sometimes my conscience tells me I ought to, but I get the message at the breakfast table that if I go against Lyndon I'll be going against her—my wife, I mean."

As a man who was seeking a bipartisan consensus for all of his actions and decisions, Johnson cozied up as much to the Republicans as to the Democrats.

Once when he was twitted about dropping into the Capitol office of Senator Dirksen to partake of Scotch and soda with a number of Republicans gathered there, Johnson explained that he was only exchanging greetings with "an American group."

"These people didn't always vote with me when I was Majority Leader," he said, "but they did when I needed them most."

Dirksen, the Senate Republican leader, later was to supply the GOP support needed to curb a Southern Democratic filibuster and to win passage of a refashioned civil rights bill, a result that filled in another gap in the Johnson master plan. The fact that Dirksen then could turn around and place the name of Barry Goldwater, who had voted against the bill, before the Republican convention for its presidential nomination did not alter Johnson's relations with the many-gaited Illinois Senator.

Kennedy had got along well with Dirksen, who had saved the young President's skin on such important foreign policy matters as the United Nations bond-financing plan. Kennedy's succinct estimate to me of Dirksen was: "Good when the chips are down."

Dirksen covered a deep understanding of the nation's problems and of how Congress must grapple with them with a mellifluous-voiced, stump-evangelist manner. Johnson knew that Dirksen would be against most of his domestic proposals. But he also knew that the Illinois Senator would be on his side, and say so publicly in international crises. Besides, Dirksen liked "Ol' Lyndon," as he called him affectionately. And that mattered.

On the Democratic side, Johnson had loyal support from Senate Majority Leader Mike Mansfield of Montana. In his first days in office the new President turned frequently to Senator Humphrey, the Democratic Whip and Mansfield's floor assistant. Between them they commanded a majority of sixty-seven Democrats that often wasn't a majority at all. This was particularly true with regard to social and economic legislation so important to the new President. On such measures Southern Democratic conservatives were likely to desert the fold and join Republican opponents.

Mansfield, an ex-miner, ex-Marine and ex-college professor, was too gentle to fill the rough-and-tumble role that Johnson had made of the leadership. He knew no "magic," Mansfield said, by which he could change Senate votes. He complained that the Leader "has no real power, none at all."

The tireless, ebullient Hubert Humphrey, a liberal Democrat, stepped in to try to fill the void. A primary contender against Kennedy for the 1960 Democratic presidential nomination, Humphrey had sheathed the sharp political knife he carried for Kennedy in that year and had buckled down to strenuous efforts toward making the New Frontier's program a legislative reality. Now Johnson was grooming Humphrey for the vice presidency—but the Senator didn't know it. The effervescent Minnesota Senator tried, but not very successfully, to curb the oratorical propensities which led him to rise to the Senate floor at almost every opportunity to talk glibly for a couple of hours on a wide variety of subjects. Told by one of his colleagues that he just plain talked too much, Humphrey replied with a smile, "I can't help it. It's just glands."

If Humphrey thought he talked a lot, he really hadn't seen Johnson in action until the latter became President. Humphrey was at the White House two or three times a day. In between these visits, there were presidential phone calls.

"I've had ten calls from the man today," he said wearily at one point early in Johnson's administration. "He has a new idea every thirty minutes and he calls me about it. I can't do anything he wants done because I don't have time to get going between calls."

Dirksen had a similar complaint. "He called me up six times yesterday," Dirksen said. "I can't get my work done because he's always got me on the phone."

This type of telephone barrage was similar to that against which Johnson had complained in 1957 when Eisenhower was in the White House. Discussing a then pending measure, Johnson said acidly, "I believe we could expedite the matter a great deal if all outside forces would refrain from attempting, by telephone calls, to direct Congress in its activities."

But the view from the White House was different, and Johnson kept the lines hot as he marshaled his forces for a big push to get things done in Congress.

3 Frugality Comes to the White House

WHEN THE JOHNSONS moved in on the historic date of December 7, 1963, frugality came to the White House.

Rooted deep in the consciousness of the new President was an instinct for thrift which had been implanted in him by necessity rather than choice. In the red dirt hill country around Stonewall, Texas, where he was born on August 27, 1908, the Johnsons had practiced frugality in order to eat regularly.

He once explained that one of the reasons he became a Democrat was that "my Daddy went broke three times during Republican administrations."

So Johnson was only doing what came naturally when he began immediately to dramatize the sort of frugality calculated to establish himself with Congress as an economizer and to rob the Republicans of a major campaign issue. On his first morning at work at the Oval Room desk, Johnson received from Budget Director Kermit Gordon, housed down the hall, a three-paragraph memo. It said there was still time to refashion Kennedy's new budget into his own but there was no time to waste. The President didn't waste any.

Gordon had had a firm November 27 date with Kennedy to lay before him a $101.5 billion budget. From that mark it was almost a certainty that Kennedy would have whittled out enough to bring the over-all total conveniently below $100 billion. With his eye on the forthcoming presidential election, Kennedy already had started a political ploy Johnson proceeded to improve upon.

Kennedy had recognized the political perils of permitting the budget to reach $100 billion. It was a round figure the Republicans could mouth in their attacks on him as a "big spender" who was following "irresponsible financial policies." While he couldn't balance the budget, Kennedy was well aware of the potency of the issue, and from his viewpoint the lower the spending total the better.

The late President had sent Secretary of the Treasury C. Douglas Dillon to Capitol Hill to do some not-too-guarded talking about the possibility that the new budget might go as high as $103 billion. Dillon was not to be pinned down on this. But if he left the impression this figure was more or less inevitable, the White House might be able to supply Congress with a pleasant surprise.

Johnson determined that he would try to work a small miracle by cutting below the $98.8 billion figure of Kennedy's previous budget. This was designed to impress the millions of Americans who seemed to retain the belief that old-fashioned budget-balancing was a good thing. It also was calculated to increase confidence of businessmen in the Democratic administration. Business' estimation of the administration had been extremely low since Kennedy's enforced roll-back of steel prices in 1962.

The new President was no fool about such matters. He knew how difficult it was going to be to effect any retrenchment in spending in a nation that was growing swiftly in population and demanding more and more federal services. As he told the United States Chamber of Commerce in January, 1964, "I challenge any rock-ribbed, private-enterprise, freedom-loving member of the Chamber of Commerce to tell me his budget is the same as it was twenty-five years ago."

Proceeding according to plan, Johnson made a production out of the titanic struggle he was supposed to be undergoing. White House leaks supplied information indicating, at first, why it would be almost impossible for him to cut the total below $103 billion. Then, as the ploy developed, the total magically was reduced to $101 billion. The truth of the matter was, of course, that for the first time since the Korean war military outlays could be reduced. Kennedy had known this and Johnson soon was made aware of it by Secretary of Defense McNamara.

Spending for missiles and hardware was being phased out. Some other outlays could be transferred into the current Kennedy budget fiscal year and thus reduce the Johnson total. Some actual cutbacks could be ordered. Out of all this came Johnson's surprise announcement to Congress that spending for the year beginning July 1, 1964, would be held below Kennedy's previous year's total, to only $97.9 billion.

Employing some of the same legerdemain, Johnson was able to hold his subsequent year's budget to $99.7 billion. Even after his landslide election in November, 1964, he was unwilling to cross the political twilight zone which led beyond the $100 billion figure. Where a Roosevelt might have plunged, Johnson hedged.

One valuable product of these financial gymnastics lay in the impression Johnson made on officials under his direct command in the Executive Department. Cabinet members, as well as those in the lower echelons, found out quickly they had a boss who intended to be boss in all respects. When they protested they couldn't cut expenditures for their departments or agencies any lower, the President told them bluntly they would make reductions or else.

Johnson knew he had a good thing in his first, reduced budget and he was determined to translate it into terms understandable to the average man, who couldn't comprehend a single billion, much less $97.9 billion. So he made a production out of it when he put his signature on the document on January 20, 1964. Summoning twenty-five Budget Bureau experts to the White House, he told them:

"Somebody told me that the light bill in the White House ran several thousand dollars a month. I challenged Mr. John Valenti over there and my maid this morning when I left to turn out all those lights in those chandeliers when there is no one in the house. Mrs. Johnson had gone to New York and I was the only one there, and I didn't require that much light.

"I don't know how much we saved today. I want a bill for the last two months to see if we are making any headway.

"And see that that goes down to every government building. A stitch in time saves nine. You don't accumulate anything unless you save in small amounts."

He went on to say that he had appealed to Army commanders to be "cost-conscious and social-conscious."

"You all check the cost-consciousness and I'll check the social-consciousness," he told the budget experts.

This latter was in line with his explanation to members of Congress that what he had been able to pare from military expenditures he was putting into humanitarian projects in the budget. Thus he pleased the economizers while justifying his bid for support of the liberals who wanted more spending in the welfare field.

Republicans complained that what Johnson saved by darkening the previously brilliantly lighted White House he more than spent in long-distance telephone calls by day and night to just about any individual he happened to think of at the moment. However, there were neither light bills nor phone bills available for comparison.

November's end found Johnson lecturing the Joint Chiefs of Staff and federal departmental and agency heads about economy. He served notice that he would cut budget requests "to the barest minimum consistent with the efficient discharge of our domestic and foreign responsibilities." He exchanged letters with McNamara in which he said that he had pledged his administration "to the utmost of thrift and frugality, and to get a dollar's value for every dollar spent." To show that he meant business, Johnson said he wanted the Secretary of Defense to bear down on military contractors for reductions in their costs and to reward those who did with future business. This was somewhat disturbing to members of Congress who liked to look to these contractors for campaign donations and who felt any reduction in defense payrolls would redound against them. But they put it down to the overactive glands of a President trying to establish a position for himself and marked it as something to deal with later.

McNamara came back with the suggestion that Johnson give particular attention to reducing defense costs by supporting his department's program of "buying only what is needed," "buying at the lowest sound price" and "reducing operating costs." Johnson thought these were grand ideas and ordered them carried out.

All of this might have been highly important, but the President recognized that it wasn't the kind of operation that excited anybody but the economists. He had some other things in mind, however.

First there was the matter of government limousines. For years as Senate Leader and Vice President, Johnson had been furnished with a luxury car and a driver. Now he had a fleet of limousines on call as the Chief Executive. But he decreed that subordinate officials had to give up theirs. The economies effected were hardly apparent to inquiring reporters. The Pentagon was told, for example, to limit the number of its limousines to ten—exactly the number it was operating.

Further, Johnson decided he could do without two of the three military attachés customarily stationed at the White House. The Army representative stayed, the Navy and the Air Force were banished.

The Navy took another blow when Johnson decided he didn't need a couple of yachts always kept in readiness for presidential use. One of these was the *Honey Fitz*, on which Kennedy had found relaxation and had used at times for diplomatic conferences. The other was a smaller boat, the *Patrick J.*

The *Honey Fitz*, a ninety-two-foot cruiser, originally had belonged to Sewell Avery, a Montgomery Ward executive who gained public attention when the Army moved in in a strike dispute and carried him bodily out of his office. The Coast Guard acquired the vessel in 1942, the Navy in 1945.

Harry Truman named the craft the *Lenore* and used it as an escort vessel for the *Williamsburg*, then the presidential yacht. Eisenhower banished the *Williamsburg* and had the smaller vessel reconditioned at an estimated cost of $140,000, renaming it the *Barbara Anne* for his granddaughter. Taking over, Kennedy rechristened the craft the *Honey Fitz*, the nickname of his grandfather, the late Mayor John J. Fitzgerald of Boston.

When Johnson, definitely not a seagoing man, said he had no use for the *Honey Fitz*, it went into dry dock. How much was saved out of its estimated $10,000-a-year maintenance cost afloat was not divulged.

Johnson had promised he would bring about a reduction in the federal payroll, a subject dear to the heart of Senator Byrd, who must be mollified to get the tax cut bill out of the doldrums into which it had slipped.

The President told all government departments and agencies "to establish new end-of-year targets" to hold federal employment levels below those of the then current fiscal year covered in Kennedy's final budget. As it turned out, the budget Johnson submitted in January, 1964, called for a payroll reduction of 1,200, leaving expenditures budgeted for 2,511,200 employees on July 1, 1965.

One hard decision for economy was made. McNamara got the President's approval for the closing of hundreds of outmoded, unneeded military bases. When the Defense Secretary began carrying out this program a sizable number of budget-balancers in Congress decided this was not the kind of economy they wanted.

While he was busy pinching pennies Johnson also seized on the opportunity to reassure the liberal supporters of more government spending. The opportunity arrived in the form of two bills initiated by his predecessor which were counted upon to have a heavy impact on certain segments of the population.

First to come across his desk was a $1.2 billion college aid measure he called "the most significant education bill passed by Congress in the history of the Republic." Although it failed to live up to that extravagant billing and did not contain the basic Kennedy ingredient of aid to public elementary and high schools, it represented a significant advance. Using sixty pens and taking twenty minutes to complete his signature on the measure, the new President called it a "monument" to Kennedy.

When a bill making additional funds available for retraining of jobless workers came along three days later, Johnson unaccountably slumped to thirty-four pens. But he jovially told Senator Joseph S. Clark, Pennsylvania Democrat who had been a severe critic of Johnson's Senate leadership tactics, as he handed him a pen, "You're the 'y' in Lyndon."

Things were going swimmingly in Johnson's first month in office. Negro leaders, businessmen, labor chieftains were arriving daily at the White House for conferences with the new President and going away singing his praises. Congress was creaking into action, although there was an ominous battle over foreign aid in the making. Only once had Johnson been forced to take significant political risk and he faced up to it without hesitation.

On December 2, the President had presented in a White House ceremony a gold medal, a citation and a Treasury check for $50,000, tax free, to an adjudged security risk. The recipient was Dr. J. Robert Oppenheimer, wartime director of the Los Alamos, New Mexico, laboratory which developed the atomic bomb.

Eisenhower had ordered in 1954 a "blank wall" placed between Oppenheimer and the atomic secrets he had helped develop. There had been a long series of security-clearance

investigations which the then President found showed "fundamental defects in his [Oppenheimer's] character."

Johnson made no mention of this controversial subject in
saying he took "pleasure and pride" in presenting the Enrico
Fermi Award, highest the Atomic Energy Commission could
bestow. But in his reply Oppenheimer said: "It is just possible,
Mr. President, that it has taken some charity and some courage
for you to make this award today. That would seem to me to be
a good augury for all our futures."

Within the first few days of his presidency, Johnson had
tidied up as best he could the matter of presidential succession
if anything happened to him. He wasn't worried, because Dr.
John Willis Hurst, who had met him at his home on the night
of the return from Dallas, had given him an encouraging report
on his physical condition.

Interviewed in Atlanta, Georgia, Hurst said that Johnson's
heart attack of July, 1955, was "in the distant past."

"Since that time," Hurst said, "he has done beautifully. I
don't know of anyone who gets up earlier, goes to bed later,
works harder and gets more done without trouble than the
President. He's extremely active and he tolerates stresses that
most people can't.

"He is vigorous, active and his heart is doing fine."

If Dr. Hurst and his colleagues were comfortable about a
heart victim's putting together a series of eighteen-hour days,
some other Americans were not. Eisenhower, whom Johnson
had liked and admired, wrote the new Chief Executive a note
suggesting that he take things a little easier. As a man who also
had survived a heart attack, Eisenhower suggested Johnson
follow a lighter schedule, conserve as much energy as possible
and avoid worry.

Obviously on account of medical advice which had been
passed along to her when Johnson ignored it, Mrs. Johnson
pinned a note on the President's pillow one day urging him to

slow down a bit and to take an hour and a half off in the
afternoon for a restful nap. He did a few times, but not often.
The plain truth was that Johnson wasn't a resting kind of fellow. He had always had too many brands heating in the fire
ever to sit and contemplate its flames and to engage in mellow
introspection. There were always things to do, and when there
were, Johnson intended to be about doing them.

As Democratic leader of the Senate he had been a cyclone
blowing furiously against any obstacle he encountered. As Vice
President he had been a whirlwind whipping up new responsibilities to add to the meager list vouchsafed to him by the
Constitution.

In his Senate job Johnson had been a Southerner elevated to
leadership by Southerners demonstrating the tactical superior-
ity—with the help of Westerners—they always seemed able to
maintain over the frustrated and leaderless liberals of the
North.

On the day that Barry Goldwater defeated Ernest W. Mc-
Farland for reelection to the Senate in Arizona in 1952, the
Southern hierarchy had sprung into action to fill the thus vacated Democratic leadership with one of their own. From Austin, Texas, Johnson, then the Democratic Whip, or assistant
leader, put in a call to Senator Russell in Winder, Georgia.
From Winder calls went out to key Senators in the South and
West. The word was passed that Lyndon would succeed the
defeated McFarland as the party leader. Better get on the
bandwagon. Within forty-eight hours Johnson had the necessary majority, plus several votes, to assure his election by the
Democratic conference. The party liberals didn't even get the
license of the speeding car that hit them that day.

The liberals always had looked askance at Johnson, tabbing
him as a conservative, ignoring his record of having supported
Franklin Roosevelt's New Deal while he was a member of the
House. However, in Texas many of Johnson's constituents regarded the Senator as a left-wing radical. Americans for Con-

stitutional Action, a conservative group, assessed him as a 90 per cent liberal on his Senate voting record.

Johnson made a pilgrimage daily, and sometimes two or three times a day, to the Capitol office of the late Speaker Sam Rayburn. There was the seat of political wisdom and of congressional sagacity. The old man had brought Lyndon up from a pup and the younger never ceased to listen to his advice.

Johnson maintained a frank intimacy with his opposite number, Senate Republican leader William F. Knowland of California. The Democratic and Republican leaders were political enemies but personal friends. Much of the Senate's business was transacted on that basis. There was a similar understanding between Johnson and Dirksen when the latter succeeded Knowland in the top partisan job.

The cooperation Johnson elicited from the opposition leaders contributed to reducing the partisan clamor in the Senate. But there remained for Johnson much in his senatorial life that was harassing and frustrating, just as there was in life in the White House.

Like the presidency, the Senate provided a fast-moving panorama of crises, long hours and—over some periods—few accomplishments. Senators talked when Johnson wanted them to vote. Members went off to make political speeches when he needed their presence in the chamber to get action on important legislation. The average day was one of a thousand frustrations, to be chain-smoked away fretfully.

At the time he was stricken by a heart attack on July 2, 1955, Johnson was having one of those days when nothing seemed to go right. It was the birthday of his daughter Luci. He had to pick out a couple of new suits and visit an ailing senatorial friend. He was running behind schedule and couldn't seem to catch up.

"I had the feeling that I had a million things to do and I couldn't possibly do them all, a feeling of terrible pressure," he recalled.

Johnson had chosen this particular day to massage his leadership ego with a familiarly picayune performance to which he subjected newsmen regularly. It was his habit to tot up long lists of bills the Senate had passed and to hand them out to reporters as a record of what had been accomplished to date under his leadership. Included would be several bills that reasonably could be designated as having a modicum of national importance. But along with these would be listed measures for the relief of some citizen hit by a mail truck and for the relinquishing by the government of 2.9 acres of land to some city for a park.

Congress was always being accused by the news media of dragging its feet, a charge that irritated Johnson no end. He looked upon it as an indictment of his leadership and he was determined to quash it. He was having difficulties extracting quality legislation from a recalcitrant Senate, where the time-honored coalition of Southern Democrats and Republicans called the turn and sometimes left him holding an empty bag. If there was little quality, Johnson would substitute quantity.

So he summoned correspondents to his office in the southwest corner suite on the third floor of the Senate wing of the Capitol. By Johnson standards the suite was somewhat grubby, despite its marble fireplaces and its splendid view. From the West window one could look down the expanse of the Mall toward the Washington Monument and the Lincoln Memorial, catch a glimpse of the roof of the White House and sight Robert E. Lee's home in the hills of Virginia beyond the Potomac. (Next year Johnson would move to an immense and elaborate throne room off the Senate floor which had been redone expensively since it had been occupied by the District of Columbia Committee as an office and hearing room.)

Sitting behind his well-ordered desk, Johnson ran through his list of accomplishments to date for the score or more of newsmen who filled the chairs in front of him. As was customary when Johnson spoke on such matters or addressed the

Senate briefly on some issue of the day, his staff had produced a word-for-word script. Johnson was cautious; he didn't like ad libbing in those days. When he had something to say to the Senate he thought important, he wanted it written down beforehand. This did not mean that he shied away from debate. He could rise on such occasions and deliver a blistering attack on his opponents. But he always harbored a fear that what he might say on some important subject might be inadequate and he liked to have his ammunition in hand.

At the desk where he now was reading monotonously the list of the Democratic leadership's "achievements," I had sat many times with him while he gobbled a fat hamburger, gulped coffee and talked, between mouthfuls, of his plans for some pending legislation or discussed some parliamentary maneuver he intended to make. Absent-mindedly opening a large glass jar that always sat on his right, Johnson popped a candy sourball into his mouth and, sucking on it, proceeded to outline a schedule for future Senate action. When he had concluded, a reporter asked the obvious question: What was going to happen to a controversial immigration bill in the outline of action Johnson expected the committees to take in bringing legislation before the Senate?

The Senate leader replied blandly that the legislation still was in the hands of a committee and he didn't have any information on what the committee was going to do about it. The newsman suggested that Johnson had been very specific about what other committees were going to do about other legislation. Why couldn't he be as specific about the immigration bill?

Johnson exploded.

"Don't tell me how to answer questions," he bellowed. "Now you get the hell out of here."

Gould Lincoln, venerable columnist for the Washington *Star*, stood up to protest. He said he thought the Senator ought to calm down and reconsider some of the statements he had made.

Johnson subsided at that point. His ever-solicitous press aide, George Reedy, clucked over him with a tut-tut here and a tut-tut there, shepherding the reporters out of the meeting with pursed lips. Reedy conveyed to all concerned that the Senator didn't really mean it, he was only a little overwrought.

Four hours later Johnson was in an automobile on the way to the Virginia estate of George Brown, of the Brown and Root firm, which owned and operated an industrial construction empire in and out of Houston. The Senate leader encountered what he thought was a digestive upset. Complaining about the inefficiency of his car's air conditioning, Johnson told his chauffeur, Norman Edwards, "I can't seem to breathe." He was marginally close to breathing his last at that point.

When Johnson arrived at Brown's estate, he took some baking soda and went to lie down. Brown called a doctor. It didn't take the medical man long to diagnose a heart attack. An ambulance was ordered and Johnson was whisked to the Bethesda Naval Hospital. There the heart attack diagnosis was confirmed, and it was a bad one.

Although the difference might not have registered on a casual acquaintance, Johnson was never quite the same again. In those first critical hours and in the months of recuperation that followed he gained a measure of patience—not much, perhaps, but some.

He had had an unforgettable introduction to death at the age of forty-six, and it influenced his outlook on life and his thoughts about the future. The physical accident he had suffered was a more compelling influence than generally was believed on his decision to accept the vice-presidential nomination, which for a while would remove his daily diet of frustrations and at the same time place him directly in line for the presidency.

Certain moderations were imposed on Johnson because of his heart attack. A three-pack-a-day cigarette smoker, he had his last puff before he went under an oxygen tent at the hospital. But nine years later he turned up now and then with an

unlighted cigarette hanging from his lips. This seemed akin to
the kind of compulsion which had caused the late Senator William Langer of North Dakota, banned from smoking, to chew
on a cellophane-wrapped cigar all day long without removing
the covering.

In his post-attack regimen, Johnson drank coffee without
caffeine, banned the sourballs and only rarely ate one of those
sugary Texas pralines he loved so well. He watched his diet.
His weight, which had zoomed to 220 pounds, fell back to
about 180. But he was up to 210 again when he became President.

Johnson cut the Scotch content of his highballs to one-half
ounce. He was a quick finisher of drinks and that way he could
have twice as many highballs without increasing his alcoholic
intake. His friends could attest that he handled his liquor well
on most occasions.

Dr. George Calver, Capitol physician, who made frequent
electrocardiogram tests, pronounced Johnson's heart sound after the latter became President. For years after the attack
Johnson carried around in his wallet a replica of his latest EKG
test. He would whip it out at the drop of a hat to support his
contention that there was no deterioration in his heart.

Johnson's attack, known as a myocardial infarction, was of
the type that involved a stoppage in an artery supplying the
heart with blood. This could damage the heart muscles and
leave scar tissue. On the other hand, such an attack could occur without permanent muscle damage if the collateral channels supplied sufficient blood to the heart. Johnson's electro-
cardiograms did not indicate the presence of any scar tissue.
But some slight abnormality remained detectable after he
became President.

Medical records indicated the chances were good that he
would not have another heart attack. The President's work
pace did not worry his physicians. So long as he was getting
satisfaction out of what he was doing, they felt that excessive

activity would not hurt him. And no one had any doubts about the satisfaction Johnson got out of being President.

If his heart did not worry the President, another possible ailment did. For some physiological reason never fully explained to him, he was a candidate for kidney stones. His first painful encounter with them came in the summer of 1948. At the Mayo Clinic in Rochester, Minnesota, a stone was removed by manipulation. Early in 1955 he had a very painful attack and flew once again to Mayo's. Surgery was necessary to remove a larger stone. Johnson was out of action for six weeks and for a time wore a steel brace to alleviate the pain in his back. Characteristically, the then Senator retrieved the stone from the surgeons and kept it in a box to show admiring friends.

In August, 1963, when he was preparing for a European trip, Johnson had a worrisome scare. He began to note symptoms he read as indicating the possible imminence of another kidney-stone attack. Quick tests by his physicians showed he was taking in more calcium than his system could assimilate. Too much milk was the verdict. So the Vice President cut out the milk and went his way.

Johnson had some slight bronchial trouble, and in one of his checkups as Vice President, Dr. Janet Travell, Kennedy's White House physician, had joined in the consultation. Dr. Travell, a pert, smiling woman in her sixties, had won renown as a muscle and bone expert. She had prescribed the famous rocking chair in which Kennedy relaxed during conferences in his White House office. Dr. Travell prescribed a rocker for Johnson, which he used because it was comfortable and because it was a symbol of continuity.

After he became President, Johnson suddenly decided to take up golf. As a Senator he had joined the exclusive Burning Tree Club outside Washington in 1948 and had played an occasional round. But he quit after his heart attack and nobody saw him with a club in hand until he played a round with

Kennedy late in 1960 at Palm Beach.

The bug bit Johnson in April, 1964, and he started turning up at Burning Tree to play a few holes. Usually his friends there had just completed eighteen holes but they were glad, even if weary, to accommodate him with a game. Where Kennedy shot in the 70s and Eisenhower in the 80s, Johnson's scores were a state secret. One of his companions once observed that while the President sometimes smacked some creditable drives, most of the time he hit down on the ball "like he was killing a rattlesnake."

Johnson felt that he was in the pink, physically, when he entered the presidency. He told all those who inquired that he never had felt better. It was not a subject which he felt needed to be explored publicly but at a news conference on May 6, 1964, he went into the matter in response to a question.

A curious reporter wanted to know the last time the President had had a physical examination and if the doctors advised him to slow down the furious pace he still was setting. The President's reply was:

"The doctors, I think—as a matter of fact I read a report from some doctors, I don't know which one, and I have been examined frequently since I have been in the White House and the last six months, and sometimes at greater lengths than I am being examined here today—they tell me that my blood pressure is 125 over 78, that my heart is normal, and that I don't have any aches and pains.

"I feel fine. I get adequate rest and good pay and plenty to eat. I don't know of anyone who is concerned about my health. Certainly none of my doctors are concerned about it."

Johnson's physical endurance systematically was promoted as a legend by the doctors he chose to examine him and by all of his White House associates. He was, by all accounts, the physically indestructible man. In a 1964 year-end report, Rear Admiral George C. Burkley, the presidential physician, said his patient was in excellent health and predicted he would withstand another four years in the White House "in outstanding fashion."

But late in January, 1965, the nation was jerked to attention when the President was taken to Bethesda, Maryland, Naval Hospital in the early hours of the morning with a respiratory infection that kept him confined for four days. Johnson, who confided to reporters that he had had pneumonia several times, took occasion to deny that his appearances without hat or over-coat during his inaugural period had anything to do with his illness. He had been wearing cold-resisting underwear in what seemed an obvious effort to present himself to the people as a healthy specimen who braved the elements without fear of physical punishment. He said he got too warm when he danced at the inaugural balls, and his temporary illness was attributed in some quarters to this.

Whatever the reason, there remained an uneasiness about the President's health. Men in their mid-fifties were subject to strokes, and eight U.S. Presidents had been killed by them, either in office or after they had retired. In the twentieth century Warren Harding and Franklin D. Roosevelt had died in office as the result of strokes and Woodrow Wilson finally had succumbed after he left the executive post.

No man who had not been elected by all the people to the office of Vice President had ever succeeded to the presidency. But the possibility that an individual who had not had the endorsement of the national electorate might become the Chief Executive had existed each time a Vice President succeeded a stricken President.

If it had been politically possible, Johnson would have liked to change the rules which made seventy-two-year-old Speaker McCormack his in-line successor so long as there was no elected Vice President.

There was legislation pending in Congress which Johnson secretly favored to revamp the line of succession. But the President could not open his mouth about it because McCormack had made it abundantly clear that he would regard any effort to by-pass him because of his age as a personal affront.

Johnson's earthy assessment of the situation was that this legislation would not get anywhere in the 88th Congress because most Democratic members of the House "wouldn't go to the men's room without consulting the Speaker first."

McCormack, who had lived his mature lifetime in the House, was highly respected by his colleagues. The white-haired, bespectacled legislative fox from Massachusetts was a valuable man who found his job as Speaker rather restricting because he couldn't talk except on special occasions when he made a partisan ceremony of it. As the Democratic leader of the House he had been accustomed to sounding off almost daily. But a Speaker didn't do that unless there was a vital issue up for debate.

An intensely religious Roman Catholic who never drank, McCormack was a graduate of a poker group that had met regularly in the White House when Truman was President. It was recalled that he once won $1,000 from Truman—who really couldn't afford that kind of stakes—in a night's sitting.

The Speaker, who left school before finishing the eighth grade because his mother and two younger brothers needed the $3.50 a week he could earn as an errand boy, never had felt comfortable with the erudite Kennedys. He had read law at night to pass the bar examinations when he was twenty-one years old. Harvard was ideologically as far away from his beloved Ninth District in Boston as it was from Austin, Texas. The McCormacks had warred with the Kennedys in Massachusetts politics and, except for the Speaker, they usually had lost.

There was an air of companionship between McCormack and Johnson that had been lacking in the Speaker's relations with Kennedy and the New Frontiersmen.

If McCormack's attributes failed to add up to the requirements American voters liked to think their Presidents possessed, it was not something that Johnson could do anything about. Accordingly he treated McCormack as he later did Humphrey, cutting him in on National Security Council Sessions, having him briefed by State Department and Central Intelligence Agency representatives, and generally preparing the Speaker to take over the top job if something unforeseen happened to Johnson.

With another bow to the elder statesmen of the party, Johnson decreed that Senator Carl Hayden, the presiding officer of the Senate, should attend weekly breakfast meetings of the Democratic congressional leaders at the White House.

The President had sewed vitally needed patches on the tattered garment of Democratic unity. True, the Republicans already were snapping their galluses in opposition to the Kennedy bills he was trying to push through Congress.

Surveying his recently acquired responsibilities, Johnson recognized that he was likely to have more immediate trouble with Democrats entrenched in Congress than with Republicans who might fear the reaction of opposing a President who had come into office on a national wave of shock and sympathy.

Christmas was coming and every member of Congress wanted to go home. Johnson himself felt the itch to get back to his native soil of Texas to commune a bit with nature and to forget, if only briefly, the domestic and international problems that pressed upon him. Luckily the world hadn't served up an international crisis to him yet, but he knew in his bones that one would not be long in coming.

That was one of the reasons he bore down hard in efforts to save the administration's foreign aid money bill from being mutilated in the Christmas Eve session in which he had insisted Congress remain. Johnson had had McCormack bring to the White House Representative Otto Passman, Louisiana Democrat who had been hacking foreign aid bills to pieces for years. The President talked long and persuasively but Passman wouldn't budge. Johnson was not equipped at that point to cope with Passman, but the President would remember that conference and Passman would learn several months later that he had underestimated his adversary.

Kennedy had asked for $4.5 billion in foreign aid funds. Under Passman's leadership the House Appropriations Committee had cut the amount to $2.8 billion. The Senate had upped the figure to $3.3 billion and a final compromise between the two houses put it at a flat $3 billion. This was $100 million below the total that Johnson had described as an absolute minimum.

More distressing to the President was the attachment of an amendment to the bill which would have prevented the sale of $250 million in surplus wheat to Russia through a ban on government credits for any sales to Communist countries.

During four furious days of maneuvering, the House twice had refused to lift the ban. The results had been influenced by the fact that many administration supporters had gone home for Christmas and weren't on hand to vote. Johnson got on the telephone to these absentees, making it clear to them that he regarded this a test of whether his presidency was going to be effective. The administration dispatched jet planes to pick up some members who agreed to return.

On the morning of Christmas Eve, when the House met at the unheard-of hour of 7 A.M., the Johnson forces were ready for the final test. Before they voted, House members got a memorandum from the President which said:

"The countries of the communist world are watching anxiously to determine whether the new President is so strong they will have to come to terms with him or so weak that they can start hacking away at the free world with impunity. . . ."

The political moratorium which followed Kennedy's assassination was still in effect but the Republicans weren't swallowing this overstatement of the situation. When the vote came, the credit ban amendment was carved out of the bill by a 189–158 vote. On the roll call, 187 Democrats and 2 Republicans supported the President. Voting against him were 133 Republicans and 25 Democrats, the latter mostly from the South.

He hadn't received all he wanted, but Johnson had won a fundamental victory that went far beyond the immediate issue involved. He had demonstrated—as his predecessor had not been able to do—that he could move Congress off its dead center to give him legislation he wanted.

4 The Real Johnson Begins to Emerge

ALL IN ALL, December 24, 1963, was a highly satisfactory day for Lyndon Baines Johnson. He had won his victory in Congress. He had soothed Senate and House members, irritated about being called back to work in the Christmas holiday period, by inviting some two hundred of them to the White House the day before, when the official mourning period for Kennedy had ended. On December 22, he had marked his wife's fifty-first birthday with a small party at the Walter Jenkins home. At that time he had given Lady Bird the same present he had given her twenty-nine years before when he was courting her. It was a photograph of himself inscribed, "For Bird, still a girl of principles, ideals and refinement—from her admirer, Lyndon." Only the "still" had been added.

The idea for the party for the lawmakers had come to Johnson suddenly. He wheeled his staff into action inviting members of the Senate, House and Cabinet. He threw the White House kitchen into turmoil by ordering preparations for two hundred on a little more than an hour's notice. The Christmas decorations which replaced black crepe of a month's mourning had scarcely been hung when the first guests arrived in the blustery snow that was falling.

To greet them there was the jovial Johnson they had known as a member of Congress instead of the sober-miened Chief Executive with whom they had been dealing. As a genial host he was dispensing coffee, eggnog and fruitcake. Some of the President's guests had been up most of the night, several circling Washington in planes that had not been able to land because of the storm. They missed the House vote but landed in time to come to the party.

There was a great deal of the happier side of the Johnson treatment on display that day. The President grasped old friends by the elbows, seized their arms and even clapped a few on the back. While he was socializing, he also was getting in his licks for administration programs that still remained before Congress. And he was patching some fences where he had detected a break.

Johnson took chunky Charles A. Halleck of Indiana, then House Republican leader, aside for a private chat. An anonymous White House official had leaked a complaint a few days before denouncing Halleck as an obstructionist for holding up a vote on the foreign aid bill. The President said he wanted to apologize.

"Charlie," he said, "I'm sorry if anybody here said anything ugly about you. We can disagree without being disagreeable."

Pleased by the presidential attention, Halleck told another guest that he guessed the House would pass Johnson's bill on the morrow.

Kennedy had never had much use for Halleck. The late President had told me on one occasion that he knew in advance just what Halleck would do when he was called to the White House for any bipartisan conference. The Indiana Representative would file into the Oval Room office unsmilingly, take his seat silently in the semicircle around the gimmick-loaded presidential desk. When it came his turn to express his views, Halleck usually would respond, "I'm against it," and lapse into silence.

Johnson was no old buddy of Halleck's. But he recognized the House Republican leader as a politically astute operator, a pragmatic party man and a confirmed conservative. If they couldn't agree on many issues, the President saw no sense in making that a personal matter. His attitude undoubtedly contributed to Halleck's later vital support for the civil rights bill.

Johnson's theory, as he put it to reporters at the White House party, was that "If you can't learn to live with leaders of Congress at home, you can't learn to live with the leaders of the world."

When the affair was about to end, Johnson got up on a gold cut-velvet chair in the State Dining Room to tell his guests how pleased he and Mrs. Johnson were that "we could be here this evening together." Figuratively, he patted the assembled lawmakers on the head by telling them "you have labored through the vineyard and plowed through the snow" to accomplish a worthy purpose.

As the guests were leaving the exuberant President encountered four women reporters just putting on their coats in the hall. He made a little off-the-record speech to them about the vital need for a substantial foreign aid program and bade them goodbye. They had hardly made it outside when an aide came running to summon them back. The President wanted a photograph of them with himself and Mrs. Johnson. The picture was made and the reporters started to leave.

"Hey, want to see the swimming pool?" Johnson called after them. They did, and the President led the four women on a tour of the pool area, the Oval Room office, an adjacent "think room" and the Cabinet Room.

During the round, Johnson disclosed that he had been calling Mrs. Kennedy on the telephone every day or two. He said he did this "because she is troubled, and she is a very special favorite of mine.

"She has always been," he said. "She went out of her way to have my children down to every little party at the White House and to be nice to Lady Bird."

The President closed his happy day by showing the reporters a photo which had been taken of him at the hastily called Cabinet meeting after his return from Dallas. The picture, a mood shot, showed only Johnson's head over the top of a high-backed chair with no others visible. The President remarked that "There sits the loneliest man in the world."

I had asked Kennedy once about the often published statement that "The presidency is the loneliest job in the world." It wasn't true, he replied.

"I see a lot more of my family here in the White House than I ever was able to before," he said. "I think that when people speak of the President's being 'lonely' they are thinking of it in the sense that there is a responsibility here that can't be shared. In that respect, the President is alone."

Tilting back in his rocker, Kennedy waved off also the suggestion that the presidency was a back-breaking task, one that had been described by Eisenhower as "the most wearing" assignment he ever had and by Truman as "an all-day and nearly an all-night job."

Kennedy said that the job was less strenuous physically than some he had had before. There was no comparison, he said, between the average day in the White House and one spent campaigning. He noted that the latter involved speaking several times within the space of a few hours, flying from one city to another, riding in open cars waving to crowds, shaking hands, patting children on the head, conferring with local party leaders and trying to get a bite to eat and snatch a few winks of sleep in all the uproar that accompanies a candidate.

"That's the real back-breaking job," he said, "especially in the primaries like those that Hubert Humphrey and I went through in 1960.

"It isn't the physical demands of the presidency that are difficult. It is the responsibilities, especially when things go badly in, well, you know, matters of war and peace. I suppose you could say that it is at times exhausting in that sense.

"The difference between campaigning for the job and holding it is that you can make a mistake in a campaign and it will affect you and your future adversely but if you make a mistake in the presidency it affects everybody in the country."

Johnson had had a taste of the mental and physical stresses of the presidency in his desperate efforts to reverse the House's position and get what he regarded as a workable foreign aid bill. On the Sunday night before the Christmas Eve vote he had been able to get only one hour's sleep because of his heavy involvement in trying to turn the legislative tide. Yet he said he "never felt better in my life" as he prepared to leave the White House for a working vacation at his LBJ spread at Johnson City, Texas. There the real Lyndon Johnson would arise and identify himself for the kind of President he was going to be in his own right. The era of "let us continue" was drawing to a close.

Johnson went back to doing what came naturally as soon as *Air Force One* had deposited him and his family at Austin, Texas on Christmas Eve. He boarded a helicopter and flew to the ranch of a longtime friend, A. W. Moursund. He and his host went deer hunting but the President fired no shots, although he got out of his car twice and leveled his rifle. Some does were in the way and he couldn't get a clear shot at the bucks.

But the Texas air made Johnson feel better. As he remarked, "I've just been here an hour and I feel better already."

Perhaps this was psychological, but the 438-acre LBJ ranch was home to him as the White House perhaps never would be. There he could relax, lounging about in khaki slacks, Texas boots and cowboy hat. He could take off on horseback for an inspection tour of his herd of white-faced Herefords. Or he could stroll through the hills along the Pedernales River. Johnson loved the old thirteen-room wood and limestone house which had been built in his grandfather's time. It had been allowed to decay in an era in which his father had encountered economic ill fortune, but he himself had been able to restore it.

He had installed a kidney-shaped swimming pool, enclosed behind a horse-country fence stretching down two sides. A nearby guest house took care of the overflow visitors who could not be accommodated in the four bedrooms of the main building.

This was no Hyde Park estate, nor could it compare with the Kennedy compound at Hyannis Port. But it had the solid quality of comfort and livability for a family which scratched its way up the economic ladder until it had reached a multi-millionaire status.

It had been a relatively peaceful and quiet retreat while Johnson was a Senator. There had been some big parties there when Johnson, as Vice President, had entertained visiting diplomats.

But it was difficult to preserve the bucolic atmosphere when a President was occupying the premises. Electronic equipment to keep him in touch with developments in the most remote corner of the world was strewn about. A couple of helicopters rested nearby. And when Chancellor Ludwig Erhard came to visit in December, 1963, he was greeted with a welcoming portrait, and the orange and black flags of West Germany fluttered along the driveway.

Even on such an occasion, the efforts of the Johnsons were directed toward emphasizing the homely virtues of neighborliness and hospitality of ordinary folk who had been elevated to a lofty office but had maintained the common touch. Mrs. Johnson confessed, however, that the ranch didn't seem as much like home as it had before the family was accompanied everywhere by staff aides, the Secret Service and two hundred representatives of the press.

Mrs. Johnson, whose height of five feet, four inches, and weight of 114 pounds made her seem tiny beside her tall husband, dressed modishly in Washington. But she really preferred the skirts and sweaters and low-heeled shoes she could don at the ranch.

Johnson was proud of his wife's abilities as a mother, a politician and a businesswoman. He once remarked, "I don't see how Lady Bird can do all the things she does without ever stubbing her toe. I'll just never know, because I sure stub mine sometimes."

It was the consensus of their mutual friends that while Kennedy might have become President without his gracious Jacqueline, Johnson could never have made it without Lady Bird. From the beginning, Mrs. Johnson had assured herself of a good press by making her doings available to the women reporters. They had always resented Jacqueline Kennedy's decision to keep her personal life and that of her children as private as possible. The women reporters were particularly incensed when Mrs. Kennedy's orders separated them from guests at White House social functions, dealing them out of the chit-chat and gossip on which some of them thrived.

Because she felt some had taken advantage of her by means of telephoto lenses, Mrs. Kennedy at times was difficult with the photographers and thus stored up no credit with that hardy breed of individualists. When she did permit pictures of her children and interviews, the privilege went without exception to friends of pre-White House days.

In contrast, Mrs. Johnson was the most accessible of First Ladies since Eleanor Roosevelt had bounded about with inexhaustible energy in her endeavors for countless causes.

Strangely enough, Johnson was the one who gave photographers most trouble among those in the new White House family. Kennedy had docilely gone along with every request for a shot from a different angle. He had drawn the line only against pictures of him wearing a cowboy hat (he said "no" in Fort Worth on the day of the assassination) or some gag shots he felt might demean the presidency.

Johnson, on the other hand, had convinced himself that his left profile was his best and he insisted that he be shot from an angle to display it rather than from the right side of his face.

Before he became President he had always insisted that photographers at a news conference finish their work before he began talking. He wanted no candid pictures that might catch him twisting his mouth for emphasis when he talked, a habit he labored mightily to lose.

On the banks of the Llano river not far away from the LBJ ranch the President had a hideaway at what was known as the Haywood ranch, which he had purchased while he was Vice President. There he had a motor cruiser and hunting equipment. The press was not supposed to find out about this retreat, which the President and his family reached by helicopter or by driving about twenty-five miles over dirt roads. But neighbors reported that Johnson had been seen towing his daughter, Lynda Bird, on an aquaboard, trying to teach her to water ski. After four dunkings, Lynda Bird gave up. The privacy which Johnson strove for just about vanished when photographers with telescopic lenses snapped him standing aboard the cruiser with his ample stomach bulging over his swimming trunks. The President didn't care at all for those pictures.

The Johnsons brought a teen-age era to the White House, where the Kennedy grade-school and pre-kindergarten set and their animals had competed for publicity with the relatives who had dunked each other in fashionable pools in nearby Virginia. Daughter Lynda Bird, a tall brunette, already had been engaged before her father became President and had broken it off after she had spent a few months in the White House. Just emerging from her teens, Lynda Bird was the Johnson family's representative on the platform at every occasion that involved young people. She complained at times about having to be "an American model for youth," but she was a good soldier.

Luci Baines, three years younger, had a lot of fun with the Secret Service men assigned to guard her. The girls at National Cathedral School in Washington, where she was studying, oohed and aahed over the handsome young men of the Secret Service who were only a couple of steps behind her wherever she went.

The President's assessment of his daughters was to the point: "Lynda Bird is so smart that she'll always be able to make a living for herself," he said. "And Luci Baines is so appealing and feminine that there will always be some man around wanting to make a living for her."

While Lynda Bird was acknowledged as an accomplished speaker to youth groups, Luci Baines surprised the family one day in San Francisco when she was called upon at the age of thirteen for some remarks at a civil rights gathering.

"I don't know what to say to you folks," Luci said with engaging frankness. "But I often think of my mother, who has dark hair and brown eyes. My Daddy and my sister do too, while I have blond hair, white skin and blue eyes. But we all get along fine together.

"If we do, in the same family, why can't everybody, without thinking of the color of people's skin or hair or eyes or even how they worship God?"

Luci was technically a blond, with fair skin and hair only a little lighter than her mother's. Her hair darkened as she grew older.

Her father, the President-to-be-in-the-future, could hardly have topped his daughter's speech. Luci had also a mind of her own. She decided after a few months of being the President's daughter to substitute "Luci" for "Lucy," the name she had been christened with. It was more chic.

Lynda brought along to the White House a collection of dolls including a hundred-year-old antique which had belonged to her grandmother and others gathered up from all over the world by her traveling parents.

Luci brought along two beagle puppies, appropriately named Him and Her, which were to get her father in trouble later when he picked them up by their ears. The family's dog, naturally named Little Beagle Johnson, had died of old age at fifteen.

Both of the President's daughters are expert divers and swimmers. Lynda, who was having a bit of trouble with her figure, complained a few months later when the photographers caught her with telescopic lenses when she went on a skin-diving excursion in Hawaii.

The White House was not exactly a novelty to the Johnson girls when they moved in. Both had been favorites of Mrs. Kennedy and they were there often for parties when young people were invited. Once when their parents had gone to Texas and left them behind in Washington the girls were invited by Mrs. Kennedy to a formal dinner the President was giving for the President of Sudan. Hurried checking disclosed that, indeed, this was no mistake. Mrs. Kennedy wanted them to come.

Excitedly, the girls called Mrs. Johnson at the ranch. What were they to do? Their mother's advice was succinct, as usual.

"Read all you can find in the encyclopedia about the Sudan and don't drink any of the wine at dinner," she said.

If these girls seemed like average teen-agers, casual and friendly, there were some differences that Mrs. Johnson had wrought.

Their mother had cautioned them long before the White House days began that "Daddy's in the spotlight, not you." She had said it was up to them to meet the requirements of responsibility and independence and not to expose their father to ridicule because of them.

Even before they became teen-agers, the girls had been given their allowances and had established their own bank accounts. They bought their own clothes and if they wanted little extras they managed them out of their available finances.

Mrs. Johnson handled the matter of dating on the basis that the girls had been taught to have good judgment and there was no need for her to put a curfew on their partying. She was rewarded in that respect by their exercise of good judgment.

As a wife, nobody was going to accuse Mrs. Johnson of favoring Parisian clothes designers over American, as they had Mrs. Kennedy. Even as the First Lady, who could pick and choose the best in clothes that world designers offered, she stuck with the native clan. And when she went to New York for a speech and to get in a little shopping too, she fell back on an old habit. When she was the wife of a lowly House member who had only his salary to live on, she had ridden the Pennsylvania Railroad's coaches to New York. As the President's wife, she took an Eastern Air Lines shuttle to New York, saving a net of $3.25 on the trip.

When the Smithsonian Institution asked her, shortly after her husband became President, for a gown to exhibit in its First Ladies Hall, Mrs. Johnson replied, "I'd better wait awhile unless I can work out an arrangement to borrow the dress back from the museum after closing hours."

As a hostess, Mrs. Johnson did not try to bat in the same cultural league as Mrs. Kennedy, who had invited such a wide variety of guests that her husband once remarked with a wry grin, "It isn't difficult to get an invitation to the White House these days."

The Kennedys had put such artists as Pablo Casals and Robert Frost on the front pages. The Johnsons felt a duty to maintain the patronage of the performing artists. But in fact they were in unconscious agreement with Emerson, who had said that "culture ends in a headache."

It was now better to be a Texan and to relish "jailhouse" chili than to be a Bostonian who insisted on creamed clam chowder. The chowder they served in Dallas and Houston had tomatoes in it. If you were willing to assault your stomach with the highly seasoned deer-meat sausage that came yearly from the LBJ ranch and could assimilate in stride the sugary pralines that were made in Austin, you had passed the first door of acceptance in the new administration. Of course, if you wore spit-and-polish cowboy boots, the low kind, that is, the White House gates almost automatically opened at your approach.

These were only the symbols of the natural change that had shipped the Harvard accent back to the precincts of its origin and had installed the nasal Texas drawl as the language of the court. They were the outward manifestation of the undeniable fact that the presidency had come down out of the intellectual clouds to the rather earthy earth.

Mrs. Johnson's inevitable parting line, when the party was over, was: "You all come back soon now, you hear?" Her guests went away feeling that she really meant it.

This woman, a dark-haired, brown-eyed charmer who had been christened Claudia Alta, had come a long way from the time when at the age of fifteen, a product of the piney woods country of East Texas, she had been so shy that she managed to avoid making the highest grades in the Marshall, Texas, high school so that she wouldn't have to stand up and give the valedictory address.

Graduated from the University of Texas in 1934 with a bachelor of arts degree in journalism and liberal arts, she met Lyndon Johnson shortly thereafter in the office of a friend in Austin. Lyndon asked her to have breakfast with him the next morning, told her all about himself and how much insurance he carried.

When she took her beau a few weeks later to meet her father, a storekeeper and landowner who was known affectionately in those parts as "Mr. Boss," she got this accolade from him: "Daughter," he said, "you've brought a lot of boys home. This time you've brought a man."

Two months later they were married in St. Mark's Episcopal Church in San Antonio. Some critics said this was about the last time Johnson went to church until he became President but, of course, this was not true.

Just before the wedding began his diminutive bride turned to tall Lyndon and asked anxiously, "You did remember a wedding ring, didn't you?" Snapping his fingers in chagrin, Johnson replied that he had forgotten to get one. Dispatched to a convenient jeweler, a friend came back with twelve rings. The bride-to-be tried them on and chose the one that fit her finger best. Never after that would she replace it with a more expensive ring.

If Mrs. Johnson was not as dedicated to the arts as her predecessor, she nevertheless was well grounded in literature and well informed about other cultural pursuits. She had read the classics in the family home library at Karnack, Texas, where she was born on December 22, 1912. If Mrs. Kennedy could charm local audiences around the world speaking in either French or Spanish, Mrs. Johnson at least could make herself understood in the Spanish she learned after her husband became Vice President.

What she lacked in classical accomplishments Mrs. Johnson made up in practical matters. Unlike her predecessor, she was intensely interested in politics and wanted to participate personally. She also was a businesswoman, with a head for figures that any Wall Street accountant might have envied.

She had had her first taste of active politics in 1937, when she borrowed $10,000 from her father to finance her husband's first campaign for Congress. Running as a complete outsider in a "sudden death" election, Johnson conceived the idea of supporting Franklin D. Roosevelt's court-packing plan to draw attention to his forlorn candidacy.

It drew enough attention to elect him, and Roosevelt was delighted—in a year in which he was getting his comeuppance for having tried unsuccessfully to purge party members who opposed him—to welcome a newcomer to the faltering fold. Cruising on the Gulf of Mexico at the time, the President invited the Representative-elect to join him at Galveston and ride the presidential train through Texas. In that era was born the fidelity to Rooseveltian ideals that, nurtured through his years as a House member, Johnson carried into the presidency.

In 1948, when he ran for the Senate after a previously un-successful bid for the job, Johnson trailed in the first primary by 100,000 votes. Lady Bird really swung into action at that point. She flew all over Texas to represent her husband at women's gatherings. She called every friend she could remember at the University of Texas, and those that Johnson had known at Southwest Texas State Teachers College, to ask each of them to work and vote for her husband. She lined up his mother and three sisters to call on the phone every person listed in the Austin telephone directory. Johnson won the round by eighty-seven votes.

In the 1960 campaign, when Johnson was running for Vice President, she logged 30,000 miles, making as many as sixteen speeches a day for the Kennedy-Johnson ticket in two hundred meetings in thirty states. Her verdict was: "Campaigning is the greatest adventure one could have.

"I like to go campaigning with Lyndon whenever I can," she explained. "I find it interesting and exhilarating. I learn a lot. I feel it's important to go. I think people can assess a man a little in relation to the kind of wife and family he has. They are interested in the total man, and that includes his family."

She had some minor troubles with Lyndon. He had firm ideas about the kind of clothes he thought she should wear. She confessed that at times she had to steer him around the purchase of some "perfectly awful" choice that he might have made.

If he wished to pick out her clothes, Johnson left about everything else in their family life to Lady Bird.

She ordered him the right kind of breakfast, making sure there was saccharin available and "reminding him of his diet without being obnoxious." This was only part of what she conceived to be her job of managing the mechanics of their lives. The President was a great man for saying that he wanted something and leaving it up to her to provide as best she could.

"He wants me to handle everything I am capable of handling," she said. "He's a little incensed if I want help on trivial things. I think sometimes he thinks I am more capable than I am, which, in a way, makes me grow more capable."

If she was a paragon as a wife, mother, social hostess and political companion, Lady Bird was also the woman who made her husband independently wealthy, pulling the strings that made the Johnsons second only to the Kennedys as the richest White House family in modern times. The Kennedys had inherited their wealth. Lady Bird had scratched and maneuvered for the Johnsons'.

When Johnson first was elected to the House in 1937, his income consisted of his salary and nothing else. This at least was an improvement over the pay he had received since 1931, when he began serving as a congressional secretary to Representative Richard M. Kleberg, one of the owners of the fabulous King ranch in Texas. Nevertheless, the Johnsons still had to rent out their living quarters in Washington when they went home to Texas for the summer and make the round trip by car to save on expenses.

All of this changed when Mrs. Johnson belatedly received a $67,000 family inheritance, left by her mother who had died in 1918, and which included 3,660 acres of pine lands in Autauga and Chilton counties in Alabama. Part of this land subsequently was rented out at $5 a month to Negro tenant farmers, whose rickety homes were visited by Republicans armed with cameras after Johnson became President.

The bulk of the family wealth grew from a $17,500 investment Mrs. Johnson made on February 16, 1943, in KTBC, an Austin radio station which was operating part time, without network affiliation, and losing money. In July of that year the company operating under its new ownership won approval by the Federal Communications Commission of its application for a new frequency, a doubling of its power, and permission to broadcast full time. By August the station had affiliated with the Columbia Broadcasting System and in October it got FCC approval to boost its power from 1,000 to 5,000 watts.

In 1947, with assets of $213,140, including $82,191 in undistributed profits, Mrs. Johnson formed a new company known as the Texas Broadcasting Corporation. She took back most of the stock of the new concern plus $80,000 in debentures which paid her 6 per cent a year interest.

On March 14, 1952, the company applied for a television license, which was granted by the FCC on July 11. The station won affiliations quickly with all three major TV networks. Texas Broadcasting branched out later to acquire interests in other Texas stations and one Oklahoma station. A 1959 balance sheet filed by the firm, which had been renamed the LBJ Company, showed March 31 assets of $2,569,503 and profits the preceding year of $430,432.

Husband Lyndon in the meantime had been buying Texas grazing land, stocking it with cattle and sheep. The estimate was that he and his wife owned 4,000 acres under the community property laws of Texas when he became President. These landholdings were roughly evaluated at a minimum of $600,000. Nobody could guess exactly what the Johnsons were worth. The estimate ran up, however, to $9 million. This was only about $1 million short of John F. Kennedy's holdings when he became President.

The $9 million guess of actual current value of the Johnson holdings was considerably higher than the $3,383,098 net the accounting firm of Haskins and Sells placed on the Johnson holdings in an August 19, 1964, statement released by the White House. The accountants had figured the value of real estate on the basis of cost, less allowance for depreciation of improvements.

The then Republican National Chairman, Dean Burch, called the accounting "most peculiar" and said it fixed an "incredibly low" total for the Johnson wealth.

Haskins and Sells put Mrs. Johnson's net worth at $2,126,298 and Johnson's at $378,081. Lynda Bird's wealth was put at $490,141, and Luci Baines' at $489,578. In ten years Mrs. Johnson's salary as an officer of Texas Broadcasting Company had been $570,856. Johnson had earned $409,730 while he served as Senator, Vice President and President.

Kennedy's wealth had come from the $1 million trust fund his father had settled on him at the age of nine. The late President had given his $100,000-a-year salary as Chief Executive to charity. He had about that much coming in from his holdings, plus the $40,000 a year all Presidents get in nontaxable allowances for entertainment.

Shortly after Johnson became President, he and his wife put their holdings in trust, where they would accumulate dividends and add to the principal while the President remained in office. In the White House, they lived off his salary and emoluments. The Johnsons, who had learned in their earlier days that a dollar was hard to come by, would have plenty of them to spend after they left official life.

Mrs. Johnson divested herself of control of the TV-radio empire in Texas late in 1963. She filed a statement showing that she owned 52.8 per cent of the stock, with 30.9 per cent administered for her two daughters, and she gave up to the trustees the right even to inquire how the company was faring financially. The trustees were A. W. Moursund, of Johnson City, Texas, and J. W. Bullion, of Dallas. She assigned them authority to "hold, manage, invest and reinvest" all of her TV-radio holdings. They were without bond and without liability for "mistakes of error of judgment or negligence but only for their own wilful misconduct." She would get no income except that necessary to pay taxes. But the increment of capital would go on.

It had to be noted that although many of the Johnson family transactions were accomplished while the President-to-be was a member of the House and Senate and of its Commerce Committee—which rode herd on the FCC and its decisions—inquiring reporters could find nowhere on the record any special plea for the Johnson stations. But as John Barron of the Washington *Star* said, the FCC always seemed to approach the Johnson applications with a benevolent attitude.

Johnson, of course, was a personal participant in the family TV-radio ventures. As a multiplicity of witnesses could testify, he was on hand personally when some of the profitable deals were made.

Johnson liked to pretend, however, that he regarded himself as a stupid oaf in business dealings who had been rescued from abject poverty by the good business sense of his wife. He was vocal in praise of her as "the best businessman I ever knew." He bragged often that no man ever took her financial measure. But no one ever need think that the man in the family didn't have his finger on what was going on.

He was fond of reciting to his reportorial friends all of the advanced, social-minded thinking that went into the Johnson TV-radio operation. The Johnson employees got stock in the company, bonuses and profit-sharing incentive. They were made to feel they were partners in an enterprise designed primarily to give all involved a better and more satisfactory life.

From an old college friend who had gone to work for them after a brief career with International News Service I got first-hand testimony that the Johnsons took care of their own. When he was seriously ill for several months, they sent him at their expense to California to rest and recuperate. This man's estimation was that there was no fairer employer than the Johnsons. This was a part of the innate feeling the President and his wife had for their fellow beings. Perhaps it was a small example, but it was not to be overlooked in assaying their character.

While Johnson was the Senate's Democratic leader the Austin operation was only beginning to get going. There was one memorable day in his office when the talk turned to the recurring proposals of some Democratic liberals—whom he regarded with suspicion mixed with open hostility—that all Senators bare the sources of their income. Johnson was against this. But he assured the intimate group present that it was a matter of principle. He would be glad to publicize his income, he said. He had nothing to hide. Dipping down in his lower desk drawer, he fished out a copy of the income tax return he had made jointly with Mrs. Johnson. When he read off figures they disclosed that Mr. and Mrs. Lyndon B. Johnson had had a taxable income of about $40,000 that year. This included his senatorial salary and the income from the Texas TV-radio operation that just then was beginning to burgeon. This, of course, was in a great degree attributable to the fact that the FCC had not let a competing television station into Austin, a city of some 200,000 persons, up to the time that Johnson became President.

After Johnson became Vice President he was burned to cinders by a remark Barry Goldwater had made in Austin. Goldwater was campaigning for Republican John G. Tower to fill the Senate seat the former Democratic leader had left vacant by insisting on running not only for Vice President but also for the Senate in the same election. Goldwater flew in his own plane, and he got a roar from the crowd when he said that he had no difficulty in locating Austin, because it was the only city of its size and the only state capital with only one TV tower.

All of these family and financial matters were pushed into the shade, however, as Johnson luxuriated for the first time in his Presidency in the informality of his beloved ranch life. For the first time since Kennedy had died, he felt he could be himself. He had to talk to Chancellor Erhard, of course, and he had Rusk, McNamara and others coming for necessary conferences. But, yippee, he was his own man again, even if it was only for a brief interlude.

5 Something for Everyone

Almost from his first day in office Lyndon Johnson had been thinking about and working at odd hours on a State of the Union message which would outline his political platform for the 1964 presidential election campaign. It would be designed to transform the sympathetic approval the people had given him during the early transition days into the less emotional and more substantial support he would need to remain President nine more years.

Johnson knew what he wanted to do. He wanted first to put his own mark on the presidency. Secondly, he wanted to identify himself at home as a man of compassion and a champion of equality. Thirdly, he wanted to convince the world that he was a man anxious to negotiate—but willing to fight—for peace. In the course of this he would offer frugality to the conservatives and social progress to the liberals. Thus there would be something for everyone in this message.

A week after he designated Sorensen to draft the framework of the speech, the President handed over to his aide ideas that he had jotted down, often in his bedroom at night when sleep was elusive. Cabinet members and other staff aides came through with contributions.

Just before he left for the Christmas work-and-play vacation at the ranch, Johnson had given Sorensen a final rundown of what he wanted. He had insisted that the mass of material which was almost swamping his aide be boiled down to 3,000 words. In his day, Johnson had heard many State of the Union messages that seemed to run on and on, leaving the members of Congress yawning in their seats before it was all over. He wanted to avoid this.

The new President desired punch lines. He knew the value of applause as it thundered up on the television and radio sets. If the members of Congress were applauding often, many people who might not be able to recall afterward anything much about what the President said would mark it off as a satisfactory performance.

Sorensen went to work, traveling to the ranch after Christmas, and by December 30 he had completed what he regarded as a satisfactory version. White House Secretary Nancy Larson typed it and late that night it went to the President.

This was only the beginning. Johnson came up with some new ideas. He suggested changes in phrasing. In the next week aides reported that the speech had been redrafted sixteen times. On January 6 Sorensen thought the job was done. Reporters had been promised advance copies, to be held for release, the following day. But it turned out that Johnson required some more revisions. It was not until late in the afternoon of January 7 that the President walked from his living quarters to the Oval Room office with the final version on which he had scribbled changes. It ran 3,050 words, shortest since Franklin D. Roosevelt's 2,500 words in 1934.

All of this changing of the script was analogous to the doctoring of a play. But Johnson knew that when he stood at the rostrum of the House to deliver his message, he would be on trial not only with the Congress but with the millions who might view and hear him on television and radio. It was up to him to put across his lines.

For all the world like an accomplished Shakespearean actor, Johnson expertly paced his remarks, providing the pauses to elicit a maximum of applause. Democrats responded, sometimes enthusiastically and sometimes dutifully. Republicans sat on their hands except when he mentioned cuts in expenditures. The loudest outburst of handclapping, punctuated by a few cheers, came when Johnson, obviously speaking to Soviet Premier Nikita Khrushchev, declared, "We intend to bury no one—and we do not intend to be buried."

When the President had concluded and was leaving the podium, an old Senate friend pressed his hand and congratulated him on making a "marvelous" presentation. Johnson nearly floored his former colleague with the whispered observation: "Yeah, I was interrupted by applause eighty times."

That was precisely the number of interruptions logged by reporters in the galleries in their meticulous check of each manifestation of approval. It seemed the new President needed no clerk to tally for him the fact that he had registered nearly twice as many applause breaks as Kennedy had with a similar message a year earlier.

Johnson called on Congress to do more to sustain civil rights "than the last hundred sessions combined." He urged the "most far-reaching tax cut of our time." He asked for hospitalization insurance for the elderly and proposed that Congress vote more funds for housing, schools, libraries and hospitals than any previous session had provided. He demanded reform of "our tangled transportation and transit policies" and said the lawmakers must "achieve the most effective, efficient foreign aid program ever."

But his major effort was a declaration of "unconditional war on poverty." Pointing to the $97.9 billion budget he was submitting, Johnson said the "war" could be carried on "without any increase in spending."

There was an echo of the "one-third of a nation ill-housed, ill-clad, ill-nourished" of Franklin D. Roosevelt, his patron political saint, when Johnson said, "Unfortunately many Americans live on the outskirts of hope, some because of their poverty and some because of their color, and all too many because of both. Our task is to help replace their despair with unconditional war on poverty in America. . . ."

The broad outlines of the anti-poverty program had been a legacy from Kennedy. The late President had been gathering together information to formulate an anti-poverty policy based on an effort to alleviate the conditions under which some Americans lived in West Virginia and other areas of what came to be known as Appalachia. Kennedy had been elected to Congress in what could have been classified as a slum ward of Boston. There he had gone out to meet these people on the streets, had climbed the stairs to cold-water flats, had seen them rally in their corner saloons at night to partake of a bit of the beer when it was foaming.

But he had never seen anything like the abject surrender to poverty, the inability to get or qualify for any job, that was exhibited by the unemployed miners of West Virginia and Kentucky. One had only to view those ghost communities, with rickety shanties all but falling off the hillsides to which they were attached, with gaunt children playing on the alternately barren and wildflower-dotted ground, to understand the shock that had overtaken him.

Kennedy had been planning a large-scale attack on poverty. Nothing really new or daring had occurred to him, as it did not to Johnson. But as the late President's brother testified in House Committee hearings on April 7, it was Kennedy who pointed the way.

"President Kennedy was totally committed to confronting and dealing with these problems and [with] involving the national administration to a greater extent than ever before," Robert Kennedy said. "President Kennedy saw the national administration's role as providing leadership, pointing the way, finding answers and stimulating local communities, state and private interests to step up their efforts and to run their own programs."

This so completely outlined the Johnson program that there was little doubt left where it originated. Yet where Kennedy had discovered abject poverty only in West Virginia, Johnson had been able to recognize its liabilities all his life. And the new President put behind this a hunger for education that Kennedy had felt only vicariously.

If it had not been for the perseverance of his mother, Lyndon Johnson might have wound up as a highly respected supervisor of a section of Texas highways. Johnson's mother, Rebekah Baines Johnson, died in 1958 at the age of seventy-seven. The President's estimate of her: "My mother was a saintly woman. I owe everything to her." And in a practical sense he did.

Mrs. Johnson, a graduate of Baylor College and a former teacher, had taught her son the alphabet from blocks before he was two years old. At three he knew all the Mother Goose rhymes, as well as snatches of Tennyson and Longfellow poems. At four he was reading simple sentences. But when he started to school, it was his mother's coaching and not his own inclinations that kept him at his studies.

The oldest of five children in the family, the future President was graduated from high school at fifteen. Naturally, he was the president of his class of seven. But at that point the young man had had it in education. He had shined shoes in the local barbershop to help make his way through high school and now he wanted to see the world, or at least a non-Texas part of it. So he joined five friends in an expedition to the promised land of California. There he made his way down the coast southward waiting tables, washing dishes, doing farm work and everything else that came to hand. In this period, young John Kennedy was just beginning his schooling at Dexter, a private, nonparochial school in Brookline, a suburb of Boston, where Joe Kennedy's family then lived.

When young Lyndon Johnson hitchhiked his way back from California to the Johnson City homestead, he was so thin from his haphazard diet that he barely cast a shadow in the Texas sun. Nevertheless, he took a job on a road gang, shoveling gravel, driving a truck and pushing a wheelbarrow.

Mrs. Johnson kept after her son to get more education. She drove home to him the contention that "education opens up everything." Johnson was to stress this theme as President. Yielding to his mother's entreaties, Johnson finally said he was ready to try for more education. Fearing to leave her son more time to consider his decision, Mrs. Johnson phoned a friend who was an official of Southwest Texas State Teachers College at San Marcos, a town forty miles from Austin, and arranged his entry in February, 1927.

Johnson later described his years at San Marcos as "the most formative period in my life." Somehow the gangling farm boy picked up the name of "Bull." This seemed attributable more to his organizing abilities than to his physical appearance.

It is recorded that Johnson got an early lesson in budget-balancing by borrowing $75 at the Johnson City bank to finance his matriculation at San Marcos. This was at about the time that Joe Kennedy was settling a $1 million trust fund on his nine-year-old son John.

At college, Johnson got a job as janitor, work that irked him so much he determined that he would get a degree in less than four years. He wangled a job as editor-in-chief of the *College Star*, the campus newspaper, which brought him in $75 a month. He studied hard for the first time in his life.

"I took forty courses and got thirty-five A's," he once said. He joined all kinds of campus organizations, but his main love was debating. From his coach, Professor H. W. Greene, Johnson soaked up a great deal of information about political events and trends.

At this point the young man was beginning to formulate some of the ideas that would shape his future course. He wrote in the campus newspaper:

"Personality is a trait that transforms a man or woman from a commonplace being into a compelling and attractive figure. It is the difference between the ordinary and the remarkable.

"Personality is power. It has force and strength, charm and attraction. The man with a striking personality can accomplish greater deeds in life than a man of equal abilities but less personality."

This was pretty good going for a young man from a cotton patch who didn't intend to remain there. Johnson had obviously determined at this relatively early age that he was going to be a personality. How well he succeeded was attested to by his political rise.

The young Johnson was attracted by sincerity. The older Johnson spoke of it often. As he said in one of his youthful editorials:

"One of the virtues of life is sincerity. One reason it is so great is that it is so rare. Most of us like to make ourselves out as bigger than we are. . . . Nine times out of ten the poser poses too much and ruins the picture he tried to paint."

All the evidence suggested that the hurry-up, let's-get-it-done man who came to the presidency was born in this college. Lyndon Johnson had found at first hand what education could do for him. He felt that what it could do for him it could do for any individual who might for the lack of it have less than an equal opportunity to compete with his fellows in a lopsided world that offered much to those who least needed the encouragement to learning and almost nothing to those who so required its help.

When he received his degree in August, 1930, Johnson turned by instinct—and by necessity, too—to teaching. He had taken a year out of his short course to teach seventeen pupils in the fifth, sixth and seventh grades in a rambling brick school at Cotulla, Texas. This had brought him in the $100 a month he needed to complete his own education.

In his activities as a teacher, Johnson developed the stern-taskmaster quality he was to carry into the presidency. But the youthful instructor earned the admiration of his rigidly regulated pupils as he was to inspire loyalty among his overworked staff employees when he was successively a Representative, a Senator, Vice President and President.

Manuel Sanchez, Sr., one of Johnson's students at Cotulla, remembered thirty-four years later that the new President "put us to work.

"But he was the kind of teacher you wanted to work for," Sanchez explained. "You felt an obligation to him and to yourself to do your work."

Mrs. Juanita G. Hernandez called Johnson a "down-to-earth, friendly teacher," but she added he was strict.

"If we hadn't done our homework, we had to stay after school that day," she volunteered.

In an area where Spanish was primarily the home language, Johnson decreed that students must speak English at all times. When Juan Gonzales stumbled over the language and didn't pass the high-school entrance test, Johnson took the boy home to Johnson City for the summer to tutor him. The lad made the grade the next fall.

In sun-broiled Cotulla, a South Texas ranching area midway between San Antonio and Laredo, Johnson came face to face with the problems that minority citizens encountered daily. His experiences in attempting to elevate the status of the Mexican Americans there made an indelible impression on him. The young teacher who had rubbed elbows with inequality found it repulsive.

From San Marcos the broad-browed young man, who parted his wavy hair in the middle, went to the growing city of Houston to teach high school public speaking and debate. There he encountered and helped iron out animosities between Mexican-American and Anglo-American pupils.

From there Johnson went to a secretaryship for Representative Kleberg in 1932. But Representative Sam Rayburn, who was a coming man in the House, had his eye on young Lyndon and got him appointed as Texas State Administrator for the

National Youth Administration in August, 1935, at the age of twenty-seven.

There, while he busied himself helping 18,000 young men and women through high school or college and landing about 12,000 of them with some kind of job, Johnson formulated some economic ideas that stayed with him into the presidency. He was not likely to forget the day in 1936 when Roosevelt came personally to inspect some of the charges he had lined up at the side of a road with their shovels at "present arms."

To Lyndon Johnson, President Franklin Roosevelt was, and remained, the Great Man. Yet as President he was not ready, as his critics said, merely to return to the palliatives that Roosevelt had recommended. He would say in a New York speech, shortly after he had laid his anti-poverty program before Congress, that "we must not operate a WPA nuclear project just to provide jobs." Many of his younger listeners were unable to identify his "WPA" reference as Roosevelt's Works Progress Administration. But Johnson had not forgotten its failures. He was a man of the middle years, neither old enough to glorify entirely the FDR experiments nor young enough not to have experienced them.

Deep in his heart, Johnson felt that nothing really very effective had been done for the poor since FDR's time. Fifteen months before he became President he told a Jacksonville, Illinois, audience there had been no "concentrated effort toward improving our national life at home" since Roosevelt had lived. He called this a crying shame.

"When Americans aren't talking politics," he said, "there is very little difference between us about the kind of life we want for all of our people. We don't want slums and sweatshops. We don't want poorhouses and potters' fields.

"We may not want the other fellow to be richer than we are but we don't really want anyone to be poor or sick or unemployed or denied justice and opportunity because of his color and creed."

Although Kennedy had laid the groundwork for the anti-poverty legislation, Johnson made it his own. Walter W. Heller, then chairman of the Council of Economic Advisers, had pulled together the outlines of a program. The bespectacled, academic-looking Heller had pushed the Kennedy administration toward greater liberalism than the then President was willing to accept.

A former chairman of the Department of Economics at the University of Minnesota, Heller was regarded as a "fiscal policy" advocate, one who believed that taxes and the federal budget could be employed to "get the country moving." When he became President, Johnson had some doubts about the Heller theory that the way to balance the budget eventually was to reduce taxes when there was a deficit. But he bought Heller's theories—and Heller. The fact that Heller had had to borrow $16,000 to get along in Washington on his government salary was later made the basis of an appeal by the President to Congress for higher pay for top-level government officials. Congress answered by raising salaries.

If legislation to advance racial equality and to attack the problem of poverty occupied the main stream of his emotions in his second month in office, the necessity of obtaining the tax cut recommended by Kennedy pressed closely upon the President after his State of the Union message.

Johnson had considered for a time in December, 1963, asking Congress to stay in session continuously until the then-beleaguered $11.5 billion tax reduction bill could be passed. He had put his political chips down on this measure as the most likely means of promoting national prosperity in the coming election year. He was convinced that if the economy continued on the upgrade his chances for election would be greatly enhanced.

The President canvassed Democratic congressional leaders about the idea of continuous sessions. These practical-minded gentlemen protested that he just couldn't get a tax bill passed in the time remaining before the Christmas recess.

Johnson didn't give up with that. He got on a phone to his old friend, Senator Clinton P. Anderson of New Mexico, a Senate Finance Committee member. Would it be possible, Johnson asked, to cut the tax bill in half and get action on the rate-reduction section, leaving the remainder of the adjustments until after the first of the year? Would Anderson undertake to introduce such a stripped-down bill in the Senate as an amendment to a House-passed revenue bill and plug for immediate action on it?

The canny Anderson replied that he would like to help the President but he wouldn't move unless Senator Harry F. Byrd of Virginia, chairman of the Finance Committee, agreed to go along. He couldn't possibly get a truncated bill passed if Byrd opposed it, he said.

Under pressure from Johnson, Anderson went to Byrd. The doughty Virginian said "no." That ended that, but as Johnson often remarked in such situations, "You can't win 'em all, but you can sure try."

The President's next action was to summon Byrd to the White House on December 5 to talk the matter over. Kennedy had tried this tactic earlier in the fall. After a chat with the Virginian, the then President strolled out arm-in-arm with his old Senate colleague to announce in the White House lobby that they were in "general agreement" on the terms of the tax reduction measure and how it would be handled in the Senate.

Byrd's subsequent verdict, delivered to a reporter: "We didn't agree on a damned thing."

Byrd, whose control of the committee rested primarily on Southern Democratic and Republican support of the governmental economy positions for which he was noted, had his own ideas about the timing of the tax bill. He was determined to stall it until he could have a look at the new budget Johnson would have to submit to Congress in January.

Unable to prod the Senator into immediate action, Johnson compromised. He would give the Virginian an advance look at the new budget, then being put into final form, if Byrd would agree to speed up action on the House-passed bill when the Senate met again in January. The President promised Byrd some pleasant surprises in expenditures cuts and the Senator bought the deal.

Personalities and experiences of the past played their part in this agreement, as they would with many others Johnson would make with members of Congress. The two men were fond of each other. Beyond that, Byrd had gone all out for Johnson, when the latter was running for the presidential nomination in 1960, to force Virginia Democrats to endorse the then Senate leader and to give him their convention votes. On the other hand, when Kennedy was nominated, Byrd preserved some of his famous "golden silence" and Virginia gave its electoral votes to former Vice President Richard M. Nixon in November. The same Byrd silence, however, did not prevent Johnson from carrying Virginia in 1964.

This ability to deal with the Southern satraps of political power was a tangible asset to Johnson in his relations with a Congress in which Dixie members predominated in the control of important committees. Some of the same men who would have been vocal in criticizing Kennedy's policies in 1964, or who would have remained silent, were eager to make every political excuse for Johnson. He was, after all, the first Southern President in a hundred years. In their estimation, he might have been a sorry representative of their viewpoint, but he was one of them.

Johnson and everybody else knew that the tax reduction was going to be approved by Congress. The President was interested in end results. He wanted action yesterday and he pounded away incessantly for speed and more speed. One of the chief ingredients of the Johnson treatment was persistence. He just never seemed to let up. When he went after a man, he never left him alone until he got what he wanted. He was no respecter of time or place, either.

Senator Dirksen told of encountering the President at a luncheon given by Italian President Antonio Segni in the Italian embassy on January 16, 1964. Seizing Dirksen by the arm, Johnson said, "I'm glad I ran into you. When am I going to get my tax bill?"

Dirksen, a member of the Senate Finance Committee, which then was considering the legislation, told the President he would have his bill in due course. He added that Johnson ought to have a bit of patience, that such things weren't accomplished in a day.

The President snorted that it was costing the economy millions of dollars for every day's delay. He launched into a long harangue about how ways could be taken to speed up the Finance Committee's work.

"He just wouldn't quit," Dirksen recalled. "He kept on bringing up one argument and another until I told him, 'Look, Mr. President, you and I are guests here. Let's talk about this some other time.' " With that, Johnson subsided. But he had Dirksen on the phone again the next morning.

A week later, while he was having lunch at the White House, the President got an emergency call from Lawrence O'Brien. Dirksen had done the administration in by getting the Senate Finance Committee to adopt his amendment to end $445 million in excise levies on cosmetics, jewelry, handbags and wallets, luggage and furs. Johnson wanted to reduce taxes but not those particular ones. He needed those levies continued, as a matter of fact, to keep his budget from becoming that much more unbalanced.

The President picked up the telephones, plural, and put in a barrage of calls. He called every member of the Committee, Democrat and Republican, to argue against this action. This version of the Johnson Treatment varied according to the man who received it. With some Democrats the President was rough and tough, calling their vote for the Dirksen proposal a personal double-cross. With Republicans he argued the point that they were budget balancers. Would they like to have him say it was their fault that the deficit was going to be bigger than he had anticipated?

One Democrat who had voted "wrong," in the view of the White House, confided later that Johnson really didn't need the phone at all. "If he had opened the window of his office, I could have heard him without any telephone," this Senator remarked.

The bespectacled, red-haired O'Brien engaged in some fast footwork. After the President had called a member, O'Brien or one of his aides sought out the Senator to be sure that the pressure was still on. In a couple of hours, O'Brien was able to report back to his boss that the necessary two votes had been changed. When the Committee met again in the afternoon, a majority dutifully rescinded the excise repealer before formally approving the tax reduction bill.

The wheels were slowly beginning to turn in Congress. On January 20, Johnson sent to Capitol Hill a message in which he stated that the economic state of the Union was good. He predicted even better things ahead. He followed it up the next day with a message fixing a spending figure of $97.9 billion for the fiscal year beginning July 1, 1964.

The Republicans didn't have much to argue about so far as the economy went. But they were quick on the draw about the budget, calling it "a figure-juggler's dream . . . contrived out of mathematical malarky and bookkeeping bamboozle."

The GOP members of the House Appropriations Committee, who fired this volley, clearly had some points when they criticized "the gimmicks, the illusions, the sleight of hand that exist within the budget." They said Johnson claimed to have reduced spending by $165 million "simply by terminating the requirement that government agencies pay the Treasury interest on money borrowed during the Korean war." They added that "in reality, of course, no saving at all is effected since the money merely goes out of one government pigeonhole into another."

They noted that the President had whacked $610 million off farm spending on the assumption that new legislation would be passed and had upped income estimates by claiming the Treasury would receive $2.3 billion on government-held export-import bank loans and home mortgages to the public. They said the income estimate involved a "risky assumption."

The heart of the matter, however, was that Johnson was boxing in his critics. He had robbed the Republicans of their budget thunder. He had coaxed "Judge" Howard Smith—who thought at that point that Johnson would carry the South against Goldwater or any other Republican—into relaxing his grip on the civil rights bill, on which he had been holding hearings since January 9. The measure would come out of the House Rules Committee's storage vault January 30. The President would sign the $11.5 billion tax reduction bill into law February 26, using sixty-four pens to do it and making a special trip to deliver three of them to Mrs. Kennedy and her children.

But the anti-poverty measure was taking some doing, even for a President skilled in the ways of Congress. It had taken the administration's experts until March 16 to come up with a bill to carry out the State of the Union declaration of the "war on poverty." There began then some of the most intensive administration lobbying that Congress had ever encountered.

Johnson had put Republican opponents on the defensive because it was difficult for any lawmaker to be counted as in favor of poverty. Here was a bill the President said was a first step toward eliminating some of its causes, especially the lack of education and training among young people, particularly Negroes. It incorporated provisions for self-help for individuals, small businesses and communities. It offered a work-training program for 200,000 potential school dropouts and subsidies for needy college students. It would set up a job-training corps of 40,000 young men and young women, in addition to establishing a domestic Peace Corps.

Republicans attacked this as an election-year gimmick. They

said that Johnson, who was always telling all who would listen how prosperous the country was, was working both sides of the street by emphasizing how poverty-stricken was a substantial portion of the population.

Because his Democratic majority there was more reliable than in the House, Johnson decided the bill would run the gantlet in the Senate first. There the question was not so much whether a bill would pass but whether it would be riddled with amendments. Johnson was on the telephone several times daily, telling old friends that his prestige was at stake, that he needed the anti-poverty bill to win in November and that he would put down a star in his book for those who not only voted for it but who got others to do so. If Hubert Humphrey didn't win the most stars, he deserved them for the long hours he spent trying to compromise crippling amendments and arguing with his colleagues to go along with the President.

There were some cliff-hangers when the Senate got down in late July, 1964, to the business of voting on individual sections of the measure. Republican Senator Winston L. Prouty of Vermont came up with an amendment which would have permitted governors to veto community action programs in their states. This was adopted, 45–44, on the first roll-call vote. When Republicans and their Southern Democratic allies tried to nail this down, however, they found that Humphrey, as the Democratic Whip, had dug up another supporter. The parliamentary situation was such that a subsequent 45–45 tie vote left the Prouty proposal open to further action. Humphrey spaded up another supporter to defeat the Prouty proposition on a third roll-call vote, 46–45.

This really sealed up the major provisions of the bill for its final test. Goldwater, who had been nominated for the presidency at San Francisco by the Republicans, came back to the Senate to receive a bipartisan ovation in the midst of the battle. The Arizona Senator had denounced the anti-poverty program as a "Madison Avenue" stunt by Johnson to get votes in November.

But when the roll call came on passage, Johnson had the horses. The count was 61–34 in favor of the measure. Goldwater and twenty-one other Republicans voted against it, along with Senator Frank Lausche and eleven Southern Democrats.

The President won the support of fifty-one Democrats and ten Republicans. All of the latter classed themselves as liberals. This was a victory but it was only half of the battle.

For four months Johnson's representatives had been working quietly in the House. Speaker McCormack had helped convince Representative Phil M. Landrum of Georgia, third-ranking member of the Education and Labor Committee, that he ought to sponsor the legislation. This broke the ranks of influential Southern Democrats inclined to oppose the bill. Landrum coveted a seat on the all-powerful House Ways and Means Committee. He had been defeated when there was a previous opening, despite administration support, because of his authorship of legislation that organized labor didn't like.

Johnson turned the heat on Southern Democrats with the result that when the showdown came on July 28, the traffic-directing Rules Committee voted 8–7 to send the measure to the House floor. On that vote, two Southern Democrats, Chairman Howard W. Smith of Virginia and Representative William W. Colmer of Mississippi, joined five Republicans in opposition.

The lobbying went into high gear then. Johnson's liaison men and representatives of every interested governmental department and agency swarmed the House halls. The Speaker's office was clogged all day long with members who were being called in and given various forms of the Johnson treatment. It was administered personally by administration aides to supplement what the President was doing in the White House conferences and on the telephone with the lawmakers.

Representative Charles E. Goodell, New York Republican, told the House when the bill was finally brought before it that "unprecedented pressure" had been brought on both Democratic and Republican members to support it. Goodell, an opponent of the measure, said that those who wouldn't back the legislation were asked to "take a walk" and not vote against it. Representative James Roosevelt, California Democrat, challenged Goodell to name names. The Republican declined.

Landrum, in the center of this maelstrom, remarked at one point, "If I live through this without getting two ulcers, I'll be lucky."

The pressure was so intense that sponsors of the legislation in the House yielded to a demand of the North Carolina delegation and accepted an amendment specifying that Adam Yarmolinsky, McNamara's special assistant, who had helped draw up the measure, would have no part in its administration.

This was an aspect of the Johnson treatment that was not comforting to look upon. Johnson had ordered the sacrifice of Yarmolinsky, a short, black-haired, abrasive New Yorker, whose Russian-born father, Avram, was an editor and translator, and whose poet-translator mother, Babette Deutsch, was a signer of left-wing petitions.

Landrum himself pronounced sentence on Yarmolinsky by telling the House he had assurances from the highest authority that "this gentleman will have absolutely nothing to do with the program."

By sacrificing Yarmolinsky, Johnson gained a problematical thirty Southern votes for the bill. Yarmolinsky, who had been loaned by the Pentagon to the drafters of the program, had been publicly attacked by Segregationist Governor George C. Wallace of Alabama and General Edwin Walker, who had been relieved of his command in Germany after political statements to his troops.

Yarmolinsky had been expected to become deputy director of the anti-poverty program, since he had been responsible for pulling together its divergent aspects. But the trouble was that he seemed to personify a potential campaign issue in the South and Johnson had to have Dixie votes to pass the bill.

It came to the point of a showdown in Speaker McCormack's

office, with all sides represented. Representative Harold D. Cooley of North Carolina and Representative Mendel L. Rivers of South Carolina told R. Sargent Shriver, designated by Johnson to head the anti-poverty program, that he would take his choice between having Yarmolinsky or having a bill. This possibly was not far from the truth, although no one would ever know with exactitude.

Shriver resorted to evasive tactics. He could not speak for the President, he said. He couldn't say in advance that he would or would not recommend Yarmolinsky. Cooley and Rivers had been through all this before. Call the White House, they suggested. With no other way out, Shriver did. He reported back that "The President has no objection to my saying that if I were appointed, I would not recommend Yarmolinsky."

Yarmolinsky had been an intelligent, loyal aide. But he was under attack from the far right. Johnson had to have the anti-poverty bill. If the aide's connection with it was going to cost the threatened thirty votes—which would have defeated the measure—then the President's decision was that Yarmolinsky would have to go back to the Defense Department.

When Landrum got a 228–190 vote to substitute the Senate's version of the bill for that of the House, Johnson and his aides breathed easier. This was only a preliminary test, however, and they were not out of the woods. Elderly "Judge" Smith, who had opposed action in the Rules Committee, caught them napping momentarily with a motion to strike out the enacting clause, a move which would have killed the measure. This motion won approval on a standing vote but a roll call was demanded which gave administration forces time to rally their absentees and defeat it.

The following day, August 8, 1964, the House passed the bill by a 226–184 vote. It had taken Johnson exactly eight months since he first formally recommended it, but he had his anti-poverty bill. He had demonstrated that he was a "can do" President who could get things accomplished in Congress.

On the domestic scene everything was coming up political roses for the President. But while he was absorbed in this aspect of his stewardship, from the storm-shrouded world outside there had come an ominous crack of thunder and the unexpected flash of lightning violence, striking near home.

6 An International Crisis Arrives

WHEN RIOTING EXPLODED into bloodshed in the Panama Canal Zone less than seven weeks after he took office, President Johnson was caught with his diplomatic guard down. He didn't even have an ambassador in Panama, although it had been four months since Joseph S. Farland had resigned his post there as an outgrowth of a series of disagreements with the State Department which caused him to believe that his warnings of increasing anti-American sentiment were being ignored.

A long-simmering dispute had come to a head in Panama on January 9. The old question of sovereignty over the Canal Zone—which had been left shadowy in the treaty signed with Panama after Teddy Roosevelt had promoted a revolution against Colombia and obtained the ten-mile-wide strip—was wrapped up in the flying of Panamanian flags in the Zone.

Former President Eisenhower had decided there should be "visual evidence" of Panama's "titular sovereignty" over the Zone and had directed that the Panamanian and U.S. flags be flown at a single site—the U.S. Canal Zone Building. A year later the two nations agreed their flags should be flown together, and only together, throughout the Zone.

In December, 1963, after Johnson had become President,

Zone officials directed that, beginning in January, no flags would be flown in front of schools. On January 7, a group of American students hoisted a U.S. flag at the American high school at Balboa, at the Pacific end of the Canal. The school principal hauled it down but students raised another and it stayed.

Incensed Panamanians marched on the Balboa school January 9 and planted their flag there. American students drove out the Panamanians and reportedly defiled the latter's flag. Rioting broke out. Hundreds of Panamanians tried to storm into the Canal Zone. Snipers on the rooftops wounded four Americans, and U.S. troops began then to return the fire. When the hostilities stopped, there were twenty dead, including three Americans, and hundreds had been injured. President Roberto Chiari of Panama severed diplomatic relations with the United States and demanded "complete revision" of treaty provisions against which Panama had been protesting, including the issues of sovereignty and of U.S. payments to Panama.

Johnson's reaction was predictable. He called in an aide and said, "Get me the President of Panama—what's his name—on the phone. I want to talk to him."

"Mr. President," the aide protested, "you can't do that. It isn't protocol. You just can't do things like that."

"Why in the hell can't I?" Johnson asked. "Come on, now, get him on the phone."

When the connection was made, Johnson said he understood the Panamanian executive's position because he had an election coming up, too. But he said the matter could be discussed on a diplomatic level and he intended to send one of his best men, in whom he had complete confidence, to see if the difficulties couldn't be ironed out. Chiari agreed this was a sensible course and said he would talk to Johnson's representatives.

With that Johnson hurried off a group of Latin-American experts. They were headed by Thomas C. Mann, a former ambassador to Mexico, whom he had appointed in December as Assistant Secretary of State for Inter-American affairs. Mann had orders to overhaul U.S. operations in and relations with South American countries. Before he had become President, Johnson had felt there was great weakness in the Kennedy administration's contacts with the Latin Americans. But he kept his silence as Vice President under his rule that he would not give advice unless it was specifically asked for. In this case it wasn't.

Falling into a common executive error, the new President planted one of Mann's feet in the White House, for direct reports to him, and the other in the State Department. Secretary Rusk, who otherwise was being upgraded rapidly by Johnson, knew immediately he could whistle for all the practical direction he would have over Mann's activities.

Johnson's dependence on Mann to solve the Panama crisis was in line with his general theory that if any particularly vexatious problem arose, the way to dispose of it in an orderly fashion was to assign a staff member to investigate all of the pros and cons. After that the Master Planner could move his ducks into a row and decide what was to be done to salvage the situation.

A native of Laredo, Texas, Mann had learned Spanish as well as English in his early boyhood. But his delegation ran into difficulty with the translation of an English-Spanish version of a proposed agreement which said in English that the United States would "discuss" a possible revision of the Panama treaty and said in Spanish that the two powers would "negotiate" a new treaty. Chiari wanted a U.S. pledge to negotiate, to help in his campaign to elect a chosen successor as President of Panama. While Johnson understood the political necessities of the Panamanian President, he was not going to incur the thunderous dissent he felt would follow any action of his that might lower the American flag in Panama.

Matters rocked along until March, 1964, when efforts of a five-nation negotiating team of the Organization of American States (OAS) seemed about to produce an agreement.

At that point, Johnson called in his old friends from Con-

gress to consult with him. He asked them, in effect, what they
thought he ought to do. This Kennedy never would have done.
He had learned the hard way that all he was likely to get from
such conferences was disagreement. But Johnson still felt that
he could "reason" with his former colleagues and get a unani-
mous agreement. It didn't work out exactly that way.

Senators Mansfield, Humphrey, J. William Fulbright, of Arkansas, chairman of the Senate Foreign Relations Committee,
and Wayne Morse of Oregon, chairman of the Latin-American
Subcommittee, took the position that the United States should
not refuse to participate in discussions of whether there were
some bad features in the old Panama Canal Treaty.

They, along with others present, opposed any advance concession that the treaty would be renegotiated, as Chiari was
demanding. They generally supported a proposal drafted by
Ellsworth Bunker, U.S. representative to the OAS, under which
diplomatic relations with Panama might be restored and talks
could go ahead.

There was, however, some Democratic and Republican pressure on the President which he did not feel he could ignore in
advance of his own election against any advance admission
that there were features in the treaty that might need revision.
Kennedy had run into this performance in semantics, with all
of its corseted unrealities, and he much preferred transacting
business in the phonetics of practicalities.

But Johnson was feeling his way at this point in an unfamiliar field and he wanted the reassurance of backing from his
old colleagues. He got what might have been called a split
decision. Senators Dirksen, Bourke B. Hickenlooper, Iowa Republican, Russell and Representative Halleck were against any
discussions. They voiced the view that discussions could only
lead in time to U.S. concessions. Johnson knew this was where
the arrow was aimed but he wasn't certain what to do about it.

Last on the list to be called upon at the round-table discussion, Dirksen told the President he did not believe the United

States should move at all while Panama continued to demand commitments in advance on any talks.

"Hell, Mr. President," he said, "if we give an inch we will be saying to every little country in the world that the way to get something out of us is to break off relations, attack our embassy and make demands on us."

Influenced by this division within the ranks, Johnson reacted furiously when Chiari sent him a message urging substitution of the word "negotiate" for the word "discuss" in a proposed declaration by the two Presidents on the treaty.

The OAS committee felt it was getting close to a two-President statement leaving the dispute open to some future settlement. Mann had said the proposed agreement looked all right to him and the OAS committee was assured by Panamanian Ambassador Sanchez Gavito that Chiari would approve it. Members went ahead with a news conference announcement that an agreement had been reached.

But the White House promptly torpedoed this by putting out an announcement denying that Johnson had given the statement his approval. The following day the President told a ceremonial OAS meeting there had been "no genuine meeting of minds" with Chiari.

This was not in the mold of what might have been called decisive presidential action. Thus the Panamanian situation was left simmering on the back burner until after the presidential election. Diplomatic relations had been restored and there was relative peace in the Canal Zone.

Characteristically, however, Johnson had a stick in the closet. Before he commissioned Robert B. Anderson, a Texas Republican who had served Eisenhower as Secretary of the Treasury, as a negotiator, the President ordered a study of the feasibility of a sea-level canal which might, or might not, be built through Panama. This would mean the practical abandonment of the present canal, with its dependable revenues for Panama. The implications were not lost on the Panamanians.

It was not until December 18, 1964, that Johnson felt the situation was well enough in hand to announce that the United States had decided to proceed with the building of a sea-level canal in Central America or Colombia. He said he would propose "the negotiation of an entirely new treaty on the existing Panama Canal." Rebuilding of the existing canal was regarded as entirely feasible.

At first, Johnson had reacted to his initial international crisis as if it were a sort of side-line development to the domestic affairs that pressed in upon him. After his original phone conversation with Chiari, the President spent the following day holding two conferences on domestic matters. He had an unhurried chat with James A. Farley, who had once been FDR's campaign manager, and because he was behind time getting to lunch he had to forgo his usual 1 P.M. swim in the White House pool. (He bragged he could cross this pool six times without stopping.) But in the afternoon he found time for a nap.

This relaxed reaction to trouble in the field of foreign affairs contrasted sharply with Kennedy's response to his first engagement with an unsettled world. It would be unfair to compare the Panama flareup with the disastrous Bay of Pigs affair, but in each case a predecessor President had left behind a legacy of an unsolved problem which had to be grappled with by the man who came after him.

In Kennedy's case, Eisenhower had bequeathed him the decision on what to do about the refugees who were being trained for an invasion of Cuba. Eisenhower, at what he described as a "little meeting" at the White House in 1960, said the decision had been made to "go ahead and train these people." It was, he said, "never anything more than that."

It was obviously nothing more than a time bomb being fused but not connected to the charger. This put the firing pin in Kennedy's hands and, inexperienced as he was in the role of Chief Executive, he felt he was committed to go through with the operation. The thought obviously was in his mind that if he called off this risky venture, the Republicans would say that Eisenhower had worked out a fool-proof plan to regain Cuba and Kennedy had vetoed it because of his reputed leanings to the left.

Kennedy, a new and uncertain President as Johnson was in the Panamanian crisis, felt constrained to take the judgment of the Chiefs of Staff and the experts he had read about in gee-whiz magazine articles but didn't know intimately.

Admiral Arleigh A. (Thirty-knot) Burke, then Chairman of the Joint Chiefs, came to sit in the chair by the President's desk and say that to him the proposed strategy of invasion seemed to have a reasonable hope of success.

The late President, however, was personally bitter about the advice he got from Allen W. Dulles, head of the Central Intelligence Agency (CIA).

"He sat there," Kennedy said, pointing to a chair next to his presidential desk, "and he told me that he was more confident about this invasion of Cuba than he had been of success in Guatemala when we went in there.

"But I don't blame him or anybody else for the Bay of Pigs disaster. It was my fault, and only mine, for ordering them to go ahead. I just didn't know how to evaluate the advice they gave me."

In the final analysis, however, the late President said that the experience had been of benefit to him. He had learned, he said, not to depend on any man's public reputation but to examine his recommendations minutely before acting upon them. He said this had helped him immensely in the Cuban missile crisis of 1962.

Johnson had been through this latter crisis with Kennedy. As Vice President he had attended all except one of the many meetings of the EXCOM, the executive committee of the National Security Council. He had watched the cauldron of presidential advice boil up, explode into tangential proposals and then subside into the relative calm of agreement on a short-of-war action. Johnson was fond of saying that the "coolest man in the room" in this crisis was Kennedy.

But he never got around to the point of promising that if he were faced with a similar eyeball-to-eyeball confrontation with the threat of nuclear destruction he would follow the same process. Indeed, those who knew him best felt Johnson was more likely to act finally on instinct, although he would listen to what others had to say before making up his mind.

Comparing the operations of the two men, an aide who worked for both characterized Johnson and Kennedy as "political men who exercised great wariness" in approaching any problem.

"They both liked to get up and walk around a problem, to see all sides of it for themselves," he said. "They both wanted all of the information they could get. I thought Kennedy was a great man on the phone in digging out facts, but Johnson is even more so."

Basically, Johnson's approach to world problems was similar to that he followed in handling domestic matters. He felt that if men could just talk together candidly they could be counted upon eventually to reach an understanding. He told the Washington diplomatic corps shortly after he became President, "We must try to understand what the other man's problems are and communicate that understanding to each other with integrity. We must be alert to points of danger, but equally alert to points of common interest."

Johnson liked the levelheaded manner and the astringent language in which Rusk put international problems in perspective for the American people. And he applauded Rusk's ability to "understand the other man's problems."

The President told with relish an incident that occurred one day when he, Rusk and Secretary McNamara got on a State Department elevator to go up to the top floor for lunch.

The young man at the elevator buttons at the moment became flustered in the presence of all this brass. Instead of pushing the "up" button, he pushed "down." As the elevator descended, Johnson glowered at the culprit.

Rusk stepped into the breach.

"You know," he said to the embarrassed young man, "this happens quite often. I've got on this elevator many times and have gotten confused, pushing the 'down' button when I meant to go up. This happens to all of us."

The young man grinned in gratitude and the President relaxed with a smile.

"That's the kind of a man Rusk is," Johnson said appreciatively in discussing the incident. "He makes people feel at ease. And he's the same way in dealing with nations. They think he understands their problems and they appreciate that."

Johnson added that when he had told his wife about the incident, she had said, "Now, Lyndon, that's the way you ought to be."

Rusk was a man who said he didn't want to "embrace adjectives." There would never be for him the "agonizing reappraisal," the "brinkmanship" or the "massive retaliation" John Foster Dulles had coined. He eschewed Dulles's moral platitudes and he declined to indulge in Acheson's caustic wit. He was, under Kennedy, the soul of self-effacement and of caution. But Johnson had other needs. He wanted Rusk to say his lines in the limelight and the Secretary dutifully doubled under Johnson the number of news conferences that he had held while Kennedy was in office.

With Kennedy, Rusk's primary job had been to "clear away the underbrush" for presidential decisions. Johnson could use that quality, but he also needed some of the finesse of which the Secretary was capable and with which the President was not notably equipped. You did not twist foreign ministers' arms, as you did senatorial limbs, and extract the same satisfying results.

As Kennedy had been before him, Johnson was pleased with Rusk's favorite quotation, which came from a circuit-riding preacher in the Secretary's native Georgia: "Pray as if it were up to God; work as if it were up to you."

But for all of their admiration for Rusk's qualities, neither Kennedy nor Johnson was willing to leave any final decision to the Secretary of State, as Eisenhower had to Dulles.

Harry Truman once said that "the President makes foreign policy." When I asked Kennedy where it was made in his administration, he grinned a little, shifted his weight in his rocker, pointed a finger at the floor and replied, "I guess when you're talking about foreign policy, we make most of it here."

Rusk subscribed fully to this theory. He said he did not believe any President should relinquish his role of what John Marshall called "the sole organ of the nation in its external relations." In that connection, Rusk observed, "It is possible for the President to delegate too much power to his Secretary of State."

While he was invariably cordial, Kennedy always addressed Rusk as "Mr. Secretary." Perhaps because they were closer personally, Johnson always saluted the big, balding two-hundred-pound Secretary as "Dean."

In hewing out policies, Kennedy was likely to call in a dozen officials, without too much regard for rank, into a seminar in which ideas were tossed about freely. What the late President wanted primarily from the men about him was a freshet of ideas. They might be good or bad but he felt competent to sort them out. When he had heard them all, he went into an intimate conference with Brother Bob and then he made his decision. It could be debated whether this method of decision-making was good or bad, but, as Bob Kennedy pointed out to me, the essential element was that Bob could differ with the President, be overruled in a final decision and lose no face, as would any other adviser whose recommendations had been rejected.

There was no brother act in the Johnson administration, however. Lacking such an alter ego, Johnson preferred to meet with Rusk, Bundy, McNamara and other advisers in small groups. He didn't want any seminar, where he felt a great deal of time was wasted by each individual's feeling that it was necessary for him to speak up to justify his presence. Johnson wanted what he considered the best advice and not too much conversation about it. In this latter respect, he was like Kennedy in that the man who put his proposition succinctly got attention while the individual who traced circles in the air with "ifs," "ands" and "buts," quickly lost the President's ear. This was true in Kennedy's relationship with Adlai E. Stevenson, the chief U.S. representative to the United Nations. Because he was a highly intelligent man, for Stevenson there was no black and no white. Kennedy recognized this, but he was impatient with Stevenson's roundabout approach to any problem. As Bob Kennedy put it, "Stevenson was not a man my brother would have chosen to ride around the world with on a tandem bicycle."

Johnson, on the other hand, accepted Stevenson's reflective approach with a great deal of respect. He had found the United Nations Ambassador fully cooperative with him and he, who then was President by accident, appreciated the deference accorded to him by a man who had been nominated twice by his party for the highest office, even if he hadn't won it. Stevenson and Kennedy perhaps had occupied the same intellectual plane too long not to be somewhat suspicious of each other. There was no such feeling between Johnson and Stevenson, each of whom was somewhat amazed at the other's abilities.

Johnson began his international career as President in December, 1963, when he called in Dean Acheson, who had been Harry Truman's Secretary of State and who had served Kennedy in an unofficial capacity in such crises as those involving the Russian introduction of missiles into Cuba. Giving Acheson an outline of his ideas, he asked his long-time friend to draft a speech for him to deliver before the United Nations.

When the draft came back, Johnson sent it to the State Department for changes. Then he gathered together his most trusted advisers, tossed the script on the table in front of them and invited further changes. After an hour of competitive inter-lineations, Johnson had a final draft that only needed to be retyped.

When he went to New York on December 17, Johnson told the United Nations General Assembly that the assassin's bullets had not altered the American course; that his administration would continue the Kennedy course in world affairs.

"We are more than ever opposed to the doctrines of hate and violence, in our own land and around the world," he said.

"We believe more than ever in the rights of man, all men of every color, in our own land and around the world.

"And more than ever we support the United Nations as the best instrument yet devised to promote the peace of the world and to promote the well-being of mankind."

As Johnson was well aware, the world was in transition, with nationalism breaking through the thin crust of the military alli-ances. These had been a shield behind which the war-logged nations of Western Europe crouched while they laboriously rebuilt their economies and gathered defense strength of their own—with American help. By late 1963 these countries were emerging from behind this shield, exhibiting a new confidence in their ability to manage their own destiny and either petu-lantly or suavely notifying the Americans to stay out of their business.

While the United States remained for all practical purposes the ultimate guardian of a peace continually threatened by Communist aggressiveness, it no longer was the unchallenged leader of the Free World. American aid still was welcome, but American ideas considerably less so.

A case in point was General de Gaulle, who was to say a few months later that Europe must free itself from "subordination" to the Americans. U.S. allies continued to trade with Cuba and with Communist China despite American protests. There was, indeed, a spirit that almost amounted to anti-Americanism in many countries which had received aid.

Kennedy had assessed these developments as calling for a fundamental change in the paternalistic American attitude that the world must be made over in the image of the limited U.S. democracy. As he said in Salt Lake City, Utah, in the fall of 1963:

"We cannot remake other nations in our image, nor can we enact their laws, nor can we operate their governments, nor can we dictate their policies. . . .

"We must recognize that every nation determines its policy in terms of its own interests. . . . The purpose of foreign policy is not to provide an outlet for our sentiments of hope or indignation; it is to shape real events in a real world.

"Our interest is best served by preserving and protecting a world of diversity in which no monolithic power can acquire the ability to dominate freedom."

Threshing about in the unfamiliar swampland of this world of diversity, Johnson found temporary footing on the doubtful theme that Americans were loved by all of the peoples of the globe. He told a gathering of Internal Revenue Bureau officials early in 1964:

"All of these [international crises] are distresses, and from time to time you will hear alarmists and people who like to jump on their government, people who like to criticize, people who find it quite impossible to be affirmative and constructive. They will join with some of our opponents, and they will be almost as much a problem as some of our other enemies. . . . So, regardless of what you hear and what some belly-achers say, we are a much-beloved people throughout the world. . . .

"Freedom prospers through the fair discussion of honest differences. Both at home and abroad we welcome such discussion. But neither at home nor abroad is there any need for twisted arguments that damage the good name of our country. . . . "

The we're-loved-by-all theme subsequently gave way to one of policy proliferation. Johnson said in a January television broadcast, "I think, as long as we are living in a world with 120 nations, that we have got to realize that we have got 120 foreign policies." Republicans ridiculed this prescription and the President quickly abandoned it.

To preserve the unofficial détente Kennedy had been able to establish with Russia, Johnson quickly took up the personal correspondence his predecessor had carried on with Khrushchev. Rusk had thought this unwise, but Johnson insisted on it. The new President was not the kind of man who ever would concede that he could not hold his own with a Russian dictator. Kennedy had felt the same way, but after his Vienna meeting with the Soviet Premier, he was not so certain of it.

Khrushchev began 1964 with a flurry of cordial messages and greetings to Johnson and other Western leaders. He arranged an interview in which he said, among other things:

"We want to see the development of relations of peaceful cooperation, good neighborliness and friendship between the people of the United States and the Soviet Union." He followed this up on January 2 with a twenty-one page note to every government with which Russia maintained diplomatic relations. He proposed an international agreement renouncing the use of force in settling territorial and frontier disputes.

There was nothing new in this, but it made no difference if the man had said it twenty times before. If he came out on an occasion like this, he would get world attention from the majority of citizens who couldn't remember what he said previously. But the administration had napped again on the propaganda front. The best the State Department could do in this case was to call the Russian message "a disappointing response to President Johnson's call for progress toward peace" in the Chief Executive's New Year's statement.

The Christmas conference with Chancellor Ludwig Erhard of West Germany at the Johnson ranch was Johnson's first presidential in-depth adventure in personal diplomacy. Erhard had suffered through all the folderol of a Southwestern barbecue with the usual overcooked, oversmoked meat (and no good German beer) because he knew Johnson had a special, personal interest in Germany.

This had begun when Kennedy had sent the then Vice President to Berlin in 1962 after the Communists had erected their wall. The grim necessity for some American show of strength there had been emphasized at the time by a report to the White House that there was in West Berlin "so little will to resist that the Communists could virtually walk into West Berlin and take it over."

Kennedy had been indecisive about whether to try to knock the wall down and risk Russian intervention in behalf of the East German regime. The weight of subsequent opinion seemed to be that if he had reacted quickly with military force the Communists might have backed down. But that was only hindsight. After his Bay of Pigs disaster, Kennedy was in no mood to bring on a showdown on nuclear war.

Johnson had done a tremendous job in lifting the morale of West Berliners on his visit. Anyone who saw, as I did, the vast outpouring of humanity that greeted him as a symbol of liberty on a seven-mile walk and ride through the war-scarred streets of that city could not gainsay his triumph for Free World morale. As though he were campaigning in Texas, the Vice President got out of his car, walked the overcrowded streets, shook hands, patted children on the head, waved to those hanging out of building windows and generally deported himself as a man would who was running for office in the United States.

The Berliners loved it and when Johnson spoke from the local parliament building, to say that the United States would stand firmly behind West Berlin, 100,000 citizens who had packed themselves into the square cheered him thunderously.

So when Erhard came to the Texas ranch to talk, he knew

how this new President of the United States felt about his country. In the comfortable den of the ranch house, the two men arranged themselves in front of a white brick fireplace with a raised hearth. Interpreters flanked them as Erhard settled his ample frame into a rocking chair with brown padded cushions and Johnson lounged in a straight chair covered in brown and green chintz.

Johnson began the conference with a question.

"What is it," he asked, "that we can do in East-West relations that we have not done?"

Erhard's face broke into an expressive smile.

"You know, Mr. President, that was precisely the question that I planned to put to you," he said.

From there the two men went on to explore in their relatively brief meeting what new formulas might be evolved to reduce tensions with the Russians over West Germany and Berlin. They found no ready-made answers. But they seemed agreed that the climate they had established would at least stimulate thinking on the problem in their two countries.

The sad fact, of course, was that these heralded meetings between heads of state seldom produced any definitive ideas that might lead to positive action. It was not until six months later, when Erhard made another visit to Washington in June, 1964, that the two men talked turkey. Erhard then had brought along the idea of opening negotiations for economic relations with Communist China. The Chancellor abandoned this thought after Johnson told him this would complicate efforts to maintain the Western World's position in Asia.

This had been an outgrowth of the January intelligence—later substantiated by action—that De Gaulle intended to establish diplomatic ties with Peking. As a man of Congress, Johnson had participated in innumerable rituals in which the lawmakers registered opposition to any recognition of the Chinese Communists. He had been bound by the political necessities to support the untenable theory that Chiang Kai-shek represented the millions of Chinese and one day would return to the mainland (but not with American assistance) to restore his type of democratic government.

As President, Johnson still was tied to these shibboleths. He could only be horrified and react vigorously against a fact of life—that Red China existed—which had been avoided with determination by the American people en masse. Mao Tse-tung ruled some 700 million people who would make their weight felt in world affairs no matter how much the white American might deplore it.

Peking, engaged in a basic conflict with Moscow over which type of Communism would subjugate the world, was reaching out for allies. It stood to gain one that had been a staunch friend of the United States since the days of Lafayette. And there was literally nothing that Johnson—or any other President, for that matter—could do about it.

To attempt to mediate one Asian crisis, Johnson called in then Attorney General Kennedy and asked him to go as a personal envoy to talk with President Sukarno of Indonesia to try to dissuade him from his announced intentions to "confront and crush" the new Federation of Malaysia.

Kennedy had decided after a short skiing vacation at Aspen, Colorado, that he would stay on as Attorney General for a time. He was recovering gradually from the shock of his brother's death and Johnson's request was by way of a presidential pledge that the ties with the Kennedy administration remained solid.

Bob Kennedy had dropped in on Sukarno in Jakarta two years previously and had won the volatile Indonesian leader's promise to pursue a more peaceful course in his demands for the Netherlands East Indies. Acting on Johnson's suggestion, Kennedy flew off to Tokyo to see Sukarno, a frequent visitor there. In two preliminary meetings over the teacups there some progress was made. When he met Sukarno again in Jakarta on January 22, after having talked with the leaders of the Philippines and Malaysia, Kennedy got from the Indonesian President an agreement for a cease fire in the Borneo guerrilla war and a promise to consult with the other two countries at the foreign minister level. But a few hours later Sukarno was exhorting a youth rally with the words: "Onward, never retreat! Crush Malaysia! Indonesia may change her tactics, but our goal will remain the same."

When Kennedy came back to report to Johnson, he found that everything was changed. On his return from previous trips of this nature, the Attorney General and his brother had closeted themselves for intimate discussions before any others were summoned to get a briefing. But when Bob Kennedy walked into Johnson's office to make his report, he found a group of members of Congress flanking the President. What would have been a bark-off discussion between him and his brother, if the latter had been alive, became instead a delicately restricted account of what Kennedy had learned and had accomplished on his mission.

The Johnson methods were his own. While his world objectives matched those of Kennedy's, the new President approached them differently, just as he would introduce some elements of his own into his handling of domestic affairs.

7 In the Market Place

BUSINESSMEN are politically stupid—big businessmen."

With that acid declaration to me late in October, 1963, John F. Kennedy summed up one of his principal frustrations in the presidency. As he himself once remarked, it seemed he could never get business "to take 'yes' for an answer."

Kennedy's repeated assurances that he wanted the men in the market place to make a profit and that he had no intention of hamstringing their operations so long as they remained decently aware of the public interest, had never caught on. There remained in the minds of businessmen the memory of his savage steel price roll-back when, in seventy-two hours beginning at 5:45 P.M. on April 10, 1962, he had used the massive power of the presidency to reverse an industry decision to charge more for its wares.

That the late President believed he had been double-crossed after coaxing the United Steel Workers into accepting what he called a noninflationary wage-benefit settlement, seemed not to matter at all. He had merely confirmed the belief of a seeming majority of businessmen that any Democratic President was antibusiness.

Frankin D. Roosevelt had gloried in this opposition and had taunted business at almost every turn. Harry Truman had tried to seize the steel mills to enforce a strike settlement and had been turned back by the Supreme Court. Kennedy, the son of a businessman who rolled up millions, felt hurt that industrialists would not accept his assurances that he wanted to work with them and not against them.

He put his frustration into words when he told a June, 1962, news conference: "I can't believe that I'm where business—big business—wants me." He said that big businessmen were Republicans and had always been Republicans.

Lyndon Johnson's rejection of this theory and his amazingly successful campaign to enlist big businessmen in his cause provided the most dramatic demonstration of the political change-over in the presidency after Kennedy's assassination.

Johnson, who had dealt with Texas oil men all of his public life, had broadened his acquaintance with business leaders as Vice President. As chairman of the President's Committee on Equal Employment Opportunities he had come into personal contact with hundreds of manufacturers and industrialists. These men had found the Texan cooperative, patient and understanding of the problems involved in providing job opportunities for Negro workers. He had behind him the potent power to recommend cancellation of government contracts that meant the difference between profit and loss for many companies if they did not comply with the program. This was the stick behind the door, but it stayed there as Johnson pushed his doctrine that if men would just reason together they could come to some satisfactory agreement.

Johnson had applied the same methods with labor leaders in getting them to put the signatures of their unions on pledges not to discriminate against Negroes. There were no government contracts he could cancel with the unions, but he could persuade.

When the new President began calling business and labor

leaders to the White House early in December, 1963, he knew the names and faces of most of his visitors. To those he didn't know, the President was likely to say, "Call me Lyndon. I'd like to get on a first name basis with you."

This was the kind of thing Kennedy never would have done. He would have been cordial and correct but he would have viewed any such appeal as Johnson's as corny. And he had a giant-sized disdain for corn.

In the first weeks of December Johnson was missing no licks. When President George Meany of the AFL-CIO sent word he would like to see the Chief Executive, the President told him to report to the Spring Valley home where the First Family then was living, and ride to the White House with him. The new President knew such a journey would be well publicized by newsmen and photographers. The conversation between the two men dealt mainly with politics. In the course of it, labor's monetary and manpower cards were laid out. Johnson found them highly gratifying.

When he called union leaders and businessmen to the White House on December 4, Johnson was ready with an announcement that he was fixing as a goal for his administration a five million increase in jobs to a seventy-five million total. Then, in separate speeches in the Cabinet Room to members of the AFL-CIO Executive Council and members of the Business Council, the President appealed for support in getting the tax reduction and civil rights bills enacted.

When the labor leaders filed into the Cabinet Room, Meany led off with a little speech to Johnson: "We are here today to tell you that we are behind you one hundred per cent. We are citizens first and union members second."

Meany outlined the unemployment and automation problems as he saw them. He said labor's answer was the thirty-five-hour work week—which Kennedy had opposed—but said he was willing to listen to alternatives. Johnson promised to think up some.

Leading the labor leaders out into the flower garden, the Chief Executive made another impassioned speech for their support. By what they said to him at the end of the meeting, Johnson knew he had their backing. All this had been easy. He knew, and the leaders knew, that labor had nowhere else to go politically. Now the task was to win over business.

Back in the Cabinet Room, he gave the Business Council the Johnson treatment. He whipped out a list of statistics to back his contention that there had been thirty-four months of "unbroken economic expansion." He said the tax cut then "languishing before Congress" could boost the gross national product an extra $12 billion in 1964 and by $30 billion a year thereafter. He described it as "both your defense against a sagging economy and a breath of free air for our free enterprise system."

Moving the businessmen to the Fish Room adjacent to his Oval Room office, Johnson asked them to bow their heads in a moment of silent prayer for Kennedy, whom he called "one of the greatest exponents of free enterprise we ever had."

Then Johnson told the businessmen:

"I am the President, but I can do nothing without the people. You represent the people. I need you and I want you by my side.

"This administration wants to help you. We are not prolabor, or pro-business or pro-any special sector. I happen to believe that a strong, vibrant economy is as essential to our leadership in the Free World as our military hardware.

"I challenge this assembly of the finest business brains in all the world to take up arms against stagnation and delay. I challenge this group of business leaders to assault the persistent problems of our generation, and arouse yourselves to put an end to them.

"I join you in taking up this challenge."

Responding, Frederick Kappel, Council president and chairman of the board of American Telephone and Telegraph Company, read a formal statement in which he told the President he wanted to "assure you in behalf of the Council that we have undiminished confidence in the economic and moral strength of our country under your leadership."

Johnson said he intended to carry on with the programs that Kennedy had laid down. But he inspired a confidence in businessmen that his predecessor could not because business tycoons found the intellectual atmosphere surrounding Kennedy strange to their taste.

The late President had wooed businessmen assiduously. He had invited them to the White House, had seated them on the beige sofas in front of his office fireplace and almost always had opened the conversation with the remark, "I'd like to hear what you think I should do."

His callers were never averse to telling him that he ought to cut government spending, balance the budget and reduce the outflow of gold to foreign nations. He would explain at length the steps he had taken to attain these objectives. Nevertheless there was a characteristic grumble from these visitors when they were interviewed by reporters as they came out of the White House. It ran this way: "He was rough with management in the steel situation, but I haven't seen him get tough with labor."

The business world just didn't believe that Kennedy meant what he said. The fact that big business leaders credited Johnson with sincerity could be traced primarily to the new President's personal efforts to make them feel he was interested in them as important individuals and not as mere bloodless abstractions who headed equally bloodless corporations.

In Johnson they found a man who was familiar with their language of production cost, profit and loss. He also was a President who shook hands with every man in the room when he invited large groups of them to the White House. He was easily accessible on the phone and, in fact, often got them on the line with a flattering request for their advice.

The reaction of one leading businessman after a White House briefing was more or less typical. "That was most impressive," he said. "Is there a citizen's group for Johnson you can join?"

The President, of course, had a couple of other factors going for him. One was the prosperity that was rolling ahead unchecked. The other was Senator Barry Goldwater, whose views on some issues the big businessmen found somewhat frightening. But while the new President made obvious headway with the satraps of the corporations, the little and medium-sized businessmen did not fall over their feet in any rush to his banner. Many of them had been Goldwater men for a long time and they weren't about to switch. Very few of the small businessmen were on the White House invitation lists and few were consulted personally by the President.

When the "finest brains" of the early December meeting sat down for cocktails with the President and Mrs. Johnson, the cozy circle included such men as Crawford Greenewalt, head of the giant Du Pont company, who had been one of the heaviest contributors to the Republican party, and Sidney Weinberg, head of Goldman, Sach's, who had raised about $3 million for radio-TV in Eisenhower's 1952 campaign.

Roger Blough, chairman of the board of U.S. Steel, was there, too. This time he was smiling as he had not been when he told Kennedy in April, 1962, of plans to increase steel prices. (His company was to report later a 24 per cent increase in earnings during 1963.) Henry Ford II, head of the Ford Motor Company, who had been an Eisenhower supporter, also was on hand. Ford's comment on Johnson was, "I think he's terrific."

With the President sitting on one divan and Mrs. Johnson on another, the top brass of the business world enjoyed the sort of social hour that Kennedy infrequently had got around to giving them. No man was so important that he was not secretly flattered when he could fraternize with a President, especially one who told him that the fate of the country depended on such as he.

Beyond that, Johnson had an agreeable way of talking that they understood. They felt he was sincere when he voiced his views about thrift and frugality in government. He seemed to be a down-to-earth, common-sense man. One of the business leaders confided later that he liked the President's telling them that his wife had "badgered" him about keeping the family budget in balance.

The businessmen went away, however, without making any immediate commitments of support. Greenewalt expressed the view that the nation was fortunate in having a man like Johnson available to step into the presidency. Henry Ford's statement that he would support Johnson in the election came later.

But it was evident that the business leaders' first impressions of Johnson had been good when President Edwin Neilan of the U.S. Chamber of Commerce called at the White House on December 12 to invite the Chief Executive to address that organization's April convention. When he came out, Neilan said he was "very well impressed" with Johnson and his ability to cope with the country's problems.

Predicting that the new President would have the support of the business community, he added, "What he plans to do will be helpful to business."

President W. P. Gullander of the National Association of Manufacturers told the Washington Trade Association executives a couple of weeks later he believed a period of tension between government and business was ending. He alluded to previous "epithets hurled from on high, applied pressures, hostile actions, retaliations, recriminations and the like." Now, he said, "We have a new President, who has paid sincere tribute to the free enterprise system."

When Johnson sent his economic report to Congress on January 20, he bore down on the theme that while the economy was heading for new heights it ought to do better and that a shift of emphasis from the government to the private sector would help improve it.

The President went about the business of talking up the

economy at every opportunity. He announced in December that the gross national product had hit a $600 billion rate at that time, though such calculations, vague at best, usually took months to firm up. He lectured reporters at almost every news conference on how good the people had it under his administration. Early in the spring he said at a Democratic fund-raising dinner, "I tell you tonight that the American economy is stronger than it has been at any time in your lifetime."

In a March 15, 1964, television report on his first hundred days of presidential stewardship, Johnson used the occasion to tell the nation how he felt about business:

"I am so proud of our system of government, of our free enterprise, where our incentive system and our men who head our big industries are willing to get up at daylight and go to bed at midnight to offer employment and create new jobs for people, where our men working there will try to get decent wages but will sit across the table and not act like cannibals, but will negotiate and reason things out together."

Some of his listeners wondered just how many corporation heads got up at daylight and worked until midnight to offer employment and create new jobs.

Johnson went on to say that "the employer, hoping to make a little profit, the laborer hoping to justify his wages, can get together and make a better mouse trap.

"They have developed this into the most powerful and leading nation in the world, and I want to see it preserved," he said. "And I have an opportunity to do something about it as President."

Five days later, Donald Cook, head of the American Electric Power Company, a privately-owned utility, used the White House lobby to announce that his company would undertake a $1 billion expansion program in Ohio, Indiana, Virginia, West Virginia, Kentucky and Tennessee. Cook had called on Johnson to tell him the $11.5 billion tax cut and "a favorable business climate" were responsible for the decision.

It seemed, indeed, that Johnson was dispelling the hostility that had arisen against Kennedy and was well on his way to converting a political liability into an asset. Things had changed considerably when the head of a private utility could praise a Democratic President, who traditionally had been a public-power advocate.

The Republicans, caught off balance by developments they could only regard as politically alarming, had begun earlier in the year to try to fight off Johnson's infiltration tactics. Goldwater told a U.S. Chamber of Commerce public affairs conference in Washington on February 6 that the Democratic President was a dangerous liberal.

"If you think President Johnson is going to give you any better attention than you have got," Goldwater told the delegates, "you're very, very mistaken. If he's a conservative, I'm a screaming liberal."

Goldwater got a standing ovation both before and after his speech. Neilan, who was backsliding from his December praise of the President, gave the Arizona Senator a send-off as a "fabulous American" in an introductory speech that sounded as if then and there he were nominating Goldwater for the presidency.

Neilan was replaced on April 13 by Walter F. Carey, trucking executive, who had praise for some of Johnson's programs, but not all. He said it was his objective "to make the idea of a great business-government partnership less a cliché and more of a productive reality." He was cautious about any predictions of presidential cooperation in this endeavor.

It remained for Johnson himself to counter what he recognized was a softening of his hard-won friendly relations with business. In April he rode the few blocks from the White House to the DAR's Constitution Hall to stage one of his top platform performances.

Putting on his folksy manner, the President started off by telling the U.S. Chamber of Commerce delegates he was confident American business was headed into a $30 billion profit year. He recalled the earlier settlement of the threatened railroad strike, said national output was running at a $608.5 billion annual rate and noted that "the biggest tax cut in all American history" was under way.

"But I must apologize to you this morning," he said. He added after a pause, "We haven't done anything for business this week. . . . But please remember, this is only just Monday morning."

Declaring that he meant business about cutting government costs, eliminating poverty and boosting the nation toward prosperity, Johnson continued, "I do not accept the viewpoint on either side that business and government are inherently hostile opponents. We'd get along a lot better if both of us didn't have these public relations men getting out hand-outs for us."

He had the hard word, however, that when record profits were in the till he would call on leaders of industry to reduce some prices to benefit consumers.

"And then, in the same week," he said, "I am going to call in the leaders of the workingmen and tell them the same thing."

Whether he made any lasting impression on them or not, the Chamber delegates liked most of what Johnson said and the way he said it. He was interrupted by applause or laughter, or both, sixty times. That was a little short of his record for the State of the Union speech, but this was not an audience where the President could command applause merely by pausing for it after some forceful statement.

In calling for future price reductions, Johnson was offering a piece of cake to the consumers who inhabited the large cities and their suburbs where presidential elections were settled. The President hadn't been able to demonstrate that he was doing much for these consumers beyond a call by his Council of Economic Advisers for the nation to "focus special attention" on price reductions in 1964. Chairman Heller's off-the-cuff designation of automobile prices as a likely area for such reductions grated an industry already at odds with the President over his spread-the-work proposal that Congress make it mandatory to pay double time, instead of time and one-half, for extra hours worked in selected industrial fields. This was calculated to force companies to hire additional workers but the auto-makers, who were employing their men an average of forty-four hours weekly on a contractual forty-hour week, didn't like the idea of training new crews.

Johnson sent a consumer program to Congress on February 6 that did little more than repackage proposals Kennedy previously had made and which had had little consideration from the lawmakers. The President opposed a bill which would permit manufacturers to set the prices at which retailers could sell their products. He supported legislation against high interest rates, false advertising, false stock offering statements and misleading packaging. But he was too busy with other matters to apply the same kind of pressure for their passage that he used to get major legislation in other fields.

While Johnson's relations with labor leaders remained generally closely knit, some began to come up with complaints against the President's policies. In January, Johnson had reissued the guidelines set up in 1962 by Kennedy for collective bargaining. The Council of Economic Advisers had classed as inflationary wage demands exceeding the long-term national rise in man-hour output, pegging this as 3.2 per cent annually.

Meany brought union dissatisfaction about this program into the open with a sharp attack on it in a March 26 speech to the United Auto Workers in Atlantic City, New Jersey. He said he feared the guidelines would lead to unwarranted government controls.

"It is quite obvious that if you are going to have guidelines on the question of wages, the question of prices, the question of the rate of production, you'll have to go a little further," Meany said.

"If we go down this road far enough, it leads to the end of

free collective bargaining. As far as I'm concerned, I don't propose that labor at any time agree to go down this road."

If this was in the nature of an ultimatum, Johnson would ignore it when he felt he was forced to intervene in collective bargaining in the public interest, just as Kennedy had done. Kennedy had had to write most of the script for an attempted mid-1963 settlement of the dispute between the operating unions and the railroads on the issue of work rules. Involved was the featherbedding of 35,000 firemen on diesel locomotives where they had nothing to do. The size of train crews was another major issue and there were minor differences on which both sides had refused to bargain collectively on any real basis.

Kennedy could get no settlement and was forced to ask Congress for help. It enacted a statute requiring compulsory arbitration of what then were regarded as the major issues in dispute. Thus a President who owed his election in part to the solid support of the unions was forced by circumstances to press for legislation that, in effect, nullified labor's sacrosanct right to strike.

This five-year-old labor dispute came knocking on Johnson's door in April, 1964. He turned, as his predecessor had, to Secretary of Labor W. Willard Wirtz as field commander of the government's effort to head off a rail strike.

A tall, spare man with crew-cut, graying hair who puffed a pipe almost constantly, Wirtz was the personification of the indefatigable civil servant whose loyalty to his boss never came under question. Friends often wondered why the high-domed intellectual, who was a law partner of Adlai E. Stevenson, ever consented to embark on a public service career. It was obvious, however, that he felt the same inner compulsion as Stevenson to serve his country with wit and distinction. Like Stevenson, Wirtz could seldom resist the temptation to make light of his troubles.

On the day Kennedy appointed him Secretary, the Chicago and Northwestern Railway was struck. The trains did not move for three weeks while Wirtz labored futilely to win a settlement of the dispute. During this impasse a reporter asked when he expected an agreement.

"I rode the Northwestern for fifty years," he replied. "I hope they are not asking for equal time."

The railroad wasn't and neither were the unions, for Wirtz got a settlement three days thereafter.

But there was a threat to national complacency, which began on the gray, wet day of April 2 with a secret meeting in a Washington hotel of the head men of the five operating brotherhoods. The prospect was grimmer than any the Johnson administration had faced domestically. There was here the possibility that transportation of food, manufactured products, exchanges of military personnel, shipments of rocket components and the mails might be interrupted. In addition, there was the matter of the convenience of a great many Americans in getting to their work and back home, as well as the likelihood that tourism would suffer.

On that rainy day, the union leaders were searching for a railroad they could strike unexpectedly to avoid the court injunctions which had prevented them from halting traffic on two carriers previously. Their feeling was that they would never make any progress fighting a unified railroad lineup on a national basis. They wanted to pick off a patsy and get a settlement that could be amplified into a national agreement.

So, after much argument pro and con, they chose the Illinois Central, which, among other passengers, carried commuters to Chicago and home again at night. This move, the union leaders figured, would be of an importance which neither the other railroads nor the government could ignore.

Wirtz learned of this later in the morning. He also had the information that in response the railroads would post new work rules certain to force the unions into a national strike. Wirtz hurried to the White House where Johnson said that another attempt must be made to get an agreement. The President had been told by men he had depended upon in the past that Congress was in no mood to take the rap again by voting for compulsory arbitration of the remaining issues.

The Secretary of Labor got labor and management leaders together for a session that lasted until 3 A.M. and produced no results. At 10 A.M. the next day Wirtz went into mediation sessions where he faced the belief on both sides that the government would intervene to prevent a strike if they did not agree. The Secretary rather thought at that time that it would not be a bad thing to have a strike, but the President had other ideas.

Keeping in constant touch by telephone with Wirtz, Assistant Secretary of Labor James J. Reynolds and Francis A. O'Neill, Chairman of the National Mediation Board, the President decided to call the disputants to the White House and apply a measure of the Johnson treatment to them.

Heller had come in with the impressive information that a national rail strike would cause six million workers to be laid off immediately and that New York City food deliveries would be hampered severely. To meet this, Johnson had decided to ask both sides to agree to postpone any showdown for twenty days while he used his good offices to seek a settlement. So at about sundown the disputants came to the White House and were ushered into the Cabinet Room. There Johnson told them he was asking for twenty days to try to work out something. He said he realized it would be difficult, didn't know how any agreement could be reached, "but I would like to have a crack at it.

"I am your President," Johnson said. "All I want is for you to give me a chance. Just give me a chance. I want you to come into my office and tell me you'll do this for me."

When this proposal was accepted by both sides, Johnson came up with the idea of bringing in two mediators who had had no connection with the dispute. The railroad representatives accepted and the President put it to the union leaders in such a way that, after a huddle in a corner of his office, they went along. So Professor George W. Taylor of the Wharton School of Finance at the University of Pennsylvania, and Theodore W. Kheel, a New York lawyer and labor relations expert, were brought to the White House to play a central role in a drama in which the author, in the person of the President, wandered on and off stage at critical intervals.

He told the assembled railroad, union men and mediators that he had had to make some hard decisions and that was what he expected from them. Once they got into session, Johnson dropped by frequently to ask, "How ya doing?"

When the meetings were moved across the street to the Executive Office Building on April 12, Johnson strolled over from the White House to check on progress. He brought along three memoranda from Heller and made what he regarded as an inspirational speech on the basis of them. Describing the economic disaster of any nation-wide rail strike, he noted that railroad profits had been rising and then criticized the unions for their obstinacy in opposing settlements. The speech did not go over very well with the listeners, who were beginning to think that if they could just get away from the President, they might get something done.

But Johnson was not letting any opportunity go by default. He put out statements at news conferences and on every other possible occasion calling attention to the imperative need for a negotiated settlement. The alternative—which he declined to mention publicly—was that he would ask Congress to legislate to enforce mediation and arbitration, which, in this case, would have sunk collective bargaining without trace. Once denied to the rail unions, it might have been denied to steel, autos and hundreds of industries where disputes affected the national security in one way or another.

Kheel kept reminding all concerned that Johnson couldn't forever avoid the question of what he would do if the negotiations failed and J. E. Wolfe, representing the railroads as chairman of the Railway Labor Conference, was becoming mortally tired of getting union concessions only on what he said were "demands they never expected to get anyway." At this point, on Sunday night, April 19, Johnson called all of the negotiators to the White House to give them a talking to. He told the union leaders they ought to have the courage to tell their members that they couldn't get for them everything they demanded. To the railroad men he said, "Don't let the almighty dollar stand in the way of a settlement."

In a six-hour session which began at midnight, April 21, a tentative agreement was reached. During the following day the unions accepted the proposal. Wolfe asked for more time to get acceptance from the nine railroad presidents he represented.

The next morning when Wolfe went to the White House, Johnson was having his regular weekly breakfast with Democratic congressional leaders. But he came out quickly to meet with Wolfe and Wirtz. Wolfe wanted to be satisfied on the President's position on two points before he would agree to a settlement. He said the railroads wanted action on a bill, then stalled in the House Rules Committee, which would give the carriers greater flexibility in adjusting their rates to compete with other forms of transportation. Johnson replied that the administration had supported this bill and would do what it could to get it to a vote. Wolfe then brought up the second point that the Treasury had refused to permit the railroads to depreciate for tax purposes their $4 billion investment in tunnels and grading. Johnson promised a Treasury reassessment of this matter. With that, Wolfe went off to talk to his railroad presidents and to bring them back to the White House for a session with Johnson.

Coffee was passed around and the railroad men voiced their objections to the settlement. A railroad executive said these complaints didn't involve disloyalty to Johnson or disrespect to his office. The President replied that the railroads had a perfect right to reject the settlement if they wished to do so. He said he didn't know what he would do if they took that position, but he wouldn't consider that the presidency was being demeaned.

One of the rail executives began his discussion with the phrase, "Now, I'm just a country boy . . ."

"Wait a minute," the President said. "I'm just a country boy, too, and when I hear anybody say that, I know I'm about to get skinned someway."

Grinning, the rail leader resumed, "Mr. President, I was about to say that I'm just a country boy, but I think you're right and we ought to accept this settlement."

Wolfe finally capped the discussion with the announcement that the railroads were doing just that. Beaming, Johnson shook hands all around and dismissed his guests with the request that they come back thirty minutes later to participate with him in a television announcement of the result.

When the negotiators and mediators walked with him into his office, they found columnist Walter Lippmann waiting there.

"These men have just saved collective bargaining," Johnson announced to Lippmann. "They did a wonderful job for their country."

The question remained, however, just how much of collective bargaining had been salvaged from this application of the Johnson treatment. The President had made it amply clear to everyone concerned in the beginning that he intended to have a settlement, come hell or high water. Both sides knew they were negotiating with a club over their heads—the unspoken presidential intention to ask Congress for a law which would have barred any railroad strike while the government itself tried to effect a settlement. There was, in this sense, no "free" collective bargaining.

There was involved also the presidential promise for action on the then holed-up transportation bill and the implied pledge that the railroads would get a Treasury reassessment of the ruling that a hole in a mountain does not depreciate for tax purposes. This involved a $30 million annual windfall for carriers hard pressed to show any profit.

As he had in his Senate days, Johnson had twisted arms, threatened, cajoled and had held out rewards for men who would reach a compromise on a difficult issue. He had proved to the public that he—and only he—could untie the Gordian knot that had baffled Kennedy.

For five months up to that point he had been an actor on a strange stage, trying to accustom himself to the role he was playing. Now, for really the first time, he had demonstrated that the wiles he had learned in the Senate would work also in the White House. His exuberance was difficult for him to contain.

8 The Unmanaged Press

With a paper cup half full of beer in his right hand, the President of the United States gunned his cream-colored Lincoln Continental up a Texas highway over the seventy-mile speed limit as he chatted animatedly with three newswomen and a male reporter about the glories of his native Texas.

Lyndon Johnson had come home for an Easter vacation in 1964 and was relaxing accordingly. Everything in Texas was bigger than life and no highway patrolman was going to flag down a President, even if the Secret Service was having difficulty keeping up with him.

This had started out as a tour of the LBJ ranch, with Johnson zigging and zagging around dunghills and herds of cattle. At one point he had come across a sow with a dozen tiny pigs. Stopping the car, he offered to pose for photographers if they would catch one of the pigs. When the sow charged the citified lensmen, as Johnson knew she would, he laughed uproariously. A photographer finally pinned down a pig, delivered it to the President's hands and Johnson held it up for a shot while still sitting in the driver's seat.

Back on the highway from the pasture, Johnson put a heavy foot on the accelerator. A reporter noted that the speedometer said 85 miles an hour. Johnson put his hat over the offending instrument. As his car approached the crest of a hill, the President pulled out to pass a slower moving vehicle and an auto approaching from the opposite direction veered off the road onto the shoulder of the highway to avoid a collision. Without comment, the President pressed the accelerator down further and regained the right side of the road.

A reporter could not resist the comment: "That's the closest Speaker McCormack has come to being President."

Pulling up at a ranch house, Johnson asked, "Is the [Secret] Service still with us?" The Secret Service men had been left far behind, unwilling to chance the passing of cars Johnson had zoomed by.

This was the uninhibited Lyndon Johnson, the Texas rancher who wasn't going to concede that becoming President had changed his life beyond recall.

The White House press secretary, George Reedy, blandly told reporters he had no knowledge that the President had exceeded any speed limit. At a later news conference, Johnson said he himself was unaware that he had driven faster than the legal limits.

But Johnson was angry and hurt that his guests, the reporters, should so report his exuberance. He had not yet come to realize that no President can have a private life, a circumstance that the New York *World* established when it asserted in Grover Cleveland's time that "the President is public property." Indeed he was.

Woodrow Wilson, a sensitive man, resented reporters' questions about his private affairs. When speculative stories cropped up about the romantic intentions of his daughter, Margaret, Wilson exploded to newsmen that this sort of thing had to stop.

"On the next offense," he said, "I shall do what any other indignant father would do. I will punch the man who prints it in the nose."

Johnson was hardly in a position to punch anyone in the nose for the stories of his speedy ride. He had had, since he succeeded to the presidency, what could only be calculated as a sympathetic press. After all, reporters are citizens, too, and most of them wanted to see the only President they had succeed.

The new President's mistake was in assuming that when he transferred from the confining atmosphere of the White House to the free air of the ranch in Texas he could act like a private citizen. He liked to have reporters around him because he found most of them interesting people. But he didn't like to have anybody criticize him. As a Senator or even as a Vice President, he could let his hair down occasionally without repercussions. But as President he was a public figure expected to set high standards for the nation at all times.

As the Senate's Democratic leader, Johnson had been known, among the newsmen who covered his activities, as a whiner. Any story which depicted his accomplishments as extraordinary—and many of them were—drew a smile and a comment, "I liked that piece you wrote." But a critical report could set him off for days. He would call the reporter to his office and tell him how disappointed he was that an old and trusted friend had written about him in such a manner. Moreover, he would often harangue one newsman about what another newsman had written. At times such discussions would last an hour, even though the newsman would explain over and over again that he had had nothing to do with the article at issue.

As Vice President, Johnson confined his remarks largely to off-the-record and background interviews. This held until about the middle of the third year of his tenure when a spate of "What ever happened to Lyndon Johnson?" stories appeared. Then he cautiously permitted some televised and taped interviews. But he always had on the desk before him written answers to every conceivable question, just as he had carried written statements into the Senate to read to reporters who met him daily at his center-aisle desk a few minutes before that body convened.

There was in the President's background a great uncertainty and uneasiness about the press. So when he became the Chief Executive he was gingerly in his approach to the problem of dealing with media he felt he must win to his side if he was to be elected in his own right. He particularly wanted the metropolitan press of the East—which had been critical of his Texas ways as Senator and Vice President—to be kind to him. It was in the metropolitan East that he felt that his image had not been favorably presented. He must correct that image to win the electoral support he needed.

Kennedy's relationship with reporters was about as close as a President could make it and still retain the final touch of aloofness he might find it necessary to apply at times. The late President seemed to read everything that was written about him. One might get a telephone call any hour of the day or night either complaining about some phrase or complimenting one for having sized up a given situation in a way that he believed was exactly correct.

In his dealings with reporters individually, Kennedy was always realistic about what he was doing and never intentionally misleading about his objectives, although at times he clouded his methods. Along with his intellectual attainments, he was a very practical man. He never wasted time trying to sell a reporter a bill of goods. Instead he was more likely to disarm a critical newsman by being engagingly frank about his own shortcomings. "That was a lousy speech," he might say of one of his platform performances that was under critical discussion. "I guess I ought never to read a speech."

If Johnson ever admitted that he hadn't done well in some endeavor, no reporter was likely to have been around to hear it. He had, indeed, a skin thinner than a Texas papershell pecan. He suffered and demonstrated a measurable amount of agony when any uncomplimentary reference was made about him. He was particularly incensed when his methods of attaining his objectives were brought into question.

But despite his uneasiness and uncertainty about the press, reporters always found it worthwhile talking to Johnson. He knew more about how the Senate should be run than any predecessor I ever encountered and I had seen Senators Joe Robinson, James F. Byrnes, Alben Barkley and Charles Mc-Nary in action. Of them all, Johnson got things done faster and with less outward friction than those who had gone before him. Similarly as Vice President he learned more about how to be President than his predecessors had because Kennedy used his second man more intelligently than did any other President. Where Nixon had had to maneuver for recognition, Johnson had had it handed to him. To offset his frustration and restlessness in his secondary role, Johnson had gobbled up every scrap of power that the President had let fall his way.

Johnson's relationship with newsmen covered a wide range, from warm friendship to carefully concealed antagonism. For individuals like columnist William S. White, who had been host at the first party for the Johnsons when they came to Washington freshly married, there was a trusting relationship that was extended to few others. One of the muted jokes around Washington early in 1964 was that the smoothest transition from the Kennedy to the Johnson administrations had been the substitution as the White House favorite of White for columnist Charles Bartlett, who had been instrumental in bringing Jack and Jacqueline together before their marriage.

The Presidency brought Johnson some newly discovered friends—on his part—such as the New York *Herald Tribune*'s Walter Lippmann and the *New York Times*' James A. Reston. The new President found these writers, who had not had much time to devote to him as Vice President because of the very nature of their work in evaluating the actions of the President, to be fascinating fellows indeed.

There were other newsmen who knew Johnson well, and all

accepted him for what he was, a man who could be alternately aggravating and soothing, imperious and humble, demanding and understanding, petty and generous, humorous and solemn, fretful and calm, picayune and grandiose. He was, in a word, about as human as men come, and then some.

Johnson kept up his individual contacts with reporters after he went to the White House. Some newsmen were surprised with invitations for lunch. Others, interviewing him, were whisked along with the President on a spur-of-the-moment excursion to Capitol Hill. An ailing reporter who had been a friend could count on the President's putting a hospital switchboard into a dither with a personal call minutes after his flowers had arrived. For some reporters there were personal invitations to the Texas ranch. While the horde of newsmen who followed him everywhere were quartered in Austin, sixty-five miles away, the selected guest slept at the ranch and was treated to a ride around the acres the following day. If it was the deer season, the President would see to it personally that his guest got a buck, even if he had to shoot it himself.

In Washington, Johnson catered to the columnists who wrote opinion pieces about him and who had not always been kind in their evaluations before he arrived at the highest office. It was a matter he regarded as a political necessity to try to enlist these ivory-tower types on his side.

Early in 1964 columnists Marguerite Higgins and Peter Lisagor had invited Bill Moyers, a presidential aide, Carl Rowan, new head of the United States Information Agency, and Jack Valenti to lunch at Miss Higgins' home. Without invitation the President arrived with his aides.

Grasping Miss Higgins' hand with both of his, Johnson told his surprised hostess, "You didn't think that I was going to let these young men come over here and chat with old friends and leave me out of it, did you?"

Johnson was direct and unabashed in his efforts to woo reporters. During the presidential election campaign newsmen assigned for the day to ride the "pool" in *Air Force One*, the presidential plane, found themselves the center of Johnson's attention on flights of any duration. These "poolers," as they were called, were rotated, usually twice a day, so that eventually every individual would have the opportunity of making personal contact with the President.

Almost as soon as the big jet had taken off, Johnson would stroll out of his rear compartment, take a seat in the middle of the plane where the newsmen worked and start talking. Everything he said was "off the record" or "for background" or, at times, "for very deep background." This meant generally that reporters could pass along the information they gathered to their fellow newsmen, could report it on a confidential basis to their bosses, but could not write or broadcast it as in any way attributable to the President.

At some of these sessions, Johnson singled out some of the younger members of the press to tell them he was going to pass along information to them which would make them stars in their chosen field. Somehow the information didn't always live up to its presidential billing. But nevertheless it was flattering to have the President put his arm around your shoulder or invite you and the other "poolers" to have a meal with him in his quarters.

Johnson's operation paralleled in many ways those of other Presidents who had sought a favorable press in personal contacts with reporters or in their news conferences.

Teddy Roosevelt had had favorite reporters he called in to give exclusive news to. He had ordered the first White House press room installed when, looking out the window one day, he saw a couple of newsmen standing disconsolately in a pouring rain at the gate of the grounds, waiting for an important visitor to come out so they could pump him about the President's views. Roosevelt was a great man for trial balloons. He tried out some of his ideas on the reporters. If they backfired, he denied everything and denounced the newsmen for printing what he had told them.

Wilson had held news conferences for a while but abandoned them during World War I. Harding, a newspaperman who once bragged that he could put the White House's business "to bed" at 3 o'clock in the afternoon—just as he had his paper in Marion, Ohio—started strong in his meetings with newsmen. But a couple of bloopers by the ill-informed President brought a rule that all questions would have to be submitted in advance in writing.

Calvin Coolidge kept this rule but never answered any pertinent questions. Leafing through a stack of them one day, he launched into a dissertation about Washington's parks, ending the meeting by bidding his callers goodbye and walking out. Herbert Hoover was another who required questions submitted in advance.

When Franklin Roosevelt came along, the news conference bloomed. Reporters crowded into his Oval Room office twice a week, collected about the President's desk and shot questions at him from all sides of the room. There was an invariable signal to FDR's mood. If the cigarette in his holder was pointed toward the ceiling and his head was thrown back, the news would be good, from Roosevelt's standpoint. If he was hunched over his desk and the cigarette pointed downward, look out, somebody was going to get hell.

Roosevelt could not be quoted directly, unless he specifically gave his permission, as he did on the day he tossed his "horse and buggy" phrase at the Supreme Court. And he thought so much of his relationship with the reporters who covered him that he once refused to give a House committee a transcript of what had been said at one of his news conferences.

Truman started with the same Oval Room office format, with reporters clustered around his desk. But he soon switched to the Indian Treaty Room of the Executive Office Building across the street from the White House. In this same room, Eisenhower permitted the movie cameras to come in and newsmen were allowed to quote him directly. Later they could get a transcript, infrequently corrected by Press Secretary James A.

Hagerty, to check the President's quotes.

It remained for Kennedy to put this show on the road in a national way. His was a full-scale production in the auditorium of the new State Department Building, involving live television and requiring an intensive briefing of the Chief Executive on minutiae of almost every activity of government. It would not do for him to say "no comment" as other Presidents had, he thought. A President had to appear knowledgeable about everything that was asked of him, and sometimes only the Lord could guess what would be asked. As an expert on Congress and domestic affairs, Johnson had sat in on the tedious briefings and had joined with Kennedy in lamenting the expenditure of time and energy involved.

Johnson had viewed these Kennedy performances with awe and secret admiration. He felt compelled to delay as long as possible any comparison in the public mind of what he was afraid would be his own less sure performance.

As a consequence he determined on December 7, 1963, to break the news conference barrier in his own way. It was a rather quiet Saturday afternoon at the White House. So he told Pierre Salinger, who had stayed on as his press secretary, to invite the regular reporters in for coffee and a little chat. It was lucky that he didn't have much to impart that was new because the agencies and the newspapers covering definitely were understaffed. Besides, most of the columnists had gone out of town for the week end, and some of them complained about instant news conferences of this kind, without proper warning. But Johnson did it again on December 18. When the regulars filed into Salinger's office for a briefing, the cigar-chomping secretary was grinning like the canary that had escaped the cat.

"The President," he said, "will now have a press conference."

Fifty surprised reporters trooped down the corridor to the President's office, where Johnson stood behind his desk.

"You mean," the President said as the newsmen crowded

about him, "I have that many friends out there that I have been missing all of these days? I thought everybody I knew had been in here."

In the course of a wide-ranging flow of questions, the President was asked if this was the type of press conference he intended to hold or whether this meeting with the press was only an interim one.

"I would say," he replied, "that we are going to maintain an adequate flow of information to the press at all times in the best manner we can. We will do what comes naturally. Maybe it will be a meeting of this kind today, maybe a televised meeting tomorrow, with maybe a coffee session the next day. We don't want to be too rigid. We always want to be flexible. One thing, though, that we are determined to do is to let you know as much about what goes on in your house and your government as we possibly can, consistent only with the interests of our country and self-preservation of our country."

The verdict was mixed on this effort. Lippmann said he was sure there was no one wholly satisfactory way of a President's conducting a news conference. Chalmers Roberts of the Washington *Post* observed that Johnson had "concentrated on creating a mood and an atmosphere, rather than on giving out hard news." Columnist Joseph Kraft thought that if Johnson was experimenting on ways of meeting the press "he can stop right now" because he had found the correct format.

After he conducted his next news conference from a bale of hay at his Texas ranch, Johnson let the press simmer until January 23, when he called another quickie meeting. It was notable in that in it the President took the occasion to offer his explanation of the Bobby Baker case, of which the Republicans made much in the presidential campaign.

This involved a senatorial investigation of the outside activities of Robert G. Baker, who had resigned from his position as Secretary to the Majority in the Senate. Baker had been elected to that post at the age of twenty-five when Johnson became the Majority Leader. On a salary of $19,600 a year, Baker was said by the Senate Rules Committee to have pyramided his outside holdings into a couple of million dollars.

The Committee released testimony, taken behind closed doors, in which Don B. Reynolds, a Maryland insurance man and a friend of Baker who had sold Johnson $200,000 worth of life insurance in 1957 and 1961, testified that Walter Jenkins, former administrative assistant to Johnson, had persuaded him to buy $1,208 worth of advertising time from KTBC-TV, the Johnson family-owned station in Austin. Reynolds further swore that Baker had insisted that he give the Johnsons a $542 stereophonic record player. Jenkins denied the charges in an affidavit furnished the Committee.

Around the Senate Baker had been known for years as "Lyndon's boy" and "Little Lyndon." He had named his youngest son Lyndon Baines Johnson Baker. He was, by all odds, the field operator who carried out policy decisions Johnson made as Majority Leader. He was the young man who buttonholed Senators and cajoled them into supporting the leader's position. The relationship between the Senator and the secretary was as close as the proverbial peas in the proverbial pod. Had Baker been more careful about the distribution of his cards he, and not Valenti, would have been the new President's shadow.

But Baker had committed the cardinal error of getting himself investigated by a congressional committee. Johnson told his news conference that the stereo set "was a gift that an employee of mine made to me and Mrs. Johnson." Then he added, "He was an employee of the public and had no business pending before me and was asking for nothing and, so far as I knew, expected nothing in return any more than I did when I had presented him with gifts."

Before reporters could question him further, the President said, "That is all I have to say about it and all I know about it."

This exemplified the measure of control any President could

exert over his news conference. In formal, televised meetings with the reporters, he could pick those whose questions would be recognized. While he had no control over the queries they might make of him, he could answer them or turn them aside as he chose. And he could stop any questioning at the point where he did not wish it to continue.

In this instance, reporters wished to know a great deal more about the President's severed relations with Baker. What influence and power Baker had in the Senate—and it was considerable—stemmed primarily from his relationship with Johnson. It was supplemented by a close cooperation with the late influential Senator Robert S. Kerr of Oklahoma. But the fountain of power flowed from the Majority Leadership.

Baker had transmitted Johnson's viewpoint to individual Senators for years. An ingratiating, accommodating young man, he could see to it that those who came around to Johnson's way of thinking got their rewards and those who didn't got their deserts.

Johnson's statement in a television interview that Baker was "no protégé of anyone" scarcely jibed with his expression to the young man's parents when he made a special stop in the 1960 campaign at Rocky Bottom, South Carolina, to visit Baker's home. At that time he described Bobby as "my strong right arm, the last man I see at night, the first one I see in the morning."

With its limitations on what might be produced by it, the news conference was a convenient presidential window on the world. The Chief Executive could change the glass in it quickly, making it clear on points he wished to drive home and opaque on others on which he did not propose to divulge his intentions. But with all his innate control of the situation, the President was subject to pertinent questions, whether he answered them or not. At times an unanswered question could create an atmosphere of doubt that might be embarrassing to him in some delicate area of negotiations then under way.

Johnson tried about every conceivable means of meeting with the press. Departing from the kaffeeklatsch format at one point, he walked in one day and took over a news briefing being conducted by his press secretary. At another point he assembled reporters on the grass in the flower garden of his office. Once from the White House balcony he shouted down answers to questions by newsmen. Several times he led newsmen on hikes around the White House grounds. Curious about this latter performance, I asked a White House aide one day why Johnson did it.

"He likes to walk and he is a kind of sun-worshipper too," was the reply.

Johnson tried out the West Wing theater, the East Room itself and the basement of the State Department.

Because reporters were grumbling about his quickie conferences and television was complaining about being left out, Johnson posted a two-hour advance notice when he tried out the White House theater. A reporter wanted to know at this meeting why he had chosen to hold a conference "in a cramped little room such as this, limited to about ninety newsmen, when you have facilities available to accommodate all newsmen, such as the State Department."

"I don't have an answer to that question of yours," Johnson replied. "I thought that this would be ample to take care of your needs. I am sorry if you find yourselves uncomfortable. It was much more convenient to come here at the time that I could come, and I was attempting to satisfy the newsmen. It is somewhat difficult to do sometimes. . . ."

When he moved to the East Room, usually the scene of social functions, the President stood behind a lectern placed between the portraits of George and Martha Washington. He read prepared statements for nine minutes, answered twenty-seven questions and exited, smiling.

Where Kennedy had been intellectual and perhaps a mite supercilious in dealing with the assembled press, Johnson was homespun and old shoe. When he talked about people not wanting war and when he mentioned his concern for the poor he sounded like the average man on the street corner. But when he discussed international problems in the first few months of his presidency his answers were likely to be vague and repetitious.

Kennedy had enjoyed the theatrical atmosphere of his televised news conferences. Johnson in his first recorded sessions for TV, was uneasy, squirming too much, smiling seldom and appearing overly wary in fielding controversial questions. He had difficulty, too, in shaking off the habit of opening the meetings with a series of statements about more or less minor matters and thus chewing up a great deal of the limited time in which reporters could ask questions.

When he went on television in the early spring of 1964 for an hour's conversation with three newsmen, Johnson showed his nervousness by being edgy at the start. But as the program went along some of his natural eloquence came through.

In its way, Johnson's performance was as polished as Kennedy's had been under similar circumstances. He was patient, philosophical, full of praise for his staff and for Congress, unruffled by hard questions and as nonpartisan as the Twenty-third Psalm. He might not be a "great" President, but he would be "a people's President" whose administration would be "compassionate." All in all, it was a solid exhibition for a President who was preempting the middle of the political road.

Johnson found this sort of appearance satisfactory. He was in his accustomed groove in chatting with a few reporters. But he did not like the built-in confusion of a televised news conference where scores of reporters were clamoring for recognition and where the discussion leaped from one subject to another.

Reedy had pointed out to him—and Johnson agreed—that there was no way to develop any continuity to the questioning or to concentrate on any one topic that the President might like to put over. It was Reedy's view, in the newspaper language to which the press secretary had been accustomed, that a dozen "leads" might come out of such sessions without much presidentially-supplied substance to fill out that many stories. Reporters would be left with bare reference to some important topics without being able to pursue them in depth.

There had been other palpable drawbacks, which had shown up in Kennedy's conferences. A few in the press corps fancied themselves members of Actors Equity, hamming it up on television for the benefit of their publishers, readers and viewers. Provincial questions were asked. Some queries were tasteless and others ill-informed.

It was a confusing mess at times, but nevertheless it had intrinsic values. The spectacle of the head of a government standing up for uninhibited cross-examination by the press of his stewardship was not matched anywhere else in the world. There was in full swing here an American institution by which the people could measure the abilities and the qualities of their President in their own way, without being influenced in their decision by another's interpretation.

The President, of course, could and did use this institution to try to project to the people the kind of image he wanted them to have of him. He could and did propagandize his ideas and his programs by reading statements of his views at the opening, before the TV watchers had grown tired or confused and had turned the dial to their favorite bowling tournament.

Kennedy took into these conferences a saving sense of humor. He was always somber when discussing such matters as the prospects for a military victory in Vietnam. But when a reporter asked him a political question his eyes lighted up, a grin spread across his expressive mouth and he was off and running before the newsman had finished.

In a typical performance, he was asked about a best-seller volume that was highly critical of him and his actions as President. He hadn't read all of it, the President confessed, but he had seen it highly praised by a couple of columnists whose views he generally regarded as considerably less than friendly.

"The part I read is not as brilliant as I gather the rest of it is, from what they said about it," he observed.

By and large, Kennedy felt that what he called the "abrasive quality of the press" had some good points. As he once said, "It is never pleasant to be reading things that are not agreeable news. But I would say that it is an invaluable arm of the presidency, to check what really is going on in the administration."

Before he finally came to the point where he was willing to risk comparison with Kennedy's performance, Johnson had considered taking some kind of cram course in dealing with masses of newsmen. He wisely decided that the only kind of homework he needed was the same method of boning-up that Kennedy had done.

Five months after he had become President, Johnson took the plunge. He invited members then attending the American Society of Newspaper Editors annual meeting as special guests so he had on hand not only the Washington correspondents but their bosses.

Whereas he had been somber and notably humorless in his earlier meetings with the press, Johnson started the conference off on a light note by announcing, "I have come before you today for a regularly scheduled, televised, notified-well-in-advance press conference. I did not drive myself over here but I did have to come from an informal meeting with some tourists at the gate."

The auditorium turned out not to be haunted, after all. There were 512 individuals on hand, including the visiting editorial firemen. This topped Kennedy's high of 437 correspondents and visitors at an August 30, 1961, news conference. Johnson had set another record.

Johnson was tall in the cotton that day. Although he never liked being photographed wearing them, he put on his glasses to read an opening statement crammed with statistics about how well the country was doing. Then, slipping his glasses into his pocket, he took on questions. Some of them were tough and a couple of President-baiters tried their best to ruffle him. But he wouldn't ruffle. He appeared sure-footed and confident, in command of his job and the situation at hand. The consensus was that he had stacked up well, as they might say in Texas.

Perhaps because it was spring and perhaps because he had been in office long enough to feel comfortable in it, Johnson began exhibiting after this conference the kind of exuberance that a man might display when a heavy load had been lifted from his shoulders. On a warm April day newsmen had been invited to the south portico of the White House to see Mrs. Johnson and a party of guests. They included Carl Sandburg, the famed poet and Lincoln biographer, and Edward Steichen, an international photographer, and their wives. Johnson wasn't even supposed to there, but he was. He stood on the "Truman balcony" above them and called down to say that if the newsmen didn't think they had had enough conferences, he would be glad to field some questions for Sandburg. Someone asked about the nature of the poet's next book. Johnson relayed the question to the hard-of-hearing poet and then leaned over the railing to shout back, "Poems."

There were some questions and answers about the railroad negotiations then going on. Johnson rang down the curtain after a few minutes by throwing both hands into the air, exclaiming, "Well, back to the salt mines," and walking back into the house.

The next day he went out for a stroll around the White House grounds with reporters trailing along. In the middle of it he ordered the gates opened so a flock of tourists could join him. The Secret Service men, clustered around the President, were horrified by this development. They were jostled around by about a hundred eager tourists who followed Johnson on a slow tour of the grounds.

A gray-haired man, a camera slung about his neck, barged up to Johnson and, pointing to the expanse of lawn, asked, "Do you cut this grass yourself?"

"No, sir," the President replied, "I don't. But I'd probably feel better if I did."

When a group of late arriving photographers arrayed themselves across a driveway ahead of him, Johnson called out to them, "Now don't you all mess this up. Get out of the way."

Three days later the President took another surprise stroll after he had driven King Hussein of Jordan from the White House to the Blair House across the street. Instead of returning to his car, Johnson did what came naturally and walked back across Pennsylvania Avenue. Ducking under a rope barrier set up to detour pedestrians, the President gained the other side of the street only to be engulfed by passers-by and tourists.

When Johnson saw Captain Cecil Stoughton of the Army Signal Corps, an official White House photographer, beating a retreat away from the melee, he shouted at him, "Cecil, come back and take some more pictures."

Kennedy had worried about overexposure. He thought the people got tired of reading too many stories about and seeing pictures of the President. It would never have occurred to him to take a personal hand in promoting public relations by opening the gates to a flood of tourists. But Johnson wanted to establish physical contact with the people. He knew that a handshake, like a rock tossed in a pool, cast up widening ripples. A tourist whose hand had been clasped by the President of the United States was not likely to go home, keep that hand in his pocket and hide from his neighbors the fact that the President had taken a personal interest in him. In the nature of things, he would be inclined to regard with a fishy eye any criticism of a fine fellow like that.

Presidents were always feeling they had been unjustly criticized. In turn the press was wary of being spoon-fed information favorable to the administration and being denied access to facts about its shortcomings. There was a great outcry during the Kennedy administration about "managed news." Arthur Sylvester, Assistant Secretary of Defense for Public Affairs, was pilloried for saying what everybody with any sense knew—that truth was the first casualty in any international crisis. Sylvester, who remained to serve Johnson and McNamara, was a graying, thin-visaged Mencken without portfolio. Always a rebel as a Washington correspondent, he declined to roll over and play dead when he became the Pentagon's spokesman to the newsmen. He spoke his piece, no matter what the consequences—and some of them were bad.

The irrepressible Sylvester made a speech about the 1962 Cuban missile crisis in which he said, "News flowing from actions taken by the government is part of the weaponry. In the kind of world we live in, the generation of news by actions taken by the government becomes one weapon in a strained situation."

This was by way of justifying the bald-faced lies told to newsmen by government officials, and by Sylvester and Pierre Salinger, during the missile crisis. This shocked the editorial writers and set them off in full cry against such nefarious practices in the government. Any Washington reporter could have told the ivory-tower occupants that this was standard operating procedure. Many government officials lied or dissembled about matters of varying importance to national security. The good reporter was one who could parse the lies into the real truth.

Sylvester's subsequent statement that government officials had the right to lie if the nation were threatened with nuclear destruction added more wood to the fire. So did a spate of silly directives aimed at hemming in newsmen in their contacts with their sources. Some of these directives were repealed but others, such as that requiring all Pentagon officials to report in detail their conversations with newsmen, were held over to the Johnson administration. After Johnson had become President, a newsman preparing a feature on the Air Force band called

Bolling Air Force Base for information. He was solemnly referred to Sylvester's office for clearance on the story before any facts would be made available.

Although the Kennedy administration had been burned about "managed news," Johnson stuck a tentative toe or two into this boiling cauldron. On February 21, 1964, when Johnson spoke in California, Salinger alerted reporters in advance to a phrase in the President's speech. In his text and his later delivery, Johnson said the backers of the Communist guerrillas in South Vietnam—meaning North Vietnam and Communist China—were playing "a deeply dangerous game." The newsmen were told that this could be interpreted as a warning that the United States might carry the war to North Vietnam and possibly to China.

It may have seemed a good idea to the President at the time, but a few days later the repercussions against inviting another Korea with the Communist Chinese had built up to the point where Secretary Rusk had to call a news conference to deny that the war would be carried north of the South Vietnam border. Pained about all this, Johnson sponsored the impression that he just couldn't understand how the newsmen arrived at any such interpretation of the phrase he had used.

Salinger had liked to depict his role of Press Secretary as that of an "added reporter," who was bringing to the newsmen information about the President's thinking. The trouble was, however, that the roly-poly, cigar-puffing Salinger wasn't as well tuned in on Johnson's thinking as he had been on Kennedy's.

When Salinger grasped the opportunity to take off into politics on his own, temporarily landing in the United States Senate as a representative of California, tall, bushy-haired and hefty George Edward Reedy took over as White House press secretary. Reedy had been working for Johnson for thirteen years and if anybody could read the President's mind he could.

A former wire-service reporter, Reedy was asked by a youthful colleague in 1951 how he could bring himself to leave the newspaper field and go to work for a politician. "Because Lyndon Johnson is a great man and he's going to be President some day," he replied. "I'm hitching my wagon to a star."

A friendly pipe-smoking panda of a man, Reedy had little time for his favorite sport of fly fishing. Most of his workdays were twelve hours or more and there frequently weren't any Sundays in his week. He complained privately that he was snowed under by administrative work and had little time for constructive thinking.

Where Salinger had been out-going and bouncy, Reedy was more ponderous and less inclined to see the light side of any matter. But no one operated behind the press secretary's desk for long without encountering the whimsy of the reporters.

At one briefing Reedy was asked if it was true that he played a trombone at Chicago's Senn High School in the period from 1928 to 1934. The exchange went this way:

REEDY: Those are the kind of queries I like. I can answer those. Yes. I also played the euphonium.

Q.: That is something that you blow, or bang on?

REEDY: A euphonium is a lineal descendant of a sax horn, which is a sort of baritone horn, not a saxophone, and it is approximately a baritone version of a base tuba, except that it has two bells. There is one bell which gives you the same sound effects as a valve trombone.

Q.: George, one more thing. These dates, '28 to '34, indicate you were in high school six years. . . . What dates did you play the trombone and what dates did you play the euphonium?

REEDY: I would say the exact date would have been about . . . (long pause).

Q.: The year is enough.

REEDY: I am trying to recall. It would have been about 1931 to 1934. . . . I do wish it to be specified that that was the period in which the Senn High School band was the national championship band. Please get that in. . . .

Q.: Do you still play?

REEDY: I still play but the difficulty with that is that you have to keep in practice because it requires the development of special lip muscles, and this week my lip muscles are wasted upon you rather than upon Bach, Beethoven and Brahms.

Q.: Your wind is all right?

REEDY: My wind is definitely in fine shape. . . .

This seemed to dispose of the nation's business for the day and the reporters went away with the idea they had found one of the sources for the President's homespun humor.

Reedy felt there wasn't much danger that the news would be managed during Johnson's tenure. Having been on the other side of the fence he thought that "a highly skeptical group of correspondents, representing a wide variety of points of view" could hardly be fooled.

The press secretary righteously told the nation's editors in an appearance before them that he would consider any attempt to manage the news not only morally wrong but self-defeating.

"It obviously is morally wrong for anyone to achieve a monopoly over the sources of news in the country, and to use that monopoly to promote his own point of view or to perpetuate his own power," he said. "But when issues arise, the administration is entitled to have its viewpoint represented and I assure you that I intend to represent the administration's viewpoint."

The issues were beginning to fly as the election year campaign began to heat up and as Johnson played his political cards carefully in a game for which the grand prize might be eight more years in the White House.

9 A Southern President and Civil Rights

O<small>N THE FRIGID DAY</small> of January 30, 1964, Lyndon Johnson engineered his biggest breakthrough on one of the underlying issues of the presidential election campaign by persuading "Judge" Howard Smith into reporting the administration's civil rights bill out of the House Rules Committee for House debate. This was a high point in a remarkable campaign by the man in the White House to pass the type of legislation he had opposed as a member of the House and had come to espouse late in his senatorial career.

In twenty years in Congress—twelve in the House and eight in the Senate—Johnson had supported the Southern position of opposition to civil rights measures. He cast his first vote against an anti-lynching bill in 1937. He repeated this opposition in 1940 and 1950. He voted against anti-poll tax bills in 1942, 1943, 1945, 1947 and 1950. In 1946 and again in 1950 he voted to block action on measures to establish a Fair Employment Practices Commission (FEPC).

In a speech in Austin in 1948, Johnson said that "this civil rights program about which you have heard so much is a farce and a sham—an effort to set up a police state in the guise of liberty." In the Senate in 1949, the member from Texas op-

[159

posed an FEPC bill by telling his colleagues they ought to learn the facts of life. "We cannot legislate love," he said.

After he had become Democratic leader of the Senate, Johnson said in 1955 that segregation was something to be "settled in a number of different forums by the courts and the executive agencies . . . Congress is no longer a meaningful forum for such debate," he declared.

Even as late as March 19, 1957, he was sending constituents a form letter in which he said:

"I do not know where you could have gotten the idea that I am supporting 'the so-called bill for civil rights legislation now before Congress.' Certainly I have made no statement to that effect nor have I intimated to anyone that I plan such support.

"The bill that has been introduced is one to which I am very much opposed, as I do not believe it would advance any legitimate cause."

But there was one "legitimate cause" he believed could stand some advancing in this period and that was the nationalization of the Lyndon Johnson appeal to the voters. The time had come to turn away from Southern provincialism, and the man from Texas executed an about-face that seldom has been paralleled.

In 1957, six years before he became President, he cast his first vote for a civil rights bill. Moreover, as the leader of the Democratic majority, he helped maneuver the bill to passage, despite his comments to constituents that he was "very much opposed" to it.

It was an Eisenhower bill to begin with, and it was true that Johnson had been instrumental in weakening its provisions. Two stumbling blocks to passage had been provisions which gave the Attorney General authority to bring injunction suits for the protection of civil rights generally and a section denying jury trials in criminal contempt cases arising out of the measure.

Johnson knew that unless something was done about these provisions the measure would not pass. So did the sponsors of the legislation. When I interviewed Senator Clinton P. Anderson of New Mexico one day he informed me that he and other sponsors had decided to offer an amendment eliminating the authority of the Attorney General to bring civil rights suits on his own initiative. This was the principal source of controversy.

After I had written this story and it had been printed in the Monday morning Washington *Post*, I dropped around to Johnson's office to get his reaction. Told that I was there, the Majority Leader burst out of his sanctuary, grabbed me around the shoulders and practically shouted, "Man, you've just passed my bill for me." I protested that I had been only reporting the news, but he seemed to believe, despite my denials, that I had thought the idea up and sold it to Anderson and the other sponsors. This was typical of Johnson in those days. He regarded any reporter who wrote what he considered a piece of good news as not merely a recorder but an instigator.

When the opportunity arose subsequently, Johnson joined the majority of the Senate in striking out the provision giving the Attorney General authority to initiate civil rights suits and voted for an amendment for jury trials. Thus the bill passed under his leadership in 1957 dealt largely with Negro voting rights.

In the same vein, it was not "all the way with LBJ" in 1959 when a battle erupted over changing the Senate's debate limitation rule requiring a two-thirds majority of the membership to choke off a filibuster. Liberals were backing a proposal to permit a majority of the members to put a time limit on debate. They contended that this was essential to permit the passage of any meaningful civil rights legislation, since members from small Western states often joined the Southerners in opposing too strict limitations on debate. The Westerners felt there might come a time when they, too, might have to talk at length to protect their states from some proposal advanced by the

Senators from other areas. Helping defeat the liberals' proposal, Johnson offered a compromise which would permit two-thirds of the Senators present and voting to curb a filibuster.

It is notable that in this year of 1959 Johnson introduced his first civil rights bill. It contained provisions for federal prosecution of bombings, subpoena powers for the Justice Department in voting rights cases and an extension of the life of the Civil Rights Commission created by the 1957 measure. The Johnson measure was not passed. However, a provision for the establishment of a Federal Community Relations Service, which was contained in his measure, was included in the 1964 bill that became law with his signature.

In 1960, when he was beginning to describe himself as a Westerner and not as a Southerner, Johnson joined with Senator Dirksen in piloting through the Senate, without a debate limitation, a measure extending guarantees for Negro voting rights.

Kennedy's record of congressional voting on civil rights had been somewhat fly-specked. He had voted in the Senate in 1957 to bring the legislation before the Senate. He voted against eliminating the authority of the Attorney General to bring civil rights suits, but he joined Johnson in supporting the so-called jury-trial amendment. This provided that Southerners hauled into court for failing to comply with a judicial order could be tried before a jury of Southerners.

When the 1960 civil rights bill was up, Kennedy was so busy working at his campaign for the Democratic presidential nomination that he missed several Senate votes. But he did support a cloture move to limit debate, which Johnson opposed and which was defeated.

Because his pattern of voting had at times seemed to favor their viewpoint, the Southern segregationists had approached the 1960 selection of a Democratic presidential nominee believing that Kennedy might not be such a bad choice, after all. They knew he would be for civil rights in the campaign, but they didn't really believe he would be a crusader when it came down to cases. After all, many of them could remember that Franklin Roosevelt had talked a good civil rights case but had never sent a message to Congress on the subject. And they had not forgotten that Harry Truman of Missouri had demanded passage of FEPC and other legislation at a time when he knew he couldn't get it.

They misjudged Kennedy as a man who would propose but probably wouldn't follow through. And that was, in a way, what happened in 1961 after the new Democratic President took office as a minority President who had barely eked out victory over his Republican opponent.

Both Kennedy and his brother Robert had regarded civil rights as more of a political issue than an emotional matter. Both of them were for civil rights, but neither had been a crusader for the advancement of racial integration. For all practical purposes, civil rights had not been the most compelling national issue in the 1960 presidential campaign. Richard M. Nixon, the Republican nominee, was just as strongly for the expansion of civil rights as Kennedy had been but had failed to dramatize his position.

But Robert Kennedy related that his brother was forcefully reminded of civil rights on Inauguration Day.

"I remember at the Inaugural parade," Bob said, "the President was reviewing it and he saw the Coast Guard march by and there wasn't one Negro in the Coast Guard. He came out shortly afterwards to greet the President of one of the new African nations and they marched down in front of the Color Guard and there wasn't one Negro in the Honor Guard."

The matter was discussed at an early Cabinet meeting and the President laid down the policy that, as Bobby put it, "people of character and ability and integrity should not be denied the right of employment because they were Negroes."

It was not, as a matter of recorded fact, until the Negroes took to the streets, signaling him that bloody race riots might be in the offing, that the late President really acted to spur Congress to correct some of the injustices that had oppressed non-white citizens.

President Kennedy, who read history avidly, obviously felt at the time that he faced a situation almost identical with that of the Founding Fathers. John Adams calculated that one-third of the population was for the American Revolution, one-third against it and one-third indifferent to the outcome. Roughly this was the situation with regard to civil rights when Kennedy was caught up in the tide of insurgent Negro demands and was forced to jettison his carefully-laid plans to win Southern Democratic support for his programs in Congress by talking, and not really acting, on the civil rights issue.

In all of the presidential soundings there had been no clear warning that the Negroes were as impatient as they suddenly demonstrated themselves to be. Young, partially-schooled Negroes had taken matters into their own hands. And in June, 1963, the late President submitted his civil rights program to Congress after there had been a wave of racial demonstrations and violence.

It was by far the most stringent program of its nature ever submitted by a President to Congress. It called for equal access to public accommodations, proposed authority for the Attorney General to initiate civil rights suits and included a broad attack on racial unemployment problems by outlawing job discrimination in federally supported projects.

Before he resigned his post as White House special legal counsel at the end of February, 1964, Sorensen said Kennedy had decided in his early years in the presidency to press for civil rights action within the executive branch, "actions which he could take on his own responsibility. . . . But he did not want to make a lot of bald speeches to the Congress about civil rights which would result in no action, because he knew that would simply increase the frustrations of those who were being denied those rights." Sorensen added, "When the time came for stronger civil rights legislation, he moved."

The President moved, but Congress didn't. To the expected opposition of the Southern segregationists had been added a new element, the white backlash in the North against growing racial demonstrations. By fall a House judiciary subcommittee had complicated the administration's problem by approving a much stronger bill.

It was the judgment of the President and of the Attorney General that this bill, reported out by a liberal subcommittee headed by Representative Emanuel Celler of New York, couldn't be passed. Bob Kennedy had gone to the Hill in early October to ask the full Judiciary Committee to restore the administration's original bill and to call for a bipartisan approach to the problem. He and his aides worked feverishly to keep the Celler group's version from being approved by the full committee.

The President called a group of congressional leaders of both parties to the White House but all he could get was a promise of a week's postponement. In that week, the Attorney General and his assistants did their job well. When President Kennedy called House Republican leader Charles A. Halleck of Indiana to the White House a few days later, he got a promise of cooperation on a compromise version, which still represented the strongest civil rights bill ever to go before Congress.

Despite the impetus toward action that accompanied his entrance into the presidency, Johnson could not produce the miracle of immediate congressional movement on civil rights. But he did get the bill started by taking the unusual step of throwing his weight behind a petition to discharge the Rules Committee, headed by "Judge" Smith, from its control of the measure. Such a petition needed the signatures of 218 House members to become effective, and that number of signatures always was difficult to accumulate. But Smith announced he would begin hearings on the bill in January and everybody saved political face. Southern opponents could tell their constituents they had stalled the bill for months. Johnson could tell the nation that he had got it moving.

Smith had had a taste of "the Johnson treatment." In this case it was a mixed affair. The new President appealed as a Texan to the Virginian for Southern support of the Chief Executive. But at the same time, he reminded Smith of the petition method of taking the legislation away from the committee.

The "Judge" was convinced that Johnson meant business. So after parading the South's objections in hearings which lasted several weeks, the chairman silently permitted a bipartisan majority of his strictly controlled committee to approve the bill.

Thus the administration's civil rights measure was launched on its perilous course through the two houses at a point when Negroes in New York City were organizing a boycott against the schools because of de facto discrimination, street demonstrations were going on in Atlanta, Georgia, against restaurant discrimination and Cleveland, Ohio, Negroes were picketing public schools in protest against unofficial segregation imposed by housing patterns.

For Johnson there were political benefits. Roy Wilkins, executive secretary of the National Association for the Advancement of Colored People, came to call at the White House. Wilkins had accused Johnson in 1959 of planning a legislative program to avoid coming to grips with the civil rights issue. The Negro leader had attacked "Johnsonism," which he then defined as "the acceptance of a parliamentary tidbit containing not enough civil rights substance to fill a thimble."

After his talk with the new President, Wilkins came away expressing "very great faith" in Johnson's attitude toward civil rights. He said the new President enjoyed the respect of the Negro community in general, although he added that Negroes "naturally are skeptical of a man with a Southern background."

When "Judge" Smith turned the civil rights bill loose, the administration's workers surprised themselves by rolling up a 290–130 House vote for passage of the compromise measure on February 10. It was a bipartisan vote, with 152 Democrats and 138 Republicans in favor, 96 Democrats and 34 Republicans opposed.

With this victory under his belt, Johnson took the political risk of talking determinedly about civil rights when he made a flying trip late in the month to Miami Beach, Florida, to address a Democratic fund-raising dinner. He said his administration was pledged "to protect the constitutional rights of every American." It would, he said, "press forward with legislation, with education, and with action until we have eliminated the last barrier of intolerance."

While a Southern filibuster against the civil rights bill which had begun on March 9 ground out the weary weeks in the Senate, rioting hit the streets.

In the April Wisconsin presidential primary, Governor George C. Wallace of Alabama furnished the President with some concrete evidence that there existed a Northern backlash against the progress of the civil rights movement. Attorney General Kennedy had had some very difficult dealings with the diminutive Governor in June, 1963. He had dispatched Nicholas deBelleville Katzenbach, his six-foot-two, 215-pound deputy—who later succeeded Kennedy as acting Attorney General —to confront Wallace at the doorway of the University of Alabama to order the Governor aside and to enroll two Negro students.

Now Wallace was repaying the administration by running for President as a protest against Johnson's actions on the civil rights front. When he came out of Wisconsin with more than 264,000 votes to the 511,000 for Democratic Governor John W. Reynolds, the Democratic pros were alarmed. Robert Kennedy had sent messages supporting Reynolds, who was running as a stand-in for Johnson. The President had sent Postmaster General John A. Gronouski, whose home was in Madison, to campaign personally for Reynolds.

When Wallace followed up this feat with substantial showings in the Indiana and Maryland primaries, there was further reassessment of the backlash issue. The fact that Wallace quit the presidential race after the Republicans had nominated Barry Goldwater as their candidate served to emphasize the two-pronged political opposition building up against Johnson in some areas of the country.

The President played it cool, however. He went about the business of showing to all concerned that he intended to practice as well as preach equal rights. He invited Negroes and their wives to White House functions and appointed Carl T. Rowan, a Negro, to succeed the famed Edward R. Murrow as head of the United States Information Agency.

Furthermore, Johnson did some personal things that pleased the Negro community more than just the recognition of their race in high places.

When he journeyed to New York in December, 1963, to address the United Nations he insisted that a Negro social worker, Mrs. D'Jaris Watson, wife of Civil Court Judge James L. Watson, ride with him in his car from the airport to the U.N. building. The Watsons had accompanied the Johnsons to Jamaica in August, 1962, when the Vice President represented Kennedy at the island's Independence celebration. They had become good friends.

Johnson spied Mrs. Watson in the welcoming delegation at the New York airport, walked up to her and said, "Dee, I want you to ride with me."

But good will at the White House was no answer to the racial demonstrations that were accelerating as the weather warmed. Because of the limitations of federal law, Johnson could not intervene in many of these disturbances. When a Brooklyn group threatened to create chaos at the opening of the New York World's Fair by stalling their autos on highways leading to it, he could only warn of the damage this might do to chances for passage of the civil rights bill. He told a news conference, "I hope . . . Congress will act promptly . . . and bring these disturbances from the streets . . . into the courts where they belong."

In the Senate, Senator Humphrey and GOP Senator Thomas H. Kuchel, civil rights bill floor managers, issued a joint statement in which they said such demonstrations as the threatened stall-in—which eventually fizzled—were hurting efforts to get passage of the legislation. After nine weeks of talk, the Senate was ready on May 7 to vote on the first of a long series of amendments to the civil rights bill. Robert Kennedy had been working with Senator Dirksen, the Republican leader, in efforts to compromise terms of the measure so that when it finally was put in shape the necessary two-thirds of those voting would approve a limitation on debate. The first amendment, fought by the bill's sponsors, would have provided for jury trials for those accused of criminal contempt under provisions of the House measure. It was beaten in a cliff-hanger 46–45 vote.

Johnson had stayed discreetly out of the conferences on proposed compromises, leaving it up to Kennedy to decide what would be acceptable. The President maintained the public position, as he had from the start, that he wanted the House-passed bill without change. He knew, probably better than anyone else, that he would get no bill unless compromises were made with Dirksen.

Two days after the Senate had reached its first vote, Johnson took off for a flying trip to Atlanta, Georgia. There his reception by a street crowd estimated at a half million persons seemed to indicate that there was admiration for the way he was conducting the presidency, even if there was resentment about his civil rights stand. The President hit the issue with a warning about the dangers of continuing racial animosity.

"Democratic order rests on faithfulness to law," he declared. "Those who deny the protection of the Constitution of others imperil the safety of their own liberty and the satisfaction of their own desires."

It was paradoxical that in the November election the "white backlash" was not registered in the votes of Northern states, but Georgia went Republican for the first time in modern history.

Back from Atlanta, Johnson stepped up his contacts with

Congress on his general legislative programs. He kept the phones ringing all over the Hill. His host was one of those surprised when the President showed up on May 14 at a luncheon given by Senator Allen J. Ellender of Louisiana, one of those filibustering the civil rights bill, in his hideaway room on the third floor of the Capitol. The Senator was making a Creole gumbo. While they ate this dish, Johnson pressed the small group of Senators present for help with his legislative program, but he did not mention the civil rights bill.

In the same week, Johnson took time out to dine at the Capitol with the Texas congressional delegation and to meet in the evening with members of the House Rules Committee. At all of these sessions, as well as at his regular Tuesday breakfast with the Democratic Senate and House leaders, the talk was about moving his program along.

Early in June the "long hot summer of discontent" was beginning. The Senate was nearing a showdown on the civil rights issue as Negro teen-agers were terrorizing white passengers on the New York subways and on the Staten Island ferry. James Farmer, director of the Congress of Racial Equality (CORE), said in this period, "I think much of this behavior is related to the absence of hope and the presence of despair in young people who are uncertain of their future, regardless of color."

Johnson held a series of conferences with Kennedy and other federal officials in which there were discussions of what the federal government could do to head off further trouble. The President had talked with about two hundred businessmen, trying to enlist them in the desegregation drive. He talked with Kennedy about the possibility of stationing U.S. marshals in sensitive areas. Publicly he could only say that he was confident that Congress would enact the "strongest rights bill in American history."

On June 10, the Senate reached what Democratic leader Mansfield described as "a crossroads of history, and the time

for decision is at hand." Shortly after 11 A.M., Washington
time, a motion for ending debate, which Mansfield and Dirksen
had sponsored, came to a vote. The motion carried by a 71–29
vote, four more than was needed for the two-thirds approval to
end the talk. Thus was talk restricted after a seventy-five-day
filibuster against the bill. Johnson had won his greatest victory
in the Eighty-eighth Congress. In commenting, he said, "Today's action demonstrates that the national will manifests itself
in congressional action."

On June 19, one year from the day on which Kennedy had
sent an urgent message to Congress for action on a civil rights
bill, the Senate passed a measure containing about eighty
amendments to the House-passed version by a 73–27 vote.
There were 46 Democrats and 27 Republicans supporting it
and 21 Democrats and 6 Republicans voting against. Senator
Barry Goldwater voted against passage.

This final measure, which was accepted by the House,
barred racial discrimination in public places, banned discrimination by employers in hiring and by unions in membership,
prohibited registrars from applying different standards in dis-
qualifying white and Negro voters, clothed the Attorney General with authority to initiate civil rights suits and gave the
President authority to cut off funds for federal programs where
discrimination was practiced.

Hailing Senate passage of the bill, which he was to sign on
July 2, Johnson said the challenge was "to the men of good will
in every part of the country to transform the commands of our
law into the customs of the land."

The good will wasn't too widespread, it appeared. Johnson
had appointed LeRoy Collins, former segregationist governor
of Florida, as director of the Federal Community Relations
Service set up under the new law. Collins had given up a
$75,000-a-year job as head of the National Association of
Broadcasters to take on the new $20,000-a-year post. He previ-
ously had shifted his position on civil rights.

When Collins' nomination came before the Senate Commerce Committee for action, the administration had trouble getting enough members to attend so that an official vote could be taken. No votes could be recorded unless a quorum of members—number varying with different committees—was present.

Segregationist Senator Strom Thurmond of South Carolina, who switched from the Democratic to the Republican party during the presidential campaign, opposed confirmation of Collins. He wanted to stall the assembling of a quorum if possible, but he wanted to register his vote against Collins if enough other members showed up. So Thurmond hung around the committee room but didn't go in.

Senator Ralph Yarborough, Texas Democrat supporting Collins, challenged Thurmond to go into the committee room. Thurmond said he wasn't going to and offered to wrestle Yarborough to prove that nobody could make him do it. The two Senators grappled and down on the floor they went, huffing and puffing until Senator Warren G. Magnuson of Washington, the startled chairman, came out to break it up.

Collins eventually was confirmed. But in what he called "the big test of our time" he had only marginal success in the beginning. Governors Orval Faubus of Arkansas, George C. Wallace of Alabama and Paul Johnson, Jr., of Mississippi refused even to talk to him. But the governors of Florida, Georgia, Louisiana, North Carolina, Tennessee and Virginia did agree to discuss the issue of accepting the inevitable.

A suggestion by Goldwater, the Republican presidential nominee, brought him and Johnson together for a conference on the civil rights matter. Goldwater had said he would like to reach an "agreement that we and our associates would not, in any word we might say, add to the feelings of tension that exist today."

The White House staff had gone all out in preparation for this confrontation. George Reedy and his aides had covered every conceivable angle that might develop and had supplied Johnson with a voluminous file. A statement of the President's position had been drafted and was on his desk.

Unaccountably, Goldwater arrived early at the south door of the White House. Johnson was playing host at a reception for two hundred labor leaders in the mansion and no one was on hand to greet the Republican nominee. When James Reynolds, Assistant Secretary of Labor, happened to glance out the door, he saw Goldwater wandering alone about the south lawn.

Rushing out to greet the Senator, Reynolds conducted him into the Cabinet Room, hustled up a newspaper for him to read and assured him that the President would be along in a few minutes. When Johnson arrived, he and Goldwater greeted each other cordially and the President led the Senator into the Oval Room office.

There was a moment or two of strained silence while Johnson waited for Goldwater, who had suggested the conference, to open the conversation. When the Senator didn't, Johnson took the initiative in outlining his position that he would do nothing and say nothing which might contribute to the violence in the streets. That was fine, Goldwater said, adding that he intended to follow the same line. Johnson then read his prepared statement. He agreed with that, the GOP nominee said. He asked if he could have a copy of it and the President called for one and handed it to the Senator.

As Goldwater rose to leave he commented that he would like to have a crack at piloting the new A-11 plane that Johnson had announced had been developed. Well, the President replied, it would be another year before the plane would be ready for piloting by anybody except the test experts and there was some question about who would be around the White House then to approve such a flight.

With that the sixteen-minute "confrontation" ended.

"What a confrontation," a White House staffer chuckled later. "We had enough information in the President's hands to

choke a Sunday newspaper but all Goldwater wanted to hear
was what the President intended to say. Wish we could have
one like that with De Gaulle."

After the meeting, the White House said in a statement:
"The President met with Senator Goldwater and reviewed the
steps he had taken to avoid the incitement of racial tension.
Senator Goldwater expressed his opinion, which was that racial
tension should be avoided."

The violence did not stop. Rioting broke out in Harlem and
spread to other Negro sections in New York City. Johnson ordered two hundred FBI agents in to investigate the possibility
of federal law violations. Rochester, New York, Philadelphia,
Pennsylvania, and Henderson, North Carolina, were visited by
violence.

But there was good news along with the bad as the long, hot
summer drew near its close. Mayor Allen C. Thompson of Jackson, Mississippi, rallied businessmen behind him in July to
buck the White Citizens Council and to begin integration of
hotels, motels and restaurants in that city. It constituted a significant break in Mississippi's racial segregation pattern.

When schools opened in September, desegregation began
quietly in Montgomery, Gadsden and Tuskegee, Alabama; Al-
bany and Columbus, Georgia; and in Prince Edward County,
Virginia.

Under Johnson's leadership the nation had come a long way
in less than a year. The President himself had completed the
historic change in position he had begun late in his Senate
career. On January 23, 1964, when the anti-poll tax amendment
became law and Johnson had expressed his "great delight" at
this accomplishment, the Republican Governors Executive
Committee had been "appalled at his hypocrisy," reminding
that he had "refused twelve times since 1942 to vote for abol-
ishing the tax." But as the presidential election approached, the
Republican governors could hardly question that Johnson had
become, in the minds of the public, a champion of civil rights.

Passage of the civil rights bill alone had been a great victory. But there were other legislative accomplishments the determined President wanted nailed down before he went before the voters.

10 Congress Gets "The Treatment"

WHAT HAPPENED to Representative Otto E. Passman, Louisiana Democrat, in a stormy five-hour meeting of the House Appropriations Subcommittee on Foreign Aid on June 23, 1964, illustrated the sharp differences in the methods employed by President Johnson and the late President Kennedy in prodding Congress into action. Passman, a bespectacled, firm-jawed legislator, had made a career out of wielding an axe on foreign aid funds. In ten years at the helm of the subcommittee he had presided over the annual pruning of presidential aid requests, averaging about 22 per cent in reductions over the years.

Neither Presidents Eisenhower nor Kennedy had been able to get at Passman. It had become standard operating procedure at the White House to "Passmanize" the foreign aid request, in other words, to inflate it beyond actual needs in recognition of the reductions the Louisiana Representative was certain to engineer.

Kennedy had tried personal appeals to Passman, but nothing seemed to work. Johnson put out the charm for Passman at a White House meeting soon after he became President, but Kennedy's $4.5 billion foreign aid request nevertheless was reduced to $3 billion. Johnson obviously made a mental note at that point to do something about Passman.

Kennedy's reaction to the failure of Congress to act on his requests had been that the people chose the members of Congress as well as the President and that the legislative branch must reflect popular thinking as well as he did. As he remarked to me in January, 1963, when he was lamenting the return in the 1962 elections of so many incumbents who had been opposed or indifferent to his programs, "The people must like what Congress is doing or they wouldn't have reelected so many of its members."

Kennedy had said before he became President that any Chief Executive worth his salt "must formulate and fight for legislative policies, not be a casual bystander to the legislative process." But he had fulfilled a 1960 campaign promise by commissioning Senator Joseph S. Clark, Pennsylvania Democrat, to draft a program of civil rights legislation and had then let Clark and other civil rights advocates sit fuming in the waiting room for two years while he withheld any presidential pressure to gain legislative action.

A realist, Kennedy saw the formidable odds a coalition of Republicans with Southern Democratic conservatives offered against the passage of what he liked to term progressive legislation. He once told a news conference, "We should realize that some Democrats have voted with the Republicans for a good twenty-five years . . . and that makes it very difficult to secure the enactment of any controversial legislation."

Discussing the situation, he once told me that those in Congress who opposed his programs were, for the most part, "solidly based people. . . . A considerable number of them were elected by rather large majorities and they are what you might call impervious to reprisals. There is just no way to convince them they ought to support my programs."

Beyond this, Kennedy was bucking a complacency on the part of the country that was reflected in Congress—a complacency that was shattered by the young President's assassination.

Both Kennedy and Johnson had been men of the Congress. But their experiences there had been vastly different. Kennedy had been an attractive, glamorous figure in the House and Senate, but he had never been a member of the "establishment," the small coterie of men who ran the show. Johnson had sat in the inner circle of power. He and Speaker Rayburn had mapped the strategy for Congress. Members who needed help brought their problems to them. They often went away with their problems solved, but they knew that a day of reciprocity would arrive.

As President, Johnson was more approachable than Kennedy had been. The younger President was always cordial to members of Congress, but he nevertheless had an aloofness about him that prevented his becoming "one of the boys." One Democratic House member, musing on this, said Johnson's invitations to tourists to come in the White House grounds and walk with him, illustrated the point. "Can you imagine Kennedy walking over to the fence, ordering the gates opened and saying, 'You all come on in'?" he asked.

There was a difference, too, in the White House parties. Members of the Senate and House invited by the Kennedys would be beautifully received at a perfectly appointed party, planned in great detail in advance. In contrast, one of the congressional guests described the White House parties when President Johnson entertained as informal affairs where the Johnsons chatted with everybody and "we have fun and relax."

Johnson used just about everything in his astonishing repertory to get Congress moving—his personal contacts with old friends on the Hill, his knowledge of tactics, his immense power as the Chief Executive, plus a persistence that almost literally wore out those who opposed him.

Passman was not the type who could be cajoled or threatened successfully. Neither could he be worn down. The alternative was to run over him, and that is what Johnson set out to do in the foreign aid controversy.

Shortly after he had become President, Johnson had named an interdepartmental committee, headed by Undersecretary of State George W. Ball, to look into the possibilities of reorganizing the aid program. The committee had threshed about several weeks and reached no conclusions. Foreign aid had a bad name in Congress and Johnson, as a Senator, had been cognizant of this fact. He told the Senate on June 29, 1956, "There is no blinking the fact . . . that the American people are not convinced that today's program serves American national interest. The American people are doubtful that any interest is any longer served by continued economic assistance to many nations far from our shores. The [Eisenhower] administration has done little to allay these genuine doubts. Therefore it is imperative that we seek to do so."

When Johnson sent his message to Congress on March 19, 1964, he asked for a $3.4 billion program that would provide a billion dollars for military assistance and the remainder in economic aid. He pledged there would be "no waste" in its administration. Arguing for its approval, he said, "We will be laying up a harvest of woe for our children if we shrink from the task of grappling . . . with poverty and ignorance. These are the grim recruiting sergeants of Communism. They flourish whenever we falter. If we default on our obligations, Communism will expand its ambitions."

As a part of his plan, Johnson had not "Passmanized" his aid request by padding it. He was so successful in selling the idea to members at a White House conference that this was a barebones program that for the first time in seventeen years the House Foreign Affairs Committee approved an authorization for the full amount a President had asked. The authorization merely prepared the way for action on the actual appropriation of funds and Passman was thundering demands for a $519 million reduction.

But Johnson had been busy. He had had members of Passman's Appropriations Subcommittee in for White House breakfasts to discuss this threat and to see what could be done about it. He kept the phone lines hot to these members. He enlisted some of their House colleagues in efforts to overcome their reluctance to turn on Passman and to support foreign aid.

Johnson was fortunate in having capable David E. Bell, a Kennedy holdover, as head of the Agency for International Development, available to help convince the lawmakers that there was no fat in the President's request. And his task was made immeasurably easier by the presence of his good friend Representative George H. Mahon of Texas in the chairmanship of the parent House Appropriations Committee. Where the late Representative Clarence Cannon of Missouri—who sometimes even refused to talk to Kennedy on the phone—had encouraged Passman's axe wielding, Mahon used his prestige to support Johnson.

When the showdown came in the subcommittee, Democratic Representatives William H. Natcher of Kentucky and John J. Flynt, Jr., of Georgia, who had been accustomed to supporting Passman, went over to the other side. Passman proposed cutting $500 million off Johnson's request. By a 7–5 vote the subcommittee limited the cut to $200 million.

This action sent Passman storming out of the committee room assailing the "turncoats and renegades" he said had let him down.

"I am not a political prostitute," Passman shouted. He said Johnson had "worked tricks you couldn't even see in the circus." The full Appropriations Committee then turned back by a 26–22 vote a new effort by Passman to trim the total to $3 billion. The House subsequently passed the measure at the $3.3 billion figure and, in the end, that was what Johnson got from Congress.

The "circus tricks" employed by Johnson were none other than those available to any President adept at offering the carrot or applying the stick. There always were favors a President could do for a cooperative lawmaker. He could instruct the Budget Bureau to put say $25,000 in a public works program for a "planning study" of some project a member wanted in his district. He could offer to campaign personally for the member in the next election. If the member was recalcitrant a President could make things unpleasant for him without half trying.

To bolster his foreign aid case, Johnson had asked and had received public support from Eisenhower. The Republican former President called for approval of the original $3.5 billion program "without partisanship." He said it represented a level of mutual assistance "that cannot be drastically reduced without damaging the vital interests of the United States."

This nudge for Republican support was matched by Johnson's own patented brand of private approach to the Democrats. He told them that "this is a big year for us Democrats" and demanded, "Are you with me or against me?" This method he applied not only to foreign aid but to other measures he regarded as essential.

Not all of the Democrats responded in the expected manner to these appeals. Some had been cut too close to where they lived by the new administration. Representative Thomas (Tip) O'Neill of Massachusetts presented a case in point. O'Neill had been a stanch Kennedy administration man on the House Rules Committee. But when Johnson backed McNamara's program to close unneeded military bases and O'Neill got the word that this might include the Boston Navy Yard and the Watertown, Massachusetts, Arsenal, there were some changes made. About eighty per cent of the Watertown Arsenal's 2,000 workers lived in O'Neill's district and they were frantically interested in what might happen to their jobs. There was also the point of Johnson's June visit to Worcester, Massachusetts, on which the White House had blundered in not permitting the Congressman to announce it first. From such happenings come unexpected opposition, at times, to a President's program.

O'Neill made his weight felt by supplying the necessary margin for an 8–7 vote within the House Rules committee to sidetrack a transportation bill which would have permitted an easement of federal regulations on minimum freight charges by the railroads on perishable commodities. The railroads had wanted this badly and Johnson had promised in the threatened rail strike to help the carriers get it.

This was a part of the price Johnson had to pay for the defense economies McNamara was making. Inherited from the Kennedy administration, the Secretary of Defense had become a catalyst in the application of the Johnson treatment to Congress in the defense field, where the lawmakers could exert their most effective influence on the course of national policy by loosening or tightening the purse strings.

McNamara was the tough, resilient executive who made decisions, fought for them and usually weathered the many-sided attacks made upon him. Backed by the President—and it was the same solid support with Johnson as it had been with Kennedy—the Secretary made the decision to phase out manned bombers in favor of missiles. He cracked service heads together and ordered the production of an all-purpose fighter plane that none of them individually wanted. He cut through the arguments about performances of TFX models and picked General Dynamics to build it over Boeing's bid.

Kennedy hadn't listened much to the generals and admirals after the Bay of Pigs and they had little success in appealing McNamara's decisions to him. As one associate of the late President said at the time, "You don't see much of the Joint Chiefs around the White House any more."

Admiral George W. Anderson, then Chief of Naval Operations, crossed McNamara and found out where Kennedy's commitments lay—with the Secretary of Defense. Anderson was kicked upstairs by appointment as Ambassador to Portugal. He complained bitterly as he left Washington that there did not exist at the Pentagon "the degree of confidence and trust between the civilian and military echelons that the importance of their common objective requires." Then he fired away a broadside at McNamara, "Military men have no crystal ball that can guarantee infallible decisions," he said, "but neither do scientists, analysts, engineers, businessmen, lawyers, or for that matter computers—which must rely on human assumptions for inputs. . . ."

McNamara's bright young civilian researchers and strategists, who fed the product of their brains and computing machines to the Secretary, were assertive and often arrogant with their military counterparts. The military brass responded with deep resentment to these tactics.

When they took their complaints to Johnson, however, they found him just as squarely behind McNamara as Kennedy had been. As a Senator the President had headed the Senate's Preparedness Subcommittee and he knew where the Pentagon bones were buried. The President was likely to hear some complaint made by the military and to retort, "Hell, don't give me that stuff. I know how you birds operate. I investigated the Pentagon enough when I was a Senator. You're not talking to an amateur. What McNamara says goes."

What McNamara said went for Congress, too, so far as Johnson was concerned. Members who brought their complaints against the Secretary got conciliatory conversation but few other results. The plain fact was that Johnson intended to cut defense spending in order to be able to finance social welfare legislation under a reasonably restricted budget and McNamara was the man to do it for him.

Military outlays ate up half or more of the budget and influenced profoundly not only the pattern of the domestic economy but the course of international actions. With the acquiescence of Congress, the Pentagon generals and admirals had been running their own show, determining their own requirements subject only to the Budget Bureau's overall total and telling Congress what it must do to meet these requirements. It had become almost unpatriotic for any lawmaker to question any defense expenditure, no matter how large or how ill-conceived. And squarely behind the military was the huge industrial complex that depended on defense contracts for its life blood of profits.

McNamara, who had come up to the presidency of Ford Motor Company as a slick-haired whiz-kid with an electronic brain, changed all of that. He put the ultimate decisions on service requirements and the fixing of overall policy back in civilian hands. He insisted on sitting in on all-important meetings of the Joint Chiefs.

The military men, of course, took their appeal to Congress. They made what trouble they could for McNamara and in the case of the TFX war plane it was considerable. The Air Force manned-bomber bloc got its usual sympathetic hearing.

But the Secretary was a difficult man to corner. The generals and the admirals found themselves cooling their heels in the Pentagon when McNamara took his civilian experts along to testify on the defense budget. The military men, when they came along later, were free to voice their personal opinions in response to any questions that might be asked. But most of them were wary of straying from the administration line lest they incur a personalized form of the Johnson treatment.

Because of all of this and because he ran a tight ship at the Pentagon, McNamara generally was depicted as a cold, hard, implacable man who wore his heart under a stainless steel shield. Even Johnson joked about this image of his Defense Secretary.

"He treats me just like he treats everybody else," the President told associates. "I called him up at the Pentagon one morning about seven o'clock after I had read in the papers something I thought ought to be checked out. He answered the phone himself. When I told him who I was, he said, 'Yes, Mr. President, I know what you're calling about. I've already got my people investigating it. When I get some answers, I'll call you. Thank you for calling, Mr. President.' Then he hung up on me."

Johnson said all of this with an amused grin at the efficiency with which his Cabinet member had dispatched what otherwise might have been a lengthy conversation. But it gave a distorted picture of McNamara as a sort of computerized martinet. And he really wasn't like that at all. When his integrity was questioned beyond what he regarded as a reasonable point in the TFX war plane investigation by the Senate's Investigating Subcommittee, McNamara wept.

"Last night when I got home at midnight after preparing for today's hearing," he said, "my wife told me that my twelve-year-old son had asked how long it would take for his father to prove his honesty."

Like Johnson, McNamara was the kind who worked all hours of the day and loaded tasks on his subordinates. But he was also the kind who would call up an employee's wife, tell her the value of her husband's work, and thank her for being patient about the hours the employee had to spend at it.

One day the Secretary heard that a hard-working assistant had turned down a chance to go on a Caribbean cruise. He urged his aide to change his mind, but the latter replied that he was too busy to get away.

"All right," McNamara said, "I won't take any vacation this year either. Damned if I'll admit you're more valuable around here than I am." The assistant went on his cruise.

In a practical way, McNamara was Johnson's man in Saigon, so far as Congress was concerned. When General Nguyen Khanh first had taken over in South Vietnam two months after he had come into office, Johnson rushed McNamara to Saigon with orders to try to bolster popular support for the new regime. If he was not exactly the type for it, the Secretary went about with the Vietnamese general on village handshaking tours, patting children on the head, plowing through swarming crowds and generally acting like Lyndon Johnson in an election campaign.

Senator Wayne Morse, Oregon Democrat, who said the

United States had no business in Vietnam, called the struggle "McNamara's war." And at a subsequent news conference the Cabinet member said he didn't mind accepting that classification. He was much more willing to have it known in Congress as "McNamara's war" than as "Johnson's war."

There was no doubt about the President's appreciation of all of the services that his Defense Secretary was performing for him. Johnson made this clear when he said at one point, "I couldn't sleep at night if I didn't know that Bob McNamara, or somebody like him, was Secretary of Defense."

Johnson had an acute and unremitting need for men like McNamara in his administration, but he was having difficulty retaining other top officials because of the financial sacrifice government service entailed for some of them. Johnson determined to do something about this and set about applying "the treatment."

The late President Kennedy had tried to cope with this problem by recommending a federal pay increase to Congress early in 1963. As with so many of his recommendations, nothing much had happened. When Johnson came into office he at first was reluctant to pick up the pay bill because it offered a definite threat to his program to cut the federal budget. But in his efforts to get key officials to stay on, he was encountering the feeling, among some of them, that they had served their time and that a change of administrations offered an opportunity to get out and make more money.

Johnson decided just before Christmas, 1963, that he would back the pay increase. But he told the Budget Bureau it would have to cut an additional $544 million elsewhere in the budget to finance the measure. The President put on the heat for early congressional action, on the theory that if members moved quickly to increase their own and other government salaries, the voters would have forgotten about it by the time the fall campaign rolled around.

But it didn't work out that way. The bill carried a boost of

$10,000 in congressional salaries, raising them to $32,500. It increased the pay of Cabinet members from $25,000 to $35,000. When it came before the House in March, leaders maneuvered to ward off changes in it by standing votes, in which members would not have to go on record individually on the issues involved. But Representative H. R. Gross, an Iowa Republican who made it his business to keep a close watch on government spending, demanded and got a roll call vote. The election year fat was in the blaze when members had to go on record in voting, and the House killed the measure by a 222–184 count.

Kennedy might have given up on the proposal at that point, but Johnson wouldn't quit. He insisted, in public statements and private talks with legislators, that a pay increase was vital to efficient government. He cited instances of public officials, including Heller, who had had to borrow money because their salaries were not sufficient to cover living expenses in official circles in Washington.

Representative James H. Morrison, Louisiana Democrat, who had piloted the original bill in the House, was reluctant to try again. He and House leaders felt they would only take another shellacking. But Johnson overruled them. He wheeled his staff into action and plunged into the business of personally lining up the votes in the House. The bill had been revised so that it provided only a $7,500 pay increase for Senators and Representatives and Cabinet members. Liberal Democrats from California and New York were threatening to vote against it unless the $10,000 raise for the Cabinet was restored.

Johnson went to work on the Senate Post Office and Civil Service Committee to get an announcement that that body would put the larger increase in the bill when it acted. There was a great deal of grumbling among Senators that they were being asked to take the political rap for the House, which nearly always cut appropriations with the belief that the Senate would restore the larger amounts.

Balking House members were demanding a public statement

from the Senate Committee of its intentions. The President's men thought they had this lined up at a meeting of the Senate group. But Republicans, fully aware of what was going on, boycotted the meeting. Chairman Olin D. Johnston, South Carolina Democrat, wasn't in any position to take a vote on the issue so the House had to act without any public assurances. But Johnson and his men had done their work well. On June 11, the House voted 243–157 to pass the bill.

When the Senate acted as expected to restore the $10,000 pay increase for Cabinet members, Johnson said in signing the $558 million measure on August 14 that Congress had been "energetic, even-handed and effective."

The pay increase helped, but it did not solve the problem Johnson had encountered in trying to persuade the men he wanted to come into government or to take on some of the "distasteful, disagreeable and tough jobs" which had to be filled to make his administration a success.

Talking to members of a private, domestic counterpart of the Peace Corps, the International Executive Service Corps, in the White House flower garden on June 15, Johnson praised its volunteer members for their efforts to provide overseas enterprises with managerial skill to aid the developing countries. In contrast, he said, when he wanted men to do some job for him that would not cover them with publicity glory—and in fact might result in their becoming something like public villains—they were hard to come by. "Their wife was sick or their daughter was going off to college, or they just couldn't spare the time to save the Republic," he said.

Johnson also had been busy on another front, trying to cope with a problem that Kennedy had left unsolved. In 1963 Kennedy had sent to Congress a "do-it-yourself" farm program in which he invited the farmers to write their own regulations. He urged expanded production controls—asking farmers to approve a referendum on mandatory limits on wheat growing—and offered government subsidies on feed grains and dairy products.

Congress had kicked the program out the back door. Members declined to go along with the rigid controls that Secretary Freemen advocated. The farmers themselves dealt the administration a stunning blow by rejecting wheat controls.

The cold facts of politics were that the farmers no longer had the political power they had enjoyed so long in Congress. Freeman conceded this when he told a Worthington, Minnesota, audience in September, 1963, that "Congress today is orientated toward urban matters and there are about three hundred members [of the House] without any major farm interests in their districts."

But Johnson was not ignoring the traditional farm vote. The House previously had defeated the administration's food stamp plan, which the Congressmen in big cities liked because it helped take care of the needy in their districts. It also had an indelible federal stamp on it, which indicated that the Representative in question was working for their interests in Washington.

The President conceived the idea that he could trade food stamps off for a farm bill, thus benefiting the slum residents and those on the farms. And it worked.

In a fourteen-hour session of the House on April 9, Johnson kept the Representatives on both sides of the question hopping with telephone calls. The members were reminded that if they wanted something for their people, they had better vote for the other man's interests. To the farm state members, who were reluctant about what was being offered to them, the President said, "My ox is in the ditch and I need your help." He appealed to his listeners' patriotism and to their recognition of the Democratic party's needs for some kind of settlement of the farm issue before the presidential campaign began. The word to the city Democrats was colder: vote for the cotton-wheat bill if you want your food stamp plan; this is the only way you are going to get it.

When he signed the cotton-wheat bill, the President said it "gives us some insurance against a depression on the farm."

The bill provided about $1 billion in payments to cotton and wheat farmers and in subsidies to domestic cotton mills. That it was considerably less than a cure-all for the farm problem became evident in the fall when various farm organizations began a vigorous campaign against its terms.

The food stamp plan, an intregal part of the Johnson antipoverty program, also won congressional approval. Under it, needy families would receive stamps which could be offered as payment to merchants for the difference between an average family's normal expenditure for food and what the stamp recipients were able to pay.

Johnson had been able to hold the political allegiance of the big-city Representatives to the farm bill by giving them the stamp plan. He had overcome in this way their reluctance to vote for a farm subsidy which the consumers might suspect would increase their food prices. He had to overcome, too, the feeling among farm state Representatives that by voting for the stamp plan they would be charged at home with increasing federal spending and thus boosting taxes on the hard-working citizens of their areas to aid "shiftless" people in the cities.

While this was a tremendous accomplishment, the Johnson treatment at times fell short of producing political miracles.

All of his efforts couldn't get Johnson everything he wanted out of Congress. In addition to civil rights, the anti-poverty program, tax reduction, mass transportation and farm legislation, Congress had piled up a substantial record of action on other legislation. When he threw a White House party for all of the members of Congress late in the summer, Johnson took fifteen minutes out during a musical extravaganza to praise the lawmakers as constructive, compassionate and cooperative. Most Republicans weren't there to hear it. "This session of Congress," he said, "has enacted more major legislation—met more national needs—disposed of more national issues than any other session of this century or the last."

But it wasn't enough. The President wanted more. Despite

the fact that it was election year, he ordered congressional leaders to bring their members back into sessions after the nominating conventions. Specifically, Johnson wanted action on a $1 billion bill to aid the economy of the Appalachia area and he wanted a record made on an attempt to pass a program for health care for the elderly financed through increased social security taxes. This was the so-called medicare bill.

But Dirksen came along with a proposal to stall court-ordered reapportionment of state legislatures and offered it as a rider to the foreign aid authorization bill. That put the monkey wrench squarely in the machinery and poorly attended sessions dragged along for weeks. Halleck complained it was all the Democrats' fault for trying to cram too much through the weary Congress. "We find a situation in which this body cannot seem to legislate and, for some reason beyond my comprehension, does not know how to quit and go home," he said.

The President wasn't going to let it quit if he could help it. But in this case he couldn't. The Senate obediently put the medicare proposal on a bill to increase social security benefits, which already had been passed by the House. But the House refused to accept this action and the measure went down the drain along with the Appalachia bill when Congress finally broke the deadlock, approved foreign aid and adjourned.

There was always next year in which to grapple with such issues. But for the international problems which pressed in on the President there were sometimes only minutes or hours at most.

11 At the Risk of War

O<small>N THE SWELTERING NIGHT</small> of August 4, 1964, President Lyndon B. Johnson came face-to-face with the issue of war or peace, just as President Kennedy had faced this issue in the October, 1962, Cuban missile crisis. Naturally, there was a fundamental difference. Kennedy had been confronted with the possibility that his decision might trigger a nuclear war which would destroy the world. Johnson's was a decision that would have involved a limited war, fought with non-nuclear weapons, but one which might easily have accelerated into another Korean conflict.

Both American Presidents had decided in their own time and in their own way that they must respond to aggression. Kennedy imposed sanctions in the form of a quarantine, backed by nuclear force if needed. Johnson responded by ordering conventional military retaliation of a limited scope. Johnson's decision was simplified because the Chinese Communists did not then have nuclear weapons at their command.

On August 2 several PT boats presumed to be under the command of North Vietnam had attacked the destroyer *Maddox*, which was on patrol in the Bay of Tonkin. The bay is a sort of inland lake of large proportions nearly surrounded by

Chinese Communist and North Vietnam-held territory. The *Maddox* had fired back and had inflicted unconfirmed damage on the PT boats.

Washington viewed all of this with a great deal of alarm. There were diverse opinions on whether the action was the kind of military accident that often happens or whether it was part of a direct Communist plan to enlarge the Asian conflict. Johnson ordered another destroyer into the Tonkin Gulf and directed that aircraft carriers, which couldn't venture into such land-restricted areas, stand by in the sea outside.

While the argument still was going on in the White House and the State Department about the meaning of this attack, North Vietnamese torpedo boats, if they could be called that, advanced against the *Maddox* and the destroyer *C. Turner Joy*, which Johnson had directed to join in the hazardous patrol with shoot-to-kill orders to all concerned.

On August 3, Washington time, the two destroyers were cruising on what the Pentagon described later as a "routine patrol in the Tonkin Gulf in international waters about sixty-five miles from the nearest land" when they were approached by "an undetermined number of North Vietnamese torpedo boats."

With a turbulent sea running high, the attackers launched what a Pentagon spokesman said were "lots of torpedoes." The two destroyers returned a hail of shells, rockets and machine-gun fire. They called on the aircraft carriers standing out to sea for help. With the aid of carrier bombers and fighters, the attackers were driven off with what was reported, but not necessarily confirmed, as significant losses.

That the attackers' losses were not large was indicated by Johnson's furious reaction to the Navy's failure to "blow those boats out of the water."

"Those Navy boys need some more target practice," the President stormed, adding what an aide described as "some sulphurous language."

Johnson was confronted at this point with a major decision. There was no unanimity of opinion among high officials of the administration as to what had triggered the attacks. There was one view that perhaps this was just one of those military accidents that had a way of happening unexpectedly. Another was that the North Vietnamese believed the *Maddox* had been involved in a South Vietnamese attack on coastal islands several days earlier and they were trying to retaliate. There were other theories, one being that the North Vietnamese were making an inexpensive test of whether they would receive aid from either Peking or Moscow if hostilities developed, another that they were acting on the assumption that the cold war had immobilized Washington from retaliating.

Johnson had to guess at the motives behind the attack in order to gauge the extent of his own action. He also had to consider the possibilities that retaliation might bring a wave of Communist Chinese jet fighters into Hanoi, might trigger a southward movement of Chinese troops and might step up the Vietcong's offensive in Vietnam.

The difficulty encountered by any President in reaching a decision in a crisis was amply illustrated here. None of the factors that had been brought to his attention could be disregarded. It was necessary for the Chief Executive to weigh each one and then to decide for himself which course to take and when to take it.

Johnson announced his decision at the White House luncheon meeting within three hours after news of the attack had reached him. He summoned Rusk, McNamara, Bundy and other officials. After reviewing briefly what everyone then knew about the situation, Johnson let the others talk. He had made his decision already, but he didn't show his hand as his advisers tossed out their suggestions. When he had heard enough, the President said he was going to retaliate in a limited way for the attacks.

Johnson told a subsequent news conference that "there are

those who felt that as soon as vessels showed on radar we should start retaliating by dropping bombs around the country. . . . But I felt," he continued, "we should take a day, one day of daylight time, to find out before involving this country in serious consequences."

Participants in the conferences said there never was any consideration given to bombing Hanoi. When the National Security Council discussed what should be done, the only argument against military retaliation was a limited one by Rusk. He advocated passing up the North Vietnamese bases nearest Red China, lest some American fighter or bomber stray over the line into Chinese territory.

All of Johnson's aides voiced the belief that an attack on U.S. naval forces sixty-five miles at sea could not be glossed over. The President knew the risk of giving the Communists any excuse for enlarging the war. But he overruled Rusk and ordered an air strike made on all of the North Vietnamese bases. This had the approval of McNamara and the Joint Chiefs. Johnson specifically declared Hanoi out of bounds and sent instructions to the carrier commanders to see to it that nobody strayed off target.

Shortly after he had come into office, Johnson had told President Chiari of Panama that he was "damned sick and tired" of trumped-up attacks on American property and American interests. He had not changed his mind eight months later when he ordered the fleet into air action.

McGeorge Bundy, who had been at the hub of decision-making by Kennedy for more than three years, was full of admiration for Johnson's decisiveness. Bundy told associates that he had "never seen a man who knew so clearly what he wanted to do or so exactly how to go about it."

Bundy, who had not been a particular favorite of Johnson when the latter was Vice President, had advanced in the President's esteem to the point where there was no question among members of the executive staff that he would get top consideration for the post if Rusk ever chose to quit as Secretary of State. As one long-time associate of Johnson put it, "We'd hate to think of trying to run the White House without Bundy."

To announce his crisis decision, the President went on television-radio at 11:49 P.M., Washington time, on August 4. He said that "these acts of violence against the armed forces of the United States must be met not only by alert defense, but with positive reply." Then he added, "That reply is being given as I speak to you. Air action is now in execution against gunboats and certain supporting facilities of North Vietnam which have been used in these hostile operations."

Secretary McNamara said later that twenty-five patrol boats were damaged or destroyed and that an oil storage depot was ninety per cent destroyed.

Senator Goldwater, reached on the West Coast by telephone, supported the move. He said that what the President had done was "the only thing that he could do under the circumstances.

"We cannot allow the American flag to be shot at anywhere on earth if we are to retain our respect and prestige," he said in a statement handed to reporters before the President went on the air with his announcement.

This kind of bipartisan support for a President, when military action was called for, was traditional. When Harry Truman ordered U.S. air action in Korea in an attempt to halt the aggression which the North Koreans had launched, Senator Robert A. Taft of Ohio had argued that the Democratic President was not justified in acting without prior consent of Congress. But he added that he saw "no choice except to back wholeheartedly and with every available resource" the adventure on which the President had cast the nation.

This bipartisanship did not last long, however, and no President really expected that it would. Soon the Republicans were calling Korea "Truman's war" and denouncing America's involvement in it. Among the many reasons Eisenhower won the 1952 election was his promise to "go to Korea" and his implied pledge that he would end a war of which the American people had grown weary and which the Democratic administration could not seem to bring to a close.

Johnson faced a parallel situation in Vietnam. Most voters did not really understand why it was necessary—and many questioned that it was—for U.S. servicemen to die there to maintain a semblance of the balance of power in Asia. And if we were fighting, a great many of them wanted to know, why maintain the pretense of conducting an "instructional" operation?

Johnson did what he could to close every possible door against political criticism. He had called the congressional leaders of both parties to the White House in advance of his televised speech to inform them what he was doing. There could be no practical dissent when a President had made up his mind to act in such a situation. What alternatives could the Republicans offer from their meager knowledge of the military necessities? But as one influential Republican remarked afterward, "All of us went along, of course. We couldn't do anything else if we had wanted to, and I don't think any of us would have wanted to disagree with what he proposed to do. But that didn't mean that if things had turned out badly that we wouldn't have blamed him. In fact, I can see the time coming when we'll be campaigning against 'Johnson's war.' "

The Democratic President was able to say in his televised speech, however, that a resolution he was sending Congress to make it "clear that our government is united in its determination to take all necessary measures in support of freedom, and in defense of peace, in Southeast Asia" would have overwhelming support.

Indeed it did. There were few, except such a hardy soul as Senator Wayne Morse, Oregon Democrat, who were willing to risk criticism of the President's course. But Morse's was a voice crying out in the wilderness when he told the Senate that the Bay of Tonkin incident was "as much the doing of the United

States as it is the doing of North Vietnam." His contention was that U.S. vessels had performed a patrol mission for South Vietnamese attacks on two North Vietnamese islands within three to six miles of the Communist-held coast.

When he signed the resolution on August 10, 1964, Johnson was surrounded in the Oval Room office by the Joint Chiefs of Staff and congressional leaders of both parties. The resolution authorized the President to "take all necessary steps, including the use of armed force, to assist any member or protocol state of the Southeast Asia Collective Defense Treaty requesting assistance in defense of its freedom." To this Johnson added in a statement at the signing: "The position of the United States is stated plainly. To any armed attack upon our forces, we shall reply. To any in Southeast Asia who ask our help in defending their freedom, we shall give it."

Johnson thus had shored up a political base which Truman had ignored and to which Kennedy had paid almost no attention in his handling of the Cuban missile crisis. Johnson had followed the lead of Republican Eisenhower, who got advance approval of Congress for whatever he might do in the Formosa Straits and in the Middle East.

But at best this approval remained a Maginot line susceptible to being out-flanked by political opponents. Goldwater began this movement without much success a few days later. He criticized Johnson for not going far enough in retaliation against the attacks on U.S. ships. He declared that the United States must "prosecute the war in Vietnam with the intention of ending it." He added that the "taking of strong action simply to return to the status quo is not worthy of our sacrifices."

The Republican presidential nominee suggested also that Johnson had freed the fleet to retaliate with nuclear weapons if necessary. Squirming to get out from under the charge that he was "trigger-happy" because he had suggested the North Atlantic Treaty Organization (NATO) commanders should be given authority to trigger tactical nuclear weapons, Goldwater said that perhaps it was Johnson who really was "trigger-happy." Rusk and McNamara fired back in a few hours that no such authorization had been given. The President himself supplied later the information that the orders to the Navy had specified "conventional weapons." This gave him a welcome chance to tell a news conference that Goldwater had done "a disservice to our national security, a disservice to peace, and for that matter, a disservice to the entire free world."

Rather thoroughly rebuffed at this point, Goldwater was back knocking on the door nine days after his first charge with the assertion that Johnson had endangered the lives of American pilots by giving the North Vietnamese warning of the U.S. attack by telling the world about it before it was actually under way.

McNamara replied that the President's forewarning was intended to communicate to "others," presumably Communist China, the limited nature of the retaliation. As a White House aide later explained it: "Once those planes lifted off the carriers, we had to assume that the Communist radar would pick them up. It was important at that point to make it clear that this was a retaliatory attack on the torpedo bases and not a strike at China itself."

The Tonkin Bay incident had been of considerable domestic political benefit to Johnson. It had demonstrated to most voters they had a President who would not falter in a crisis. He had reacted as most Americans wanted their Chief Executive to react when U.S. fighting men were involved.

Johnson's handling of the crisis also had a deep impact on Europeans who still were wondering what kind of President he would turn out to be when he faced an international crisis. Just as Kennedy's international stock had rocketed as a result of the Cuban missile showdown, Johnson's went up. Whether they believed the United States had any business in the Bay of Tonkin, the world's statesmen recognized that here was a President who understood how to implement tremendous power with restraint.

In Asia the action undermined the Communist propaganda

that the United States was only a "paper tiger." Instead, it was a tiger armed with deadly claws which struck with discernment.

All of this was gratifying to Johnson. But he had studied enough history to know that opinion could turn quickly. Unless he found some solution to the Vietnam problem—and none was in sight as he ended his first year in office—his hopes for a return to the White House in 1968 could be wrecked on the shoals of Southeast Asia. Beyond that, Johnson, more than any other man, wanted to stop the slow but inexorable slaughter of Americans in Vietnam for no discernible gain.

The Democratic President knew that this issue was packed in an explosive political package with a slow fuse. He might patch and improvise to shield himself from it in the 1964 elections, as he did, but the seemingly insoluble problem would not go away in the future. Its repercussions might evaporate all of the esteem in which he felt the people held him when they gave him a landslide election victory.

It had all begun long ago at Dienbienphu when the French were forced out of the peninsula. Laos had become the chief problem of the Eisenhower administration. In the viewpoint of most Americans Laos wasn't a nation at all but a conglomeration of tribes of people who evinced little interest in whether they were ruled by Communists, neutralists or Westerners so long as their rice paddies went unmolested. Dulles had sold Eisenhower on the "falling domino" theory that if Laos went under to the Communist Pathet Lao all of Southeast Asia would fall with it. Besides, the guerrillas were filtering troops through Laos to Vietnam.

Late in 1960 Eisenhower had told Kennedy, in one of those uncomfortable conferences between the outgoing and the incoming Presidents, that he was distressed to leave his successor with the nasty problem of Laos.

"He just kind of threw up his hands and said he was sorry but I might be forced to commit troops to Laos," the late President had recalled. "He said it was my problem now."

Unfortunately Kennedy had dived overboard in the 1960 campaign with pledges that his administration would prevent the Communists from taking over Laos. These promises took on a new dimension when he had had time to sit down as Chief Executive to determine what could be done to defend the vital Plain of Jars. It was 9,000 miles from Washington, 4,000 miles from Moscow but only 140 miles from Communist China's border.

Kennedy took the extraordinary course as President of making a chart talk on Laos at a televised news conference. He told his fellow Americans that Laos was far away and the world was small.

"The security of Southeast Asia will be endangered if Laos loses its neutral independence," he said.

The White House mail failed to indicate that many Americans were aroused about the matter. The television viewers had listened to the President explain a crisis that seemed remote to most of them.

Kennedy found himself in a situation, as all Presidents must at times, where public opinion would not support any strong move. When he had held his first conference with Khrushchev at Vienna, about the only concession the American President got from the then head of the Russian state was an agreement for a cease fire in Laos.

Making the best of the matter, Kennedy sent W. Averell Harriman to Asia and then to Geneva to try for the best possible deal at a fourteen-nation conference. It was not a very good deal, as it turned out. It called for a coalition government which the Republicans freely predicted the Communists would take over in time. Even before this unhappy solution was reached at Geneva, Kennedy had had to send ground and air forces to Thailand to protect that country if Laos were overrun by the Communists.

Johnson thus inherited in his succession to the presidency—and made no outward move to change—the Democratic administration's theory that if South Vietnam or Laos fell to the

Communists, the shock waves would roll over Cambodia, Thailand, Burma and Malaysia.

The new President had to cope with the chameleon attitudes of Prince Souvanna Phouma, the neutralist Laotian Premier, who was for the West one week, for the Pathet Lao the next, and neutral the third. Johnson was forced to take some military steps in Laos. The United States sent reconnaissance planes over the country to check on Communist violations of the Geneva agreement after Phouma asked for them. When Pathet Lao gunners attacked them, U.S. carrier planes bombed out the antiaircraft-gun emplacements.

But it was in Vietnam that the great gamble lay. From November 1, 1963, when President Ngo Dinh Diem and his powerful brother had been deposed and killed, there had been little stability in the Saigon government. Each upheaval, and they occurred with monotonous regularity, threatened the American position there.

Unless the United States could maintain a stable government, it might be forced to intervene directly instead of carrying out the diplomatic formula that it was there because its help had been asked. If a neutralist government came to power, the Americans would be asked to get out. If they did not go they would be subjected to a barrage of unfavorable world opinion likely to be shared by their allies. The alternative of entering negotiations while the Vietcong still retained the military initiative seemed likely to invite an eventual Communist take-over.

From the beginning, Johnson had kept a middle course in Vietnam. He rejected Air Force pressure to bomb the supply lines in North Vietnam and to attack Hanoi itself. He had reinforced the U.S. military contingent. But the President's decision was to continue—as Senator Dirksen put it after a bipartisan White House briefing by General Maxwell D. Taylor on September 9, 1963—"to plow the long, hard furrow."

Taylor had been tapped by Johnson in June to leave his post as Chairman of the Joint Chiefs of Staff to become Ambassador to Saigon when Henry Cabot Lodge, the 1960 Republican candidate for Vice President, asked to be relieved. Johnson had also sent along U. Alexis Johnson, a career diplomat, as Deputy Ambassador.

How unpredictable the situation had become was demonstrated on Taylor's return to Saigon, after a Washington report, when there was a bloodless military uprising aimed at ousting Premier Nguyen Khanh, the thirty-seven-year-old general who then had held on to power for eight months in the American-backed government. Taylor had no inkling of any such move on his visit home to report. Khanh survived the move because his troops generally refused to go along with the 2,000 or more rebels who had marched into Saigon but who didn't fire a shot.

While he was in Washington, Taylor had explained succinctly why Johnson could not extricate the United States easily from its South Vietnam commitments. The handsome soldier-scholar, who had been brought into the administration by Kennedy as a White House military adviser and then was made Chairman of the Joint Chiefs of Staff, had won Johnson's high regard and full confidence. There was no doubt Taylor was reflecting the President's viewpoint when he told a House Foreign Affairs subcommittee why the Americans could not pull up stakes.

"It would mean first, that South Vietnam would become Communist almost at once," he said. "Second, it will prove that Ho Chi Minh [North Vietnamese leader] and Khrushchev were right in believing that they have a new tactic, the war of liberation, which cannot be defeated by the strongest nation in the world.

"After Communist success in South Vietnam, the remainder of Southeast Asia would very shortly thereafter go neutralist, possibly even Communist. Burma would be affected, India also. Indonesia would soon line up with the Communists. We would be pushed out of the Western Pacific back to Honolulu. That would be the short term effect over the next few years."

With so much at stake, Johnson tried desperately to bring

U.S. allies into the Vietnam picture. He sent Lodge off to Europe to solicit support of a policy that called for containing and weakening the Vietcong to the point where it would be on the defensive when any international negotiations were undertaken to end the conflict.

Lodge made his hat-in-hand round of European capitals. When he came back to report to Johnson in a private conference, the President made a show of satisfaction. After the conference he walked arm-in-arm with Lodge to a battery of microphones and cameras at the White House front steps.

The tall Ambassador-at-Large turned on the enthusiasm in reading a statement in which he said that, "broadly speaking, the governments which I have visited expressed appreciation for the United States efforts in Vietnam, hoped for success of these efforts and gave assurance of help.

"The outlook, therefore," Lodge continued, "is for more flags in Vietnam and for more people in the field who will share some of the dangers and discomforts involved in helping the Vietnamese in their struggle for freedom."

How much of the "dangers and discomforts" they would share, however, remained problematical. Nine of ten countries had agreed to give some aid to South Vietnam. Europeans were not eager to get involved in that far away place. All the aid they promised was of a non-military nature. The Dutch, for example, said they would bring some Vietnamese students to the Netherlands for university study.

Significantly absent from the list of nations which promised even such meager aid was France. President de Gaulle had expressed concern with the welfare of the Vietnamese people. But that was all.

Washington blamed De Gaulle and his neutralist policies for much of its troubles in Southeast Asia. Since the French had been forced out of Indochina in 1954 they had never lost hope they could return.

Senator Dirksen related how the French had tried to influence him when he visited Saigon on an inspection trip. He said that after being briefed by Diem government officials he was invited to a formal dinner at the French embassy:

"There were five wine glasses lined up beside my plate," he said. "There was consternation on the faces of my hosts when I sat down and proceeded to turn all of them upside down. The conversation was considerably less convivial than they had expected and they didn't get anywhere trying to sell me their neutralist viewpoint."

De Gaulle first openly broke with American policy on August 29, 1963, when he said in a statement made public in Paris that the people of France would be prepared to help the Vietnamese people to rid themselves of "foreign influence." Since then Paris said often and publicly that American policy was wrong.

A master at exploiting what he regarded as the inevitable, De Gaulle took the position that the war could not be won in Vietnam, drawing on French experience in that respect. And he was confident that other U.S. allies would not join in any expansion of the hostilities that could burgeon into a "white man's war" in Asia. Unfortunately, all he had to offer as an alternative was a neutralization proposal which involved an American surrender.

If De Gaulle could be ignored temporarily in Vietnam the time was approaching when he must be dealt with in Europe. Johnson recognized this and he was getting his ducks in a row.

12 The Diplomatic Hat

As HE BECAME more and more immersed in the international problems which demanded his attention at all hours of the day or night, it became increasingly clear that President Johnson was preparing the way to employ personal diplomacy on a scale perhaps never matched since the days of Franklin D. Roosevelt.

Because there was a vacancy in the vice presidency, Johnson had imposed upon himself the restriction that he would not travel outside the country. This required other heads of state and foreign ministers who wished to consult with him to meet the President either in Washington or at his Texas ranch. With the restriction lifted after his election, Johnson was likely to become a President who had plans, would travel.

But he was a cautious and prudent man. He would not go gallivanting off on on foreign junkets just to hear the cheers of the multitudes, much as he was exhilarated by them. Eisenhower and Kennedy had demonstrated that an appearance of an American President aboard could recharge good will for the United States. But there had to be more than that.

Johnson wanted results and they came only out of laborious groundwork, careful preparations and expert timing. He was tempted after his overwhelming landslide election to make a quick trip to Europe. But he rejected the idea because he felt the time was not ripe for a confrontation with Charles de Gaulle—and it would be embarrassing to pass up Paris.

One of the strongest likelihoods in Johnson's future was that, if both survived, he and De Gaulle would have to sit down together to try to talk out the differences that were threatening to splinter the Free World. So in a period in which the French leader was preaching neutralism in Asia, causing dissension in the European Common Market, opposing the Multilateral Nuclear Force and threatening to withdraw entirely from NATO, Johnson was endeavoring to find some way of approaching him.

The President had had a taste of De Gaulle's imperiousness in the timing and the manner in which the latter announced his decision to recognize Communist China. Knowing that the action would be repugnant to Washington, the French President had publicized his decision in the period when Johnson was struggling to organize his own administration after Kennedy's death.

Instead of communicating directly with the American President and without any preliminary discussion of the matter, De Gaulle sent his Ambassador around to inform Johnson that the decision had been made. This was the kind of insensitive procedure De Gaulle himself would have taken as a personal affront. It was an understatement to say that Johnson was not pleased.

In addition, the French President withdrew his country's officers from the NATO naval headquarters units. He had already withdrawn French ships earmarked for NATO duty in case of conflict. Now he was isolating France from allied planning in NATO naval councils. Johnson's reaction was that he would not fuss publicly at De Gaulle about these actions because there was no way in which he could reverse them. He would have to wait until De Gaulle had run his unilateral course.

However, Johnson was not a man merely to sit around and

wait. So he went outside of diplomatic channels in an effort to get to De Gaulle. The President's old Texas friend, Robert Anderson, who had served as Eisenhower's Secretary of the Treasury, had a long-time friendship with General Pierre Billotte, who had been De Gaulle's chief-of-staff in wartime.

In March, 1964, De Gaulle called in Billotte to discuss the rivalry between the United States and France over NATO tank designs. The French President approved a trip to Washington in April on which Billotte avoided his own embassy and arranged, through Anderson, a conference with Johnson. McGeorge Bundy was present. Johnson said he would review the matter of tank armor with McNamara. Then the President proceeded to explore with his visitor some of the differences which had cooled the two countries' relations.

Billotte went back to Paris to report at length to De Gaulle. He got the French President's agreement to see Anderson and an appointment was set for May 30. When Anderson told Johnson about it, the President decided to follow it up with an official visit by Undersecretary of State Ball, who was by way of becoming the administration's chief troubleshooter. Ball, a gray-haired, husky two-hundred-pounder with a ready wit and dogged determination in negotiations, had met with De Gaulle before. Once, in reporting to Kennedy on a frustrating conference with the French President, Ball remarked that "every time the hand of friendship has been extended across the sea, General De Gaulle has put a dead fish in it."

But this time there was more success. Anderson and Ball, who called on the French President June 5, came away with an agreement that there was need for high level discussions aimed at improving relationships. There the matter was left standing until after the presidential election.

Johnson also had been preparing for a confrontation with Nikita Khrushchev until the latter suddenly disappeared in a sea of oblivion in Russia. The Soviet upheaval, in which Alexei Kosygin was named Premier and Leonid Brezhnev Communist

Party Secretary, caught the United States by surprise and nullified all the preparations which had been made toward a possible summit conference in which the President and the Russian leader could test their individual abilities.

John McCone, director of the Central Intelligence Agency, said a month after the event that the change-over came as "a distinct surprise—not only to us but to the [Soviet] Presidium as well." McCone's view was that Khrushchev's critics "did not themselves believe they had the strength to remove him" until they had assembled in Moscow on October 14, 1964.

This development canceled out the feelers both sides had put out for a Johnson-Khrushchev meeting to discuss further advances in the policy of coexistence which Kennedy had helped nurture and which Johnson was pursuing. If any administration policy seemed to have received a mandate in the presidential election, this apparently was one. Goldwater had called for a "tough" attitude toward the Russians, including the threat of breaking off diplomatic relations with them if they did not behave as the United States wished them to do. Johnson had made it clear he expected to go beyond the limited nuclear test ban treaty in a search for the kind of accommodation with the Russians that would permit honorable avoidance of nuclear destruction.

But the disappearance of Khrushchev left the President without sound basis upon which to build toward the personal diplomacy in which he felt there was hope for agreements that might lead to the shining goal of a lasting peace. The history of Communist Russia suggested that power eventually would devolve upon one man. But which man, in this case? There was nothing much Johnson could do except await developments.

When Anatoly Dobrynin, the Russian Ambassador, called at the White House on April 17, 1964, he had been received in what presidential aides called a "very friendly" atmosphere. Dobrynin agreed with this assessment of his meeting with Johnson, McGeorge Bundy and U.S. Ambassador-at-Large

Llewellyn E. Thompson, Jr. There had been discussion of what Dobrynin called "many aspects of our relations." In other words, the opening feelers were made for an eventual summit meeting. The Russian Ambassador's official task was to deliver to the President a letter from Khrushchev agreeing to a cutback in each country's production of enriched uranium, thus paving the way for a joint announcement the following week.

But the problem of the then-current flare-up over American aerial surveillance of Cuba had come up. On an irregular schedule, the United States was sending high-speed and high-altitude planes from bases in Texas, Florida and other Southeastern states to photograph Cuba from stem to stern. Many of these were U-2's, which flew more than 500 miles an hour at altitudes up to 90,000 feet to make detailed pictures of the island.

In their 1962 missile adventure, the Russians had installed in Cuba five hundred SAM-2 antiaircraft missiles capable of knocking down U.S. jets. They had trained Cuban crews to operate these weapons. Since the Russians themselves had knocked down a U-2 over their territory—an excuse which Khrushchev had used to torpedo his Paris summit meeting with Eisenhower—and had blasted another out of the skies during the 1962 Cuban missile crisis, the problem remained of what Fidel Castro's gunners might do.

McCone said the U-2 flights over Cuba which revealed Soviet missiles on the ground in the 1962 crisis constituted "one of the greatest intelligence achievements of the present day." He added that for years the U-2 had gathered "invaluable information" about Russian military developments. After Eisenhower ordered such flights discontinued, the CIA director said other more sophisticated means were brought into use. This seemed to be a reference to "spy-in-the-sky" satellites which literally photographed about everything on earth.

When the change in Soviet rulers came in the fall of 1964, Johnson's problem was to attempt to divine whether the new

Russian regime would restrain the Cuban gunners, as had Khrushchev's, from firing on American planes. Barring such an overt act he made it clear he had no intention of taking an immediate initiative against Fidel Castro's government. He counted on economic pressure and time to topple the dictator.

This was the basic U.S. policy sketched out by Johnson in discussions with Gustavo Diaz Ordaz, then President elect of Mexico, at the LBJ ranch shortly after the U.S. presidential election. Johnson was making every effort to keep relations with Mexico, which still maintained diplomatic ties with Cuba, on a personal plane.

Of more immediate importance than Cuba, however, was the question of whether Russia's new leaders could, or even intended to, patch the wide ideological split between Moscow and Peking. Presumably, Khrushchev's adamant attitude toward the Chinese had contributed to his fall. But Chinese Premier Chou En-lai's visit to Moscow in November, 1964, seemed to have produced few concrete results toward rapprochement.

It was McCone's opinion, which obviously was reflected in the reports Johnson received, that the depth of the schism between the Kremlin rulers and Peking remained "greater than the public account." Beyond this McCone said the fundamental Russian problems were that the European satellites were "looking over the wall" at Western affluence and that there existed a "violent and uncompromising" struggle within the Soviet Union between military demands and the desire of Russians for a more comfortable life. All of this, of course, was intelligent guesswork and provided no firm basis for Johnson to make any personal contact with the Soviet leaders, or leader, as it might turn out to be.

But Johnson didn't really need the advice of Richard M. Nixon, the 1960 GOP presidential nominee, not to "coast" in Russian relations because of his election victory. Nixon, whose contacts with the Soviets hadn't been noticeable for several

years, advised Johnson in an impromptu news conference that
the danger was "infinitely greater" than it had been because the
new leaders would be "younger, hungrier and tougher than
Khrushchev."

An administration aide observed sarcastically, "We are so
glad to have this up-to-the-minute advice out of Mr. Nixon. We
presume it must be a deduction from something Khrushchev
said to him in the kitchen debate they held while he was Vice
President."

However tough the new Kremlin chieftains might get, it was
the considered opinion of Walt W. Rostow, head of the State
Department's Policy Planning Staff, that "they realize no single
country can dominate today's world."

This had been the basis on which Johnson had proceeded
ever since he became President. Five months before he died,
Kennedy had made a basic decision to work for increased accommodation with the Soviets. This marked a change from his
mood in January, 1963, when he said in his State of the Union
message that the Sino-Soviet dispute was over "means not
ends." He added then, "A dispute over how best to bury the
Free World is no grounds for Western rejoicing."

But as Kennedy continued his correspondence with Khrushchev and as he parsed each situation as it arose, he came to
believe that the Moscow-Peking split could be turned to American advantage if the methods employed were subtle enough.
He pursued with the Russian Premier the possibility of ban-
ning atmospheric testing of nuclear weapons and was rewarded
with an agreement. A year later, on August 3, 1964, Khrushchev
said that the preceding twelve months had "enriched international life with new experience."

"With a certain amount of trust stored," he said, "it is possible to advance further toward the relaxation of international
tension and toward agreement in different fields."

In his reply to Khrushchev's 1964 New Year's letter to all of
the countries with which Russia maintained diplomatic relations, Johnson outlined to the Soviet Premier his hope that the

United States and Russia could build on "areas of agreement instead of merely emphasizing our well-known disagreements."

Johnson had continued in operation the "hot line" Kennedy had installed to communicate with Moscow. This was a teletype setup for speedy transmission of messages between the two capitals. During the election campaign Johnson often picked up an imaginary telephone when speaking to the crowds and asked them whether they would rather have him or his opponent on the line "when the phone rings." This bit of byplay went unchallenged except among newsmen who felt such license ought to be restricted to the poets and not be used by politicians.

In pursuit of the coexistence policy, Johnson gave the green light to the signing in Moscow of a consular treaty. The first formal bilateral treaty ever negotiated between the two governments, the agreement authorized the establishment of consular offices outside of Washington and Moscow. What was more important, it guaranteed, so far as any piece of paper could, almost immediate access to nationals of the other country who were detained in either. Under existing conditions, an American could be arrested in Russia and be held incommunicado for nine months while he was under investigation.

On its face, the treaty seemed a common-sense agreement which would permit the Russians to establish a consulate in, say, San Francisco and the United States to set up one in Leningrad. But Republican conservatives saw some evil incursions in this. Senator Bourke B. Hickenlooper of Iowa, a GOP member of the Senate Foreign Relations committee, served notice he would fight ratification.

By all of these actions the Johnson administration was committed to a coexistence policy that appeared to be leading inevitably toward some kind of summit meeting with the Russians. But this course, and its ultimate objective, had had to be reassessed in the light of what had happened in the Kremlin. This might take months or even years.

With the Russian situation foreclosed from an early exercise of the Johnson treatment in the form of personal diplomacy, there was little in the way of success to point to in this area in the President's first year in office.

The telephone calls to President Chiari of Panama had produced pacification of the Canal Zone but no real solution to the controversy there.

Johnson had written on December 23, 1963, a personal letter to João Goulart cordially congratulating him on his election as President of Brazil. This election was hailed at the time as a major break-through toward improving U.S.-Brazilian relations. The letter pledged American cooperation toward retiring Brazil's foreign debt. It called for social reforms but praised Brazil's industrial progress.

A revolution in April, which ousted Goulart, probably saved Brazil from a Communist take-over. The situation was such at that point that if the rebellion had *not* been successful Johnson might have faced the dilemma of sending American troops or of standing by while a country which covers half of the South American continent went Communist.

Johnson's attempt to intervene personally in the bloody controversy in Cyprus perhaps was not necessarily a failure, but neither was it fully successful. It certainly did not provide the rewards of other applications of "the treatment."

In an effort to establish some base by which progress could be made toward peace in Cyprus, Johnson invited Premier Ismet Inonu of Turkey and Premier George Papandreou of Greece to separate conferences in Washington. Johnson had intervened earlier in June, 1964, to help prevent a threatened Turkish invasion of Cyprus. There had been fighting there after Archbishop Makarios, Greek Cypriot President, had changed the constitution to strip the outnumbered Turks of their veto power over government action.

Inonu came first for two days of what a communiqué described as "cordial and candid" conversations. When he departed, Papandreou arrived, angered over the previous day's

Washington communiqué which had reaffirmed "the present binding effects of existing treaties."

The 1959 treaties which had given Cyprus its independence had set up the constitutional provisions Makarios had rescinded. The Turks were interpreting the treaties as giving them the right to intervene militarily on Cyprus if the terms of the documents were not carried out. The Greeks had served notice that any such intervention would be regarded by them as aggression and would be met by retaliation. Johnson urged on Papandreou and Inonu in their separate conferences that their countries enter direct negotiations with each other.

At this point in the operation of the personal diplomacy he was using to prevent a war between the two NATO partners, Johnson had taken the calculated risk of angering both without any assurance that his suggestions would be accepted or that if they were it would produce any results.

When talks were arranged between the United Nations, Greece, Turkey and Britain, Johnson sent Former Secretary of State Dean Acheson to Geneva to represent the United States. Acheson came up with a wide-ranging plan which almost, but not quite, won approval. Simplified, it provided for Cyprus' union with Greece, Turkish renunciation of the right of intervention, compensation to Turkey in the form of a military base on the island and protection of the Turkish minority.

Acheson might have put over the plan if Makarios had not called loudly for Russian protection against Turkish air attacks. He got Greek leaders to stall the negotiations in return for his calling off his appeals for Russian intervention.

When Acheson returned to report to Johnson on September 4, the former told a news conference that the situation on Cyprus was "very critical indeed," adding that "war could break out in 25 minutes." Asked about Makarios' part in the stalled negotiations, Acheson replied, "The archbishop didn't go out of his way to be helpful. . . . He threw monkey wrenches into the machinery."

Not all of the conferences with world leaders were grim, of course, and when he had an opportunity Johnson let off steam with his foreign visitors. When Prime Minister Bjarni Benediktsson of Iceland came to the White House on August 19, the handshaking was hardly over before Johnson led his guest on a fifteen-minute walking tour of the grounds. They were trailed by a group of reporters and an unbelieving contingent of State Department officials.

Johnson described to Benediktsson the outdoor news conference he had held previously, when he had invited newsmen to bring along their wives and children. It had turned into something of a mob scene and the President insisted to his visitor that "I got a better story from the children than from these guys," gesturing toward the reporters.

Johnson pointed across the Ellipse to the Jefferson Memorial and told his visitor, "That's the Washington Monument." But he correctly identified the Lincoln Memorial.

When the entourage neared the southeast gate, tourists were peering through the bars to see what was going on. The President quickened his step and headed straight for the gate, telling the Prime Minister "these are the people we work for." Johnson reached through the bars to shake hands and autographed one man's cast after he had introduced his guest to the crowd and praised him as "a great friend of America and a great friend of NATO."

Resuming the walk, Johnson pointed out the Treasury Building.

"That's where we keep our money," he said. "We have a Republican who looks out for the money."

As the group walked back toward the White House, the gardener came out with two beagles on a leash. The Prime Minister was properly introduced to Him and Her. Then the President picked up the dogs, but not by the ears, and bore them over to the gate for the tourists to see. As he headed back toward the house, the President supplied some more information.

"Him is a little bit stubborn," he said. "He's the one who got me in all the trouble."

Benediktsson came up with a question.

"Do you still go around turning off the lights?" he asked.

"Yes, yes," Johnson replied, "it saves seven hundred dollars a month."

The President then pointed to a platform being erected for a congressional reception, which bore at its top a sign that read: SALUTE TO CONGRESS. The Prime Minister asked if the President were pleased with the members' work.

"Very pleased," Johnson replied. "You don't think I'd have nearly a thousand down here entertaining them if I weren't, do you?"

All of this was a happily gay example of the Johnson treatment and its application in personal diplomacy. But the Johnson touch wasn't always sure, especially when it had to be applied at long range by others.

There was the case of the Congo, where Kennedy had met threats of the Russians to give "all possible assistance" to the government of Antoine Gizenga by saying bluntly: "I would conceive it to be the duty of the United States . . . to defend the charter of the United Nations by opposing any attempt by any nation to intervene unilaterally in the Congo."

Kennedy had supported the United Nations' decision for the use of force to put down Moise Tshombe's secession move in the Katanga. This was a decision which had come under heavy fire from many in the United States, including Johnson's close friend, Senator Thomas J. Dodd, Connecticut Democrat.

Now Tshombe had come back to pick up the pieces of a supposedly united, but much divided, country. Because Johnson had evolved no clear-cut policy of dealing with the Congo —as Kennedy had, for better or for worse—the administration cloaked its moves in secrecy in the hope of avoiding the kind of political donnybrook the late President had experienced.

From Tokyo on June 14 came news reports authored by Peking's New China News Agency that American pilots and planes were fighting in the Congo. The following day Washington officials said they knew nothing about this. But on that same day the New China News Agency said U.S. Air Force Hercules transports had air lifted the Congolese 13th Battalion from Katanga province to Bukavu. The Chinese broadcasts had a ring of truth in them but nowhere in Washington was there confirmation until the next day. Yes, it was said then, American transports had been furnished.

The Washington *Post* spanked the Johnson administration editorially for its deviousness. The *Post* said:

The country has come to a sad pass when it must turn to Communist China's New China News Agency for reports on covert military operations being conducted by the United States. Yet this incredible inversion has taken place twice within the last week.

In Laos, Communist China claimed that American planes had flown attack missions against installations on the Plain of Jars. First the State Department refused to comment but very soon the story leaked out in quite the form the communists had charged.

In the Congo, the Peping news agency accused the United States of air strikes against rebels in Kivu province. The State Department first issued a denial and yesterday, embarrassed by news reports, confessed that Americans under contract to the Congo had flown the planes.

What in heaven's name does the United States think it is doing by trying to keep these air strikes secret? Does the government really have the naïveté to believe its hand in these operations can be concealed?

If it is to conduct or sponsor such raids, then let the matter be decided openly in terms of whether American interests require it. But let there be no repetition of the humiliating sequence whereby Communist China makes a fool, if not a liar, out of the United States.

This was not one of Johnson's favorite editorials. Its dose of harsh criticism was especially difficult to swallow for a President who was preparing to doff his diplomatic topper to put on his political hat.

13 The Political Hat

B Y ONE of those quirks of fate that always seemed
to be turning up in Lyndon Johnson's career, a political power
play he launched at the 1956 Democratic convention in Chicago was instrumental in placing him in a position to inherit
the presidency.

Johnson, then the Senate Democratic leader, hadn't really
entertained the idea that he might become President until he
won national attention by piloting through the Senate in 1957
the first civil rights bill passed by Congress in eighty years. He
could dream, of course, and had done so. But as a practical
man he had never really felt he had much chance to become
President.

Always wary about any public expression of ambition which
might spur suspicion among his party colleagues of his leadership tactics, Johnson pretended to ignore the spate of talk
that sprang up about him as a possible 1960 presidential
nominee. Questioned about his political future in this period,
he replied bluntly, "Talk about my being a potential candidate
is a lot of foolishness. I have no interest, no ambition in that
direction. I'm conscious of my limitations. I think it's fair to say
that nobody but my Mamma ever thought I'd get as far as I
am."

[219

Nevertheless, the seed had been sown. But the whirlwind he had helped start in the 1956 convention and which resulted in Kennedy's 1960 nomination, bent the plant to the ground. Fate intervened again, however, with the offer of second place on the 1960 ticket.

Despite Harry Truman's efforts to promote W. Averell Harriman, former New York governor, as an alternative to Adlai E. Stevenson, the 1956 convention had been a cut-and-dried affair. Stevenson won the presidential nomination hands down and then unexpectedly tossed the choice of his vice-presidential running mate to the delegates.

Few presidential nominees cared to take this sort of chance with a convention. It was the kind of gamble that Johnson rejected in 1964.

Stevenson's announcement brought on a wild night of campaigning for delegate votes by New York Mayor Robert Wagner and four Democratic Senators—Hubert H. Humphrey of Minnesota, Estes Kefauver and Albert Gore of Tennessee and John F. Kennedy of Massachusetts.

At one point in the disorganized proceedings I came across Kefauver at 5 A.M. making a television recording in a hotel corridor. As I stopped to listen for a moment, Kennedy came careening around a corner, tripped on a TV cable and almost fell into Kefauver's arms. Both grinned and the young Massachusetts Senator scrambled away hastily to address another weary state delegation down the hall.

Kennedy had placed Stevenson's name in nomination for the presidency and it soon became apparent that powerful forces were going for him in the vice-presidential contest. The most potent of these was Lyndon Johnson, master of the Texas delegation and the quarterback for the party conservatives mostly concentrated in the South and border states.

Young Jack Kennedy was packing some political liabilities at that point. Mrs. Eleanor Roosevelt was against him because he had not taken a stand in the Senate's rebuke of Senator Joseph R. McCarthy of Wisconsin. Kennedy was a Roman Catholic and there was fear among the delegates of the religious issue.

Where Kennedy's views were little known on the question, Senator Kefauver was regarded by Southern delegates as a renegade because he had voted twice on the side of the South and twice against it on civil rights issues. But there was a large reservoir of support for the Tennessee Senator because of the strength he had shown in contesting Stevenson in the primaries.

After a night in which the candidates had exhausted themselves and anybody awake enough to listen to them, the convention got down to voting the next day. On the first roll call, Kefauver demonstrated the breadth of his support by rolling up 483½ votes. But the surprise was that Kennedy, considered little more than an outsider, was second with 304. Behind him was Gore with 178, Wagner with 162½ and Humphrey with 134½.

Johnson decided that this was the point at which to move decisively. He sent his runners fanning out over the convention floor with the message that Kefauver had had it. It was time, they said, to get on the Kennedy bandwagon. Gore and Humphrey countered this move, however, by withdrawing and throwing their support to Kefauver.

But it was still touch and go and Johnson never lost easily. He had Southern governors jumping at his bidding as he tried to organize a blitz for Kennedy. He might have pulled it off if Kennedy, representing his New England constituents, hadn't voted against the farm bill in Congress. A key state was Oklahoma, whose Governor Raymond Gary had been a Harriman man and thus was approachable. But when the Johnson messenger reached Gary, sitting tight in his seat and holding his state's standard firmly in his left hand, the answer was negative. Kennedy had voted against the farm bill which Kefauver had supported and Gary was going for Kefauver. That ended it, for all practical purposes. Kefauver won the dubious prize of second place on a ticket that was soundly beaten.

All of this might have been merely a footnote to history if it had not given Kennedy his first exciting glimpse of how a convention nomination was won or lost. This was no ordinary young man. He had a consuming ambition that outweighed Johnson's at that point. He intended to be President and there were millions of dollars back of him to finance the effort.

Kennedy had been defeated but he had gained national attention. He had become a man to reckon with in the Democratic party. He had four years ahead of him to gain the main prize and he was going after it hammer and tongs. As he campaigned during the next forty-eight months, Kennedy often brought down the house by gravely thanking the leaders in large states for not having voted for him for the vice-presidential nomination.

Johnson's judgment on political matters usually was cold, calculating and excellent. But he slipped a cog in not recognizing earlier the young Senator from Massachusetts as a serious challenger to his own pre-eminent national position. He felt logically that he had recruited a young, vigorous ally who owed him a political debt of sorts and who could be useful to him in the future.

So the Senate leader proceeded to help his Massachusetts protégé climb the ladder which led to Senate recognition and power. An issue came up quickly. Kefauver, who had not evidenced any interest in it before, decided he wanted to become a member of the Senate Foreign Relations Committee. Kennedy told Johnson he would like to fill the vacancy on the Democratic side.

With four years of seniority in Senate service, Kefauver felt he was the natural choice in such an inner-circle contest. But the power of the Majority Leader was such that Kennedy wound up with the prize assignment. Ironically this provided the youthful Massachusetts Senator with a forum which permitted him to pose in 1960 as an expert on foreign affairs, while the Texas Senator who was opposing him for the party presidential nomination could offer no comparable credentials in that field.

Although he never commented on it publicly or privately, Johnson had to feel that in his relationship with Kennedy he had made every possible mistake except one—his acceptance of the 1960 vice-presidential nomination.

While Kennedy was gallivanting around the country mesmerizing local politicians, sewing up prospective delegates and laying the foundations for a 1960 convention victory, Johnson was going about the alternately head-cracking and soft-soaping business of getting the Senate to pass legislation he believed would convince the country that he was the man who got things done while others frittered away their time in talk.

Johnson made another political mistake in this period when he accepted the assurances of senatorial colleagues, who wished him well, that he would have their state's votes in the convention. The hard facts of the matter were, of course, that Senators and House members didn't have much to say about the makeup of the delegations their states sent to the nominating conventions. The governors and the state chairmen were the people to talk to and Kennedy spent his time with them instead of with his senatorial colleagues.

Johnson was encountering tough opposition in pushing significant legislation through the Senate in this era, but he was getting some bills passed by exerting all of his know-how. He was demonstrating that, as Senator Russell put it, "He doesn't have the best mind on the Democratic side of the Senate. He isn't the best orator. He isn't the best parliamentarian [Russell himself was]. But he's got the best combination of all of these qualities."

In a period when Kennedy infrequently was around for Senate roll calls, Johnson busied himself polishing up a "can do" image of a "prudent progressive," a term he applied to himself in the presidency. It had a nice middle-of-the-road sound, exactly where Johnson wanted to be as Senate leader and as President.

With a Republican in the White House, Johnson was persisting even in the face of the oncoming 1960 election in refusing to join in the billingsgate some Democrats aimed at Eisenhower. When he had become the Democratic leader, Johnson had laid down his precepts in these words:

"It is my belief that the American people expect continued responsibility from us. They are expecting the Democrats to be positive, to be prudent, to be statesmenlike. They do not want blind opposition nor blind support.

"Our dedication must be to the politics of responsibility—to a statesmanship which is based upon the realization that we cannot survive unless our country survives. No course will be successful unless that thought becomes our guiding star."

Following this up, Johnson said he never wanted to be classed among those who "oppose just to be opposing.

"I am a partisan," he said. "I have practiced my partisanship with enthusiasm in proper political seasons. But I have never—and will never—seek to destroy before the nation or the world the confidence of free men in the institution [the presidency] upon whom the success of freedom's cause must depend."

To the end of Eisenhower's tenure, Johnson maintained a close relationship with the Republican President, whom he regarded as a great general and a great patriot.

Once when the two men were talking in the President's office in this period, Eisenhower tossed off a prophecy. Pointing to the chair behind his desk, the President said to the Senator, "Some day you'll be sitting in that chair."

"No, Mr. President," Johnson replied with the solemn humility he always practiced on such occasions, "that's one chair I'll never sit in."

If the liberals, the labor leaders and the big-city bosses of the Democratic party had had their way, Johnson never would have sat in that chair. They could and did prevent his winning the presidential nomination, but they could not buck successfully his selection as the vice-presidential nominee once Kennedy had chosen him.

When Johnson and Kennedy were locked in battle for the

top spot, Americans for Democratic Action voiced this complaint about Johnson:

"He is a conservative, anti-civil rights, gas-and-oil Senator. He has supported all of the anti-labor legislation enacted during the past two decades—and bragged about it."

ADA and the New York Liberal party continued to fight Johnson's selection as the vice-presidential nominee. Joseph L. Rauh, Jr., ADA Vice President, denounced Kennedy's choice of the Texan as a "betrayal." When Johnson's name was put in nomination, Rauh struggled with other members of the District of Columbia delegation in a futile effort to keep them from hoisting the District banner in the Johnson victory parade around the convention floor. Much more would be heard of the Rauh-Johnson relationship.

As a matter of fact, Johnson's acceptance of the vice-presidential nomination had amazed the Kennedys. Certain that he would win the presidential nomination, Kennedy had made up his mind several days before the 1960 convention opened that he would invite Senator Stuart Symington, Missouri Democrat, who had campaigned for the top place, to join him on the ticket as the vice-presidential candidate.

Symington had avoided the bitter personal attacks on Kennedy in which Johnson had indulged. The Missourian would not have to eat during the 1960 campaign the phrases that the Senate leader had thrown at his former protégé.

Kennedy was urged to play it smart. The suggestion was made that an effort be undertaken to appease Johnson's bitterness at not winning the top prize by offering him the vice-presidential nomination. If he was elected President, the argument went, Kennedy would have to deal with the Texan as the party's leader in the Senate.

Nobody in the Kennedy camp thought for a moment that Johnson would agree to play second fiddle. He just wasn't that kind of politician. So the offer was made and, to the utter surprise of the Kennedys, was accepted.

On the night of the convention session when Johnson was nominated, the Kennedys piled into their limousine to return to the apartment Joe Kennedy had rented in Beverly Hills. A passenger reported that they were all swathed in gloom. Bob Kennedy was particularly low because he said the idealistic crusade which had brought the presidential nomination to Jack now had been punctured by what the Republicans were certain to call a cynical political deal.

Surprisingly, Old Joe was the least perturbed. He told his sons not to worry about that aspect of the situation. Lyndon would help carry the South, he said, and that could be a much more important factor in deciding the election than any criticism leveled at the ticket because Johnson was on it. The elder Kennedy was right, as it turned out. Kennedy was elected and began what looked to Johnson and almost everybody else concerned as likely to be an eight-year tenure.

Johnson had resigned himself to filling the uncomfortable role of a secondary man for another five years.

Johnson vindicated his selection in the campaign, however, when he helped keep a substantial part of the South in line for Kennedy. In this period the voters were seeing the last of the provincial Johnson, with the deep "Take-sus" drawl, the cowhand expressions and the barnyard humor. He would be folksy always, but never as much so as in 1960.

Campaigning in the South, Johnson laid it on thick. Traveling on a train with Bobby Baker as his chief functionary, the vice-presidential candidate took aboard every Democrat willing to "ride a ways and talk a bit" about how to put over a ticket with Kennedy at its top.

When the "Cornball Special," as reporters dubbed it, halted at Culpeper, Virginia, Johnson laid on a classic.

"I just want to tell you how happy I am that you would come here and howdy and shake hands with us this morning," he said. "I'd appreciate so much if you-all would come just a little bit closer. You make us feel so wonderful to come out here and look us in the eye and give us a chance to press the flesh with you. Give us your help now."

It had been scheduled as a brief stop and Bobby Baker had given the signal that it was time to be on the way down the line. As the train started to roll slowly, Johnson raised his voice to shout:

"They tell me we can't carry Virginia. I don't believe it, do you?"

Members of the crowd shouted back, "no." Johnson put on the clincher.

"When they tell you that," he yelled, "you just ask 'em, 'What did Richard Nixon ever do for Culpeper?' "

One of the first things Johnson undertook as Vice President was to polish up his speech-making. Kennedy had told him there would be a great many formal addresses ahead of him and as a Senator he got out of practice because he had neither the time nor the inclination to engage in the oratorical exercises that were so dear to some of his colleagues.

With Horace Busby as the chief drafting agent, Johnson worked out a formula for short, simply phrased speeches which would drive home the points he wanted to make. Then Johnson practiced a slow, measured delivery in which he stressed key words and phrases rhythmically, trying to remember not to shout in the microphones.

This was a small but integral part of the transformation of Lyndon Johnson, the successful politician and Senate leader extraordinary, into the "man of equality," the moderate, prudent, experienced and vigorous individual the Democratic party might want for its presidential nominee in 1968 and the people might want for their Chief Executive in that painfully distant year.

Kennedy and two terms seemed then to stand between him and the presidency, but Johnson's eyes were on it. The long highway ahead was full of hazards but the man was full of determination.

His former Senate colleagues notified Johnson quickly that as Vice President he no longer was one of them. Johnson had assumed he would continue in a command post behind the scenes. He had expected to preside over the caucus of all Democratic Senators and dispense his wisdom on legislative matters.

But Senator Albert Gore of Tennessee challenged this arrangement. Gore lost, of course, but the test notified Johnson that a significant number of Senators didn't want him butting into what was their business and not now his, except for his duties as the Senate's presiding officer. Johnson was so chagrined that when he took over the chair at the next meeting of the Democrats he immediately vacated it in favor of Majority Leader Mansfield. From that point on, he gave his advice only when asked.

Johnson had learned, as had Vice Presidents before him, that he was only an appendage—and not the traffic cop—of party action in the Senate. This took a great deal of fun out of the Vice President's life. In one of his gloomy moments, Johnson defined the vice presidency as "the one constitutional office that exists solely to assure the orderly and effective functioning of our system."

As he told friends in this period, "the Vice President is only as big a man as the President will let him be." Kennedy, who had been generally bored by the routine requirements of Senate service, recognized that when Johnson was lifted out of the vortex of political power in the Majority Leader's job and deposited in the vacuity of the vice presidency, he would have to have something to do. Kennedy looked around and found several jobs for his second man.

In return, Johnson gave full loyalty to the President. He spoke admiringly in private as well as in public of Kennedy's "resourceful leadership," his "courageous compassion for America's needs at home" and the fact that the presidency rested on "strong, young shoulders."

Johnson plainly had decided that self-effacement was the best policy in his relationship with the President. He carried this out to the extent of always standing deferentially in the background when he appeared with Kennedy. His "your obedient servant" attitude provoked amused comment among those who had observed his drill-sergeant operations as Senate leader.

Johnson was by statute a member of the National Security Council and thus was afforded an inside view of world problems that had not been available to him as a Senator. Kennedy and Johnson got the law changed to make the Vice President head of the National Space Council. The President gave his second man as much authority over the $5 billion space budget as McNamara had over the $50 billion defense budget. He took Johnson's advice in the presidential decision to shoot for the moon.

When Kennedy told Johnson he wanted him to take over the chairmanship of the President's Commission on Equal Employment Opportunities, Johnson was reluctant to do it because he thought that, as a Texan, he couldn't escape criticism no matter what he did. And he never cared much for criticism. On the other hand, there was the opportunity to outshine former Vice President Richard M. Nixon in this field. Johnson took the post, which technically he could have refused, and did a creditable job.

Thomas Jefferson had demonstrated that a Vice President could be independent if he chose. When John Adams suggested that Jefferson undertake a mission to France to patch up American relations with the newly formed republic, the Vice President replied coldly that such activities were outside his constitutional domain.

But Jefferson had no political party ties such as those which exist today and which, if for no other reason, demand that a Vice President do the President's bidding or suffer the consequences of an open break.

There had existed at the beginning of their official relationship a wariness between Kennedy and Johnson that was not dispelled by their public expressions of felicity. The two men were correctly cordial, always cooperative but never intimate. Gradually, as the President dispatched the Vice President on foreign missions, listened to his advice on legislative matters and consulted with him and others in crisis periods, a warmer relationship grew up between them.

The President knew that Johnson was laboring under some handicaps the Vice President had not encountered in years. One of these particularly galling to Johnson was the fact that after such a long period in the headlines as Senate leader, his name had almost dropped out of the papers. Johnson could talk only in a guarded way about what the Equal Opportunities Committee was doing. He couldn't discuss what went on inside the administration without laying himself open to the possibility that a "leak" would be traced to him. His speeches and international jaunts usually wound up on the inside pages.

Kennedy knew the Vice President was not temperamentally fitted for anonymity. It was with amusement that he received the news one day that Johnson wanted to go along as a representative of the Space Council, with astronaut John Glenn, for the latter's tickertape reception in New York.

"Okay," the President told an aide with a grin, "let Lyndon go along. He doesn't get on page one much."

On John Glenn's day, Johnson was beside him in every pictorial news shot and on live television.

While he might be amused by Johnson's congenital yearning for recognition, Kennedy had a great deal of admiration for Johnson's abilities. He once remarked during the 1960 campaign that if he himself were not seeking the presidency he would have been supporting Johnson. "He's the ablest man I know in American politics," Kennedy said. "And he really cares about this country as I want a President to care."

Despite this evaluation, Kennedy had shut Johnson out from

other than rather casual contact with the Democratic party machinery, except for the Vice President's own state of Texas. Kennedy's men manned the organization and knew where their allegiance lay. Nobody was going to tinker with Kennedy's hard-won control of the party. So little was Johnson taken into the confidence of the President on arrangements that were going forward for the projected 1964 reelection campaign that the matter of whether he would be on the ticket again never was discussed between them. It was not until Kennedy made a news conference announcement to this effect that Johnson could dismiss from his mind the gnawing misgivings about the possibility that he might be dumped.

When he was plummeted into the presidency, Johnson faced the immediate necessity of establishing a personal political base for himself. He had a little more than eleven months to go before the next presidential election. The time was too short to remold the Kennedy organization into the Johnson image. He must make himself indispensable to the party organization, particularly to the liberals, the labor chieftains and the Negro leaders who had only tolerated him up to that point. This required speedy action. And no President in history ever moved more swiftly.

Johnson began with the obvious, the conferences with representatives of labor, business, the Negro organizations and Congress. He moved on to educators, religious groups, bankers, almost any group which could be induced to visit the White House. But there were plenty of innovations to come.

By the second week of January, 1964, the new President had dispatched his wife on a "poverty" tour of the area around Wilkes-Barre and Scranton, Pennsylvania. This was the beginning of distaff campaigning never quite equaled by any previous President's wife, even Eleanor Roosevelt. Shaking hands, talking with every individual she could, Mrs. Johnson charmed the crowds. She told the people of this section, plagued by mine cave-ins and fires, that they had "taken me behind the cold statistics to the human needs, problems and hopes of this area."

At home in the White House the First Lady was busy escorting senatorial wives around the living quarters and enlisting some of them in helping her redecorate. She was presiding at dinner dances, at one of which, on January 23, 1964, the President asked that Senator Margaret Chase Smith of Maine be seated on his right and Mrs. Barry Goldwater on his left.

"May I have the first dance?" he asked Mrs. Goldwater. "I want to get in good with you. I may want to be invited back here sometime."

Mrs. Johnson was on call, no matter what the hour, when the President felt he needed her. A couple of weeks after the dinner dance, Johnson brought home with him from a stag dinner two senatorial friends who represented opposite ends of the political spectrum. They had a couple of drinks each in an upstairs living room and the President excused himself. It was then about one o'clock in the morning, but back he came with Mrs. Johnson.

"I knew Lady Bird was the one you wanted to see," the President said, "and so I went and woke her up." The conversation, which had been about politics, continued on the same plane.

All of this feminine activity was leading up to something, as most of Johnson's moves did. In mid-January he had had two women join his Cabinet meeting. They were Assistant Secretary of Labor Esther Peterson and Mrs. Johnson's staff director, Mrs. Elizabeth Carpenter. The latter was generally credited with selling the President on the idea that women should play a much larger role in government since there were more female than male voters. Johnson's statement at this particular meeting was that "the day is over when top jobs are reserved for men."

Mrs. Peterson and Mrs. Carpenter had been directed to bring to this meeting, and a subsequent session of the heads of government regulatory agencies, lists of fifty women qualified to hold high government posts. Johnson told the Cabinet members, and, through Labor Secretary Wirtz the agency heads, that he wanted women hired, and no foolishness about it.

Miss Mary McGrory, perceptive columnist for the Washington *Star*, unearthed some testimony from career women that they didn't want equality of treatment at all. If they didn't already have one, most would have settled for a man around the house.

But the President was not to be diverted. He chose a formal dinner of the Women's National Press Club on the once-historical presidential inaugural date of March 4 to announce that he had appointed ten women to high—well, rather high—office. He preceded this action with the observation that "I would like at this time to make a policy announcement: I am unabashedly in favor of women."

If all of this was palpably a political pitch, as the envious Republicans contended, it seemed to have been one that was effective. As the November election count showed, Johnson was a substantial choice of women voters over Goldwater, who exuded male handsomeness over the television screens.

Spring was coming to Washington at the time and Johnson began to engage in a series of capers that seemed designed to call attention to the fact that he was President and was cutting a pattern of his own. He was exposing himself to public view as almost no other Chief Executive ever had done. And, in less than six months in office, he was making the headlines, obscuring all other public officials on the television-radio networks and was keeping the cocktail circuit in a buzz. There was a miscue or two, such as the time he picked up his beagles by the ears, but he was getting himself identified with the American voters as quite a fellow in his own right.

Kennedy had been cautious about overexposure. He wanted to save his television appearances for occasions he felt counted. Johnson dismissed advice that he was showing himself too much. When learned pundits wrote that he was going to have to choose between the "folksy" and the "dignity" vote, he ignored it. He wanted both votes and was confident he could be both folksy and dignified, at appropriate times.

If his actions didn't fit the American political pattern, Johnson at least had some precedent among heads of states and was happy to cite it when King Hussein of Jordan paid a state visit to the White House in mid-April.

"His Majesty and I have found we have some things in common," Johnson announced at a state dinner party. "As you know, his Majesty in his desire to be closer to his people has been known to disguise himself and drive a taxicab through the streets of his capital.

"I have not as yet found a successful disguise for myself and the streets of our capital are sometimes crowded with cabs, but I am trying to spend the week ends lately with the people of my country who are touring Washington."

Johnson, who hadn't even conceded up to this point the possibility that he might be a candidate to succeed himself, got plainly political when he went to Chicago on April 23, 1964. His motorcade barely had started to move out of the airport after he landed, before he signaled a stop, jumped out and barged ahead into the crowds with the Secret Service men trying to keep up with him. Speaking at a hundred-dollars-a-plate dinner that night, he unloaded some carefully prepared campaign humor.

"A funny thing happened to me on the way out here," he said. "I passed Dick Nixon coming back from Vietnam and Barry Goldwater and Nelson Rockefeller going out. . . ."

In Pittsburgh the next day, Johnson jumped out of his White House limousine, walked a block in the milling crowds and then got into an open Secret Service follow-up car, his first ride in an open auto since Kennedy's assassination.

In the course of this trip, which took him and his wife into depressed areas in Pennsylvania, Indiana, Kentucky and West

Virginia, Mrs. Johnson found time to explain what motivated her non-candidate husband in these excursions. A trip of this type, she said, was like a dose of adrenalin to the President. She added it was "the sort of a day that makes Lyndon feel like going back and working harder to live up to the faith that he has found people having in him today." It did him good, she said, to get out of Washington to meet the people.

"I don't think Washington is a reliable thermometer to test the political temperature or a barometer of the way the wind is blowing," she said.

Asked if she didn't worry about her husband's safety in the crowds in the light of what had happened to his predecessor, she replied "Never." But she said she did worry about his getting his hand bruised. "People don't exactly shake," she explained. "They hold."

Whatever the fundamental reasoning was behind these jaunts, Johnson recognized that he had a great thing going for him in them. Among other things he was identifying himself with the downtrodden.

The President went off again in May for a visit to Appalachia's economically stricken areas, with a few other incidental stops.

In traditionally Republican Knoxville, Tennessee, thousands waited for him at the airport, other thousands lined the highways into town and eight thousand heard him speak at the city's Coliseum. Routed through a poor section of the city, Johnson stopped his motorcade to climb the steps of a dilapidated house and say howdy to the occupants. Harrison Moore, who lived there, looked at his right hand in wonderment as he told reporters, "He shook my hand and I shook his'n." Moore said he was unemployed at the moment.

Everywhere Johnson pounded home the message that his objective was "to free thirty million Americans from the prison of poverty." This was social welfare with a bang and the Republicans looked on helplessly. They had no single leader who could speak with the voice of authority for what they might do. In the meantime "that fellow in the White House" was campaigning the socks off them.

Not only that, but the President had taken along his twenty-year-old daughter, Lynda Bird, and she made speeches, too. At their first appearance of the day at Cumberland, Maryland, she had breezed along so well in a speech that her father, the President, had to signal her to cut it short so he could get to talking. Johnson's womenfolk seemed to take to politics naturally, including sixteen-year-old Luci. Presumably the teen-agers the latter spoke before were being indoctrinated for the 1968 election.

As the time drew near for the Republican nominating convention Johnson was as busy making political speeches as were the candidates running for the GOP nomination.

He went to Swarthmore, Pennsylvania, to denounce the "phantom fears" that the federal government had grown to the point where it menaced individual liberty, a favorite Barry Goldwater theme. In Cleveland, Ohio, he linked his program to those of Franklin D. Roosevelt, Harry S. Truman and John F. Kennedy in an address to the Communications Workers of America.

Even while the Republicans were gathering for their San Francisco convention, Johnson kept the presidency in the news. The Johnsons went to church every Sunday and were photographed from every angle. On the day the GOP convention was scheduled to reach its nominating climax the Johnsons went for a stroll, hand in hand, in Lafayette Square, across the street from the White House. Newsmen noticed that as time went on the Johnsons displayed more affection in public than had been customary between presidential couples.

Bareheaded and wearing a sleeveless dress with a beige silk scarf at her throat, Mrs. Johnson set out with her husband in the ninety-degree heat for a walk that took them first to the Decatur house, once the home of naval hero Stephen Decatur.

From there they proceeded to the monument of Baron Friedrich von Steuben, on to the equestrian statue of Andrew Jackson, across Madison Place and back to the White House. At the portico entrance the President hugged his wife and gave her a kiss. She ran up the steps and he headed back to his office.

Perhaps such performances did not compete with the unfolding drama of the Goldwater nomination, but they reminded the people that they already had a family-man President who seemed more willing each day to continue to labor for them in the vineyards.

14 The One-Man Convention

W HILE HE WORKED tirelessly for public identification and approval, Johnson toiled behind the scenes to put the Democratic party in such order that all of its elements not only would acquiesce in his nomination but would be enthusiastic about having such a leader and would unite behind him in the campaign for election.

There remained an appendage of the Kennedy administration with which the new President must deal. He was Attorney General Robert F. Kennedy, heir to the Kennedy political dynasty—a turbulent, ambitious, personable young man, who had been temporarily stunned by his brother's assassination. Johnson calculated this would not last long. He gave the Attorney General a month to regain his feet, and it took about that long.

After that this young man presented the only threat the President could discern to his nomination and to his election. The overriding necessity, of course, was to eliminate Kennedy from the ticket without causing a major disturbance. Johnson wanted no Kennedy crutch displayed at his side when the voters went to the polls. The election had to be an overwhelming Johnson victory, with no suspicion that the Kennedys even had contributed to it, beyond the measured loyalty they owed

THE ONE-MAN CONVENTION [239

to him as the elected successor of the late President. Columnist Charles Bartlett, who was close to the Kennedys, had written earlier in 1964 that Johnson told certain labor leaders he was not going to have a Kennedy on the ticket with him. Johnson's determination not to be indebted to any other for his election was reinforced by the President's belief that Bob Kennedy hadn't wanted him on the ticket in 1960.

While he was Vice President there had been published reports that Johnson observed, "I know where those 'LBJ who?' jokes are coming from—out there at that swimming pool." This was a reference to the Attorney General's penchant for assembling administration bigwigs around the swimming pool at his suburban Virginia home.

In February, 1964, the public opinion polls were beginning to show Kennedy as a favorite for the vice-presidential nomination. When Democratic Governor John W. King gave his support to a proposed write-in drive for Johnson and Kennedy in the March New Hampshire primary, reports of a feud were heightened.

Actually, Kennedy sent through Kenneth O'Donnell an offer to Johnson to issue a statement aimed at killing off the drive then building up for him. The White House judgment at the time was that it wasn't necessary. A second offer to issue a statement invoked a similar reply. But on March 6 the Attorney General acted on his own, saying through the Justice Department press officer, Edwin O. Guthman, that he wished to discourage the write-ins.

When a Wisconsin group incorporated to boost Kennedy in that state's primary, the Justice Department put out a statement that the Attorney General "calls on individuals in Wisconsin who have formed committees in his behalf to discontinue their efforts.

"As for the vice presidency," the statement said, "the Attorney General has said on several occasions that President Johnson should be free to select his own running mate."

Pierre Salinger, then White House press secretary, said that

Johnson and Kennedy had seen each other "from time to time on various matters." This was the only answer to published reports that the President and the Attorney General were not communicating with each other except through intermediaries. The important point was that Kennedy had not removed himself in his statements repudiating the New Hampshire and Wisconsin write-ins, from the field of potential candidates for the vice-presidential nomination.

In that period the Attorney General had a great deal to say publicly about how kind Johnson had been to him. On March 12, 1964, Kennedy told a group of visiting students who quizzed him that there was no substance to reports of a feud between him and the President. He added, "I have the highest regard for him." Responding to other questions about his relations with Johnson, Kennedy said, "They've always been friendly and still are friendly. He is continuing where my brother started."

Nevertheless, there remained a feeling on the part of the President that not all was well in the Kennedy precincts. There was uneasiness about political developments that might get out of White House hands. Two reasonable, pragmatic men thus were thrust into a situation where, from a standpoint of self-preservation, each had to regard the other with a suspicion neither would permit even to surface.

The United Auto Workers invited Robert Kennedy to Atlantic City, New Jersey, late in March to accept an award. Kennedy was most circumspect. He talked about the accomplishments of his late brother and predicted that they would be carried on by Johnson in the nearly nine years of potential presidency left to him.

A sizable majority of UAW members at this point seemed to be aching to endorse Kennedy for Vice President. The Attorney General skirted this issue. He said, as he had before, that the President must choose his own man to run with him. Not all of the delegates were satisfied. After he had spoken, some of them lowered a bedsheet from the rail of the visitors' gallery which said, "UAW for RFK for VP." It took some fast maneuvering by Walter Reuther to prevent an emotional endorsement of Kennedy for the vice presidency. The UAW, Reuther said, should "stick to its business" and leave the choice of a vice-presidential nominee strictly to Johnson. Its business at that point was to have no fundamental argument with the man in the White House.

When Kennedy went to Scranton on March 18, 1964, to talk to the Friendly Sons of St. Patrick of Lackawanna County, he was mobbed everywhere. Shrilling crowds of teen-agers and older women poured adulation on him. His comment was: "I appreciate it, but I think it's out of place."

On March 28 the Attorney General was quoted as saying in reference to his relations with the President, "There is no problem between us. He has said this and I say it." But there was.

From the beginning Johnson's course had been directed toward putting his own imprint on the administration and obliterating that of his predecessor. But the emotionalism that clung to the Kennedy name had to be reckoned with. If he could prevent it, the President was not going to permit it to get out of hand. He rearranged the Atlantic City convention schedule so that the nominations of President and Vice President would be made on the same night. He set back a Kennedy memorial service until the final day of the meeting. His precaution proved wise, judging from the outburst of sixteen minutes of genuine applause—unaccompanied by the organ or bands—which greeted the sad-faced Attorney General when he stood before the convention on that night. The demonstration was not so much for Bob Kennedy as it was for a shining era that had died in Dallas. Camelot was no more.

After the Republicans had nominated Barry Goldwater, Johnson had given serious thought to the matter of publicly eliminating Kennedy from consideration for second place on the ticket without giving the appearance that he was treating the younger man shabbily and without affronting Democrats to whom the name of Kennedy still had a magic ring.

The President finally came up three weeks before the convention with what was at best a clumsy contrivance. He called newsmen in to announce, without any detailed explanation, that he had decided it would be "inadvisable" to select as his running mate any member of the Cabinet or anyone who met regularly with the Cabinet. He said he had communicated his decision personally to Kennedy, Rusk, McNamara, Freeman, Ambassador Stevenson and to Sargent Shriver, director of the Peace Corps. This elaborate maneuver scarcely disguised the fact that the President's chief intention was to thumb down Kennedy.

Johnson tried his best to soften the blow to the Attorney General. He summoned him to the White House on July 29, 1964, and, as was his custom in such matters, his staff had written out in advance what he desired to say. He began by remarking that since the Republican convention he had been thinking about the vice presidency. He said Kennedy had a bright future, a great name, and he had given serious consideration to asking him to go on the ticket with him. But the President noted that the younger man had not been in politics very long.

He felt it inadvisable, Johnson said, to ask Kennedy to take second place on the ticket and he wanted the Attorney General to know what his position was in advance of the convention. Besides, Johnson said, the vice presidency was the most difficult job he ever had filled and even though he worked at it twenty-four hours a day he was miserable in it most of the time. He didn't think, he went on, that Kennedy would be happy in the Vice President's chair.

When Kennedy asked how the President planned to make his announcement, McGeorge Bundy came in with the suggestion that the Attorney General announce that he didn't want to campaign for the vice presidency. Kennedy said quietly he wouldn't do that. He was firm about it, too.

The President said he would like to have Kennedy's help in the campaign, a suggestion attuned to Johnson's knowledge that most of the machinery of the party at local levels still was controlled by men Bob Kennedy had put in the places of power after his brother had been nominated and after he had been elected. There wasn't any reason, the President continued, why Kennedy should resign. He named other Attorneys General who had campaigned. This matter, of course, was washed out by subsequent events which brought Kennedy into the New York senatorial contest.

As he walked to the door to leave the President's office, Kennedy turned for one parting shot.

"I could have helped you a lot," he told the President, in obvious reference to the vice-presidential candidacy.

"You will help me a lot," Johnson replied, with reference to his own campaign.

When Johnson closed the final door on Kennedy with his public announcement of his elimination, there were practical political reasons for his decision, as well as his desire to win the presidency entirely on his own. Developments in the eight months since the assassination had completely reversed the political field.

When he went into office, Johnson was regarded as politically strong in the South and West, but weakest in the industrial states of the East which had contributed to Kennedy's victory in 1960. The nomination of Goldwater by the Republicans had changed all of this. Now Johnson was a solid favorite in the North and the East, but Goldwater was crowding him in the South and West.

Bob Kennedy had something the President needed in December, 1963, but he was a political liability in July, 1964, because the Cabinet member was strongest where Johnson was strongest and weakest where Johnson was weakest. As a symbol of the fight for civil rights, Kennedy was a political liability in the South, without offering any compensatory assets that might otherwise be denied to the President. It was in this

period, too, that the President was perusing polls which indicated if he could run alone—without any second-place candidate—he could win by a larger margin than with any running
mate he chose.

So it happened that Kennedy, who did more than most to
make it possible for Johnson to get the civil rights legislation
he felt he must have for a successful race for a first elective
term, was denied a place in the line of succession to the Presidency he hoped someday to reach.

Perhaps all of this could have been set down as a ruthless
exercise of Presidential power. In the long view, possibly it
was. But every politician concerned recognized that this was
the man, the President of the United States, in action. And
when you were inspired to oppose a man in that position, you
generally found you couldn't cope. Whoever lived in the White
House exuded power. If he knew how to mix it with the oxygen
of politics, as Johnson did, there was not much that could be
done about it.

While he was eliminating Bobby from consideration as his
second man, Johnson also was busy patching up the hybrid
Democratic organization he needed to accomplish what from
January had been his prime ambition—to be nominated for the
presidency by acclamation—and not by even a perfunctory roll-
call vote. Even Roosevelt hadn't attained this, and Johnson was
busting to chin the bars that his hero, FDR, had not attained.

It was impossible for him to equal Roosevelt's record of being elected four times because a Republican-controlled Congress had given the starting signal for a constitutional amendment which prevented that. But he was determined to go down
in the record books as the President who had held the office the
second longest period in the history of the Republic.

The President and his staff had been engaged in a great deal
of homework for the forthcoming convention and the campaign
that was to follow. Even before the Republicans ratified Goldwater's nomination in July, Johnson had ordered the Demo-

cratic National Committee to compile a record of the Arizona Senator's sayings. With ten full-time researchers and thirty-five volunteers the committee turned out by mid-July four volumes of "what Goldwater said." Johnson took one of these to bed with him at night to mark particular passages and turned others over to Richard Goodwin and Horace Busby who were doing stints as speechwriters.

At the same time, Johnson was placing his own men in key positions in the National Committee organization. He kept Chairman John M. Bailey on as the nominal manager of the campaign. But he insisted that Clifton C. Carter, a rangy, taciturn Texan who had worked for Johnson in every election since 1944, sit at Bailey's right hand as a full-time administrative assistant. Two Kennedy men, Kenneth O'Donnell and Lawrence F. O'Brien, the remanents of the "Irish Mafia" of the Kennedy regime, were assigned, respectively, as executive director of the National Committee and director of organization.

Johnson ordered that James H. Rowe, Jr., Washington attorney who had served as an assistant to Franklin D. Roosevelt, be installed as director of citizens' activities, which fell outside of the regular party organization. Rowe had long been a political adviser of Johnson.

The President was being careful in all of this to retain his connection with the Kennedy men in the organization. But he also was making certain that his own men, those he could trust implicitly, were at the control boards when the lights went on. And of these, Carter was the man who called the shots.

What Johnson was attempting to do in this period was to evolve what might have been called a "consensus" party which could bring into its fold the liberals, who believed in big government, the conservatives, who wanted federal power diffused, the representatives of big business, big labor, the minorities most vocally represented by the Negroes and the poverty-stricken. This followed almost exactly the Roosevelt pattern that had kept the Democrats in power for twenty years.

It dismissed casually the New Frontier crusade, which wound up by making Kennedy a minority president.

More than his principal, Representative William E. Miller, the Republican vice-presidential nominee, saw the danger to the Republicans in Johnson's pitch to bring all of the voters under his tent. Miller complained that the President's actions and repeated appeals for national unity were nothing less than an effort to cut off partisan campaign debate and point the nation toward one-party rule. Miller said that Johnson was attempting to "silence criticism behind appeals for unity," as, indeed, the President was.

"Is Mr. Johnson so sensitive to criticism, is he so confident of his unquestionable leadership, that he would want to destroy the Republican opposition?" Miller asked plaintively. The answer was that Johnson was and nearly did.

In the period between the Republican and Democratic conventions, Johnson exerted himself to be kind to individual members of the opposition party.

He already had Henry Ford II on his side and he wooed David Rockefeller, brother of the New York GOP governor, assiduously. He brought in 264 businessmen as guests at a White House luncheon, the biggest in history, shortly after the Republican convention. National Airport, fourth busiest in the world, was stacked up with ninety company planes for the event.

Johnson was cordial to John Hay Whitney, publisher of the Republican-oriented New York *Herald Tribune*. He invited Henry Luce, head man of the Time-Life-Fortune empire to a White House dinner. He gave a glowing toast to Henry Cabot Lodge, who seemed for a time to be the rank-and-file Republican's choice for their party's nominee but who faded in the stretch.

All of Johnson's courtship of Republicans was coordinated in the campaign organization by Rowe, former Undersecretary of the Treasury Henry Fowler and by John Stillman, who resigned as the Commerce Department's liaison man with Congress to devote full time to electing Johnson.

Most of this activity went against the Kennedy men's grain. They didn't think big business turned out many voters at the polls. Their strength rested on labor, liberals and the minorities. But Johnson was looking beyond the 1964 election and his feeling was that he would be more comfortable running again in 1968 if he had business on his side. Roosevelt and Kennedy both had believed that it would be politically advantageous to them to be opposed by big businessmen, so they could denounce the "money-changers," but Johnson was not of that breed.

Johnson had passed the word to Democratic campaigners in the period before his party's nominating convention that bread-and-butter issues would dictate the outcome of the presidential contest. He called the Cabinet together late in July to lecture members on campaign methods. He made it clear to these officials that all of them—including those in sensitive security posts like Rusk and McNamara—were expected to give their all in the campaign. No President in history had ever demanded such political efforts from his Cabinet as did Johnson. His ukase did not exclude Adlai E. Stevenson, his representative to the United Nations. There would be no official spectators, only workers, in the President's election by a resounding majority which would give him a mandate beyond that Franklin Roosevelt possessed after 1936.

Johnson's admonition to his Cabinet was to stress the economic well-being of the country to offset the threatened backlash of voters against civil rights. One official quoted him as saying, "When the people know how good things are and are going to be, they'll stop worrying about who is going to move next door."

Johnson suggested to the Cabinet members that in their speeches they point up the fact that "this is the first administration in this century without a recession or depression in peacetime." He fished out figures he said showed that the American economy had grown more during the four Kennedy-Johnson years than it had during the eight years of the Eisenhower administration.

The President was a man of changing moods. On that particular day, he felt he ought to stand above the battle of campaigning and let his vice-presidential nominee carry the load. He reminded his Cabinet listeners that in 1940, when he was running for a third term, Roosevelt had not gone out of Washington until about three weeks before the election.

While he was instructing officials of the Executive Department under his direction, Johnson also was busy whipping up support among members of Congress who had to be coaxed and not commanded. From an old friend who went back to the days of his early tutelage under Sam Rayburn, the President got an urgently requested assist.

Representative Carl Vinson of Georgia, eighty-year-old dean of the House of Representatives and a leader of Southern moderates when he wasn't defying Presidents on military recommendations, told Southerners not to cut off their noses to spite their faces by voting for Goldwater.

"Will the South, blinded by its anger and frustration of the moment regarding its civil rights problems, reward a political enemy and punish an old friend?" he asked. "This will be the case if the South supports Barry Goldwater and opposes Lyndon Johnson."

This pronouncement was little noticed outside of those to whom it was directed. Johnson had read the political temperature in Georgia and was applying what medication he could.

He also was busy recruiting former critics in his cause. The curious case of Joseph L. Rauh, Jr., vice chairman and a guiding light in Americans for Democratic action, cast some illumination on Johnson's methods of political operations.

The tall ubiquitous Rauh, who stuck out in a crowd with his graying blond hair straggling in all directions and his bow tie bobbing as he talked animatedly, long had been a passionate critic of Johnson. Unlike some of the other liberals who were mollified after the Texan had become Vice President and seemed to be proving himself considerably less of a conservative than they had suspected, Rauh remained a die-hard.

Early in 1963, when Johnson had refused to step beyond what he regarded as his constitutional authority to help the liberals alter the Senate's rules to make it easier to kill off filibusters, Rauh said the Vice President had "demonstrated once again that his first loyalty is to the Southern racists."

It had always been Johnson's belief that if he could just reason personally with any man he could win understanding from him, if not support for his ideas. He tried this out on his consistent critic. Rauh was surprised, on the day of the funeral of the late Democratic Senator Herbert H. Lehman, to be invited to ride on the presidential plane to New York. He and the President had a few pleasant words. This was followed by an invitation to dinner at the White House, something that had never come the ADA leader's way while Kennedy was in office.

Rauh also was called in to stand, smiling, in the group behind the President as Johnson signed as a presidential witness when the anti-poll tax amendment formally became a part of the Constitution. Johnson said that "this triumph of liberty over restriction is a proud moment for me." Ignored were the ADA's previous complaints that between 1942 and 1960 Johnson had voted twelve times in Congress against legislation to abolish poll taxes.

There was no question where Rauh stood when he went to the presidential nominating convention in Atlantic City. He was a Johnson man. He bore credentials as Chairman of the District of Columbia Democratic Committee, was a member of the Convention Credentials Committee and, as an attorney for the United Auto Workers, was a spokesman of sorts for labor.

The script didn't work out exactly as it had been written in the White House, as part of the overall design for a convention that was otherwise rigidly controlled by Johnson. Always a man of multiple interests, Rauh had become the lawyer for the

Negro-dominated Freedom Democratic Party of Mississippi. This group was challenging Mississippi's "regular" delegation for seating. Everybody knew most of the "regulars" would be for Goldwater in the election. But Johnson gave orders to compromise with them, if possible, and at all costs to prevent a walk-out before the television cameras which would advertise to the nation that the Democrats were split and perhaps demonstrate, after all, he wasn't exactly "President for all the people."

The Credentials Committee, headed by former Governor David L. Lawrence of Pennsylvania, also had its instructions, and members worked diligently at compromise. Senator Humphrey took the leadership, under Johnson's direction, in working out a proposal by which the all-white Mississippi delegation would be seated and two Freedom Party members would be admitted as delegates-at-large to the convention.

To the exasperation of the President, Rauh led his group in rejecting it. Johnson's courtship of Rauh almost ended there. But the President still wanted the ADA leader's election support so he acted to calm the rebellion. He got Walter Reuther, President of the United Auto Workers union, which had retained Rauh as an attorney, on the phone and told him to get hopping to Atlantic City to straighten the matter out. Reuther, a militant foe of segregation, wasn't pleased by being instructed to get a compromise, but he did what he was told.

Working with Bill D. Moyers, a presidential assistant, and Humphrey, and reporting personally to the President, Reuther helped calm the Freedom Party rebellion. The "regulars" also had turned down the compromise but three of the latter group signed the party loyalty pledge and were seated. When five members of the Freedom group marched into the Mississippi section, the "regulars" promptly took a walk. It was a minor affair and of only passing moment. Johnson had prevented a headline-blazing incident.

In the course of this, the President had had to step on some liberal fingers. Senator Philip A. Hart, Michigan Democrat, had proposed in a closed meeting of the platform committee a plank endorsing "peaceful demonstrations" in support of Negro rights. With the threat of the white backlash in mind, the cautious President thumbed it down.

There were other examples of direct White House intervention in the platform deliberations. State Senator John Powers of Massachusetts quietly pocketed a proposed plank supporting legislative reapportionment when he was informed firmly that Johnson didn't want to be tied down on this issue. Senator Joseph S. Clark, Pennsylvania Democrat, abandoned a disarmament plank when it was brought home to him that the Republicans might seize on this to contend the Johnson administration wanted to gut American defenses without any guarantee that the Communists would disarm.

At the same time the President was occupied with these matters he was playing out a game calculated to prevent the convention from becoming a pointless and boring performance in the selection of a vice-presidential candidate.

The prudence with which Johnson approached every political decision, his genuine love for intrigue, the business of making the simple appear complex and his enjoyment of the uses of power—all these factors operated in his selection of Senator Hubert Horatio Humphrey, Minnesota liberal Democrat, as his running mate.

In the earliest stages of the game there was considerable speculation about Humphrey because of his prominent position in the party and because he would help the ticket in the areas where it then was thought to be weakest, the big industrial states with their large labor and minorities votes. But Johnson wanted a large field to choose from and he did not want to commit himself until he read the polls on his own standing in July and August. He wanted to look at the polls on vice-presidential preferences and was reported to have been disturbed when they showed early in the year that Attorney General Kennedy was favored.

The President resorted to diversionary tactics of seeming to smile on one after another potential nominee. He covered a wide field, which included Sargent Shriver, director of the Peace Corps; Mayor Robert F. Wagner of New York; Governor Edmund G. (Pat) Brown of California; McNamara; Stevenson; several Senators and President Clark Kerr of the University of California. Among the Senators, other than Humphrey, were the latter's home-state colleague, Eugene J. McCarthy, and Majority Leader Mansfield.

Nobody knew exactly what to make of all this, and when newsmen asked him almost daily if he was in the running, Humphrey could only say, "Nobody has to woo me. I'm old reliable, available Hubert."

Confessing that he was perplexed, he quipped, "Just look what's happened. The President sent Bobby Kennedy to the Far East. He sent Sargent Shriver to deliver a message to the Pope. Adlai Stevenson got to escort Mrs. Johnson to a theater in New York. So I asked the President, 'Who's going to enroll Lynda Bird in George Washington University? I'll volunteer.' "

Johnson talked to literally hundreds of people in all walks of life, sounding them out on their vice-presidential preferences. He said he wanted a man who represented the consensus, one who would be acceptable to most Americans and one who would be regarded as qualified to become President if it ever came to that.

The President had listed his requirements for a running mate at a July 30, 1964, news conference. He said the man he was looking for should be equipped to fill not only the vice presidency but the presidency itself.

"I think he should be a man that is well received in all the states of the Union, among all our people," Johnson said. "I would like to see a man that is experienced in foreign relations and domestic affairs. I would like for him to be a man of the people who felt a compassionate concern for their welfare and who enjoyed public service and was dedicated to it.

"I would like for him to be attractive, prudent and progressive. I would like for him to be one who would work cooperatively with the Congress and the Cabinet and with the President. I would expect him to be one that would meet with overwhelming approval of the delegates who have the responsibility for passing upon him."

This description fit Humphrey like a glove, with one exception, and it was an important one. Johnson had to find out how the South would react to the selection of a man with a long record of advocating civil rights causes.

Southern party leaders had not forgotten that strife-torn night at the 1948 convention in Philadelphia when the ambitious young mayor of Minneapolis had charged to the platform and had stirred the delegates with such an impassioned plea for a stronger civil rights plank that a majority threw out a compromise agreed on by the platform committee and adopted the Humphrey substitute. With Confederate flags flying the Mississippi delegation led the walkout that followed.

Still unresolved also was the question in Johnson's mind whether he should put a Roman Catholic on the ticket with him. After he had eliminated Kennedy, the President thought mostly of McCarthy, an old Senate friend, and Mansfield in this connection. Mansfield told the President bluntly he didn't want the nomination. McCarthy was willing, so the game went down to the final round of the convention opening.

The signs all pointed to majority delegate support for Humphrey. But, of course, the delegates really had no say in the matter. Johnson would pick his man and they would accept him.

A couple of days of sharing a telephone switchboard and television appearances with Humphrey had convinced McCarthy that he wasn't going to be chosen. He was weary of playing the President's game. McCarthy took matters into his own hands. He sat down and pencilled out a telegram for Johnson withdrawing his name from consideration and proposing Humphrey as the vice-presidential nominee. Wise in the ways of the

White House, McCarthy handed out the text to the press as soon as he had sent the message off. Sure enough, the White House had him on the phone as soon as the message arrived there with the request that he not make it public. Too late, McCarthy replied.

Despite this discouraging development, Johnson kept the mystery drama rolling along. Pierre Salinger, playing his unaccustomed new role of appointive United States Senator, was one of those the President called by phone—as he did scores of others—about the vice-presidential choice. Salinger suggested in the course of the conversation that Johnson really could dramatize the matter by flying to the convention and announcing his selection. Johnson, who hadn't intended to make a convention appearance until his acceptance speech, leaped at the idea.

Calling in George Reedy to tell him to set up the trip, Johnson whacked his secretary with some crackling criticism. "Why don't you ever come up with some ideas like that?" he demanded. Reedy's answer was not recorded.

Still playing it coy, Johnson called up Humphrey and Senator Thomas J. Dodd of Connecticut and told them to hop on a plane and come to the White House. Neither man knew until he arrived at the Atlantic City airport that the other had been summoned.

Managing the suspense till the last minute the President struck out on another of those walking news conferences. This one turned out to be an endurance test of fifteen laps around the south lawn, a total of 4.35 miles. During it Johnson kept insisting that he hadn't made up his mind about second place on the ticket.

After he had talked separately with Dodd, who told the President he didn't want to be considered for the vice-presidential nomination, and to Humphrey, Johnson let it be known that he would fly to the convention that night. At Andrews Air Force Base he walked over to a group of reporters to tell them, "I want you to meet the next Vice President, Senator Humphrey."

The world knew all about this in a matter of minutes. But the delegates in their seats at the Atlantic City convention who had just nominated Johnson for President, had no general knowledge of it until the President burst into their presence and made a ringing nomination speech for Humphrey.

These were the outward manifestations of the crowning of a new regent of the Democratic realm. Behind the scenes were the evidences of a take-over that was so complete that no official of the party raised a protesting voice.

At a motel across the street from Convention Hall had been installed a "Little White House," hooked onto the Washington mansion switchboard. This operation engaged half of the President's Cabinet and all members of his staff who could be spared from capital duty. The lines from this board ran to the hotel rooms of every important governor, Senator or House member Johnson might want to reach immediately. The lines seldom cooled.

On the convention platform, fifteen feet behind the rostrum, sat Cliff Carter, with J. Leonard Reinsch, director of the convention staff, at his elbow. In front of Carter were four television monitors which provided him with a view of what the three commercial networks were carrying and linked him to the convention's closed-circuit TV. Three telephones, with an elaborate console of buttons, stood on his desk. Through them he could talk to any delegation chairman or could switch all of them on simultaneously. Another telephone was linked to the National Committee and White House lines. The third gave Carter access to seven regional coordinators assigned as key liaison men for the convention.

With this kind of control, Johnson could feel the pulse of any delegate at any given moment. Quite aside from the spectaculars, Johnson was engaged in an operation aimed at attempting to prevent the South's rejection in the November balloting of the first Southern President in a hundred years. It was a sore subject when anyone mentioned to Johnson that Goldwater might carry more Dixie states than he.

Accordingly, he sent the order down that Alabama must yield to Texas for Governor Connally of the latter state to put the President's name in nomination. Alaska was ahead alphabetically and was willing. But no, it had to be a Southern state that gave way. This took some doing among the balking, walking Alabama delegates but Johnson ordered it and it was accomplished.

Then there was the matter of getting a seconder for Humphrey's nomination. Senator George Smathers of Florida, an old Johnson friend, got a White House call which was a command and not a request. He would second Humphrey's nomination. Smathers demurred.

"I really like Hubert," he explained later, "but I know the difficulty of carrying that load in the South."

Characteristically, Johnson did not mention the matter at all when he called Smathers. But a few minutes later Bill D. Moyers, a White House assistant, reached Smathers and asked him to get up and speak for Humphrey.

"I said, 'Bill, that's really putting it on me,'" Smathers said. "He said I had to, so I told him okay."

This was a bit of political side play, however, to the changes that Johnson was accomplishing within the party structure at the convention. Party organizations are such that only every four years, when a new presidential nomination is made, is there any real opportunity to change their personnel.

With a minimum of fanfare, Johnson took over the New York national party organization by installing his old friend and former legislative counsel, Edwin L. Weisl, Sr., as national committeeman to succeed the controversial Carmine G. De Sapio. This meant that the President would have his man near the core of the Empire State's political organization no matter who was mayor and who was Senator.

Amid all the excitement of his first presidential nomination,

Johnson was taking care of the precincts. His hour of triumph was complete. He had demonstrated that he owned the Democratic party, lock, stock and barrel, when it was in convention assembled. But he also knew by such change-overs as Weisl for DeSapio that he had a majority stockholder's interest in almost every state Democratic organization. What had been Kennedy's now was his. The party wore the brand of LBJ and unless some unforeseen disaster overtook him, it would continue to bear that label for eight more years.

15 The Strident Campaign

THE PRESIDENT OF THE UNITED STATES, a wide grin on his face, his five-gallon hat pushed back on his head, plunged into the airport crowd with both arms outstretched to touch the forest of hands thrust toward him.

This was Lyndon B. Johnson, consummate politician, communing with the people, displaying his compassion for them, drawing strength from them and warming his own self-assurance that he was much loved by them.

Here was a President who, by all the polls and signs, would win the election handily. For all practical purposes, all that was required of Johnson was to stand quietly by while Barry Goldwater lost the election. The Republican nominee had been so effectively tagged as "trigger happy" by his Republican critics—chiefly Governors Nelson A. Rockefeller of New York and William W. Scranton of Pennsylvania—that he was never to escape from it.

Goldwater himself said bitterly after his nomination at the San Francisco convention, "Rockefeller and Scranton hurt me more than Lyndon Johnson ever could." The core of truth in this was that, while the voters might have discounted as only campaign oratory any "trigger happy" charge made by Johnson, they were inclined to accept such an assessment by other Republicans.

Thus was born in the minds of a substantial segment of American voters a deep-seated doubt that Goldwater could be trusted with the awful responsibility of avoiding nuclear war. Whether this doubt was justified made no material difference. It was there. It alone was enough to mark him for defeat.

The Republican nominee was required to answer other indictments raised by his Republican critics. He might protest they were false but he could not quash them when Democrats repeated them in the campaign. His original statement that the social security system ought to be made voluntary, for example, never was overtaken in the minds of its beneficiaries by his campaign assertions that he was a strong supporter of the compulsory system.

Goldwater's vote against the civil rights bill and his position that this issue was primarily a moral one to be settled at the local level gave him the electoral votes of five Southern states. But it cost him nearly all of the Negro vote and drove many moderate Republicans out of his camp.

The Republican nominee's refusal to disown the far right extremists divided his party and certainly cost him support that might have given him a chance of carrying some key states. In almost every instance, moderate Republicans seeking Senate and House seats outran him substantially in their states.

Johnson hit the extremism issue early and often. The wording changed but the theme was the same as that he proclaimed in the beginning stages of the campaign when he spoke at a Democratic fund-raising rally in Harrisburg, Pennsylvania.

There he said that Goldwater offered "a doctrine alien to America . . . a doctrine that invites extremism to take over the land." He further defined it as "a doctrine that plays loosely with human destiny, and this generation of Americans will have no part of it."

Entrenched in the White House, Johnson seemed to have

everything going for him from the start.

The President had been able to avoid the kind of television debates between candidates that had enabled Kennedy to demonstrate in 1960 that he was as knowledgeable and was more pleasing on TV than Richard M. Nixon. Johnson ordered the Democratic majority in the Senate to kill a bill, passed by both houses in slightly different form, which would have paved the way for debates between him and Goldwater. The deed was done quickly.

The Republican nominee thus was denied not only the audience that he would have shared with a President but the opportunity to project what came over as a considerably more engaging personality than Johnson's.

With all of this and peace and prosperity going for him, Johnson never had a doubt from the day Goldwater was nominated that he could defeat his Republican opponent. After all, the American people weren't likely to change Presidents three times in a little more than a year. He did not need to stir out of the White House to gain victory. But Johnson wanted to see the people and he wanted them to see him. So he took to the streets, the airports, the parks and the convention halls in an unceasing drive for a landslide victory. If he could manage it, he would become America's greatest vote-getter. He would erect a monument along the campaign trail to remind men LBJ had scaled the peak.

Johnson pushed into mobs where it was impossible for the Secret Service to guard him adequately. He ordered straining, sweating police to let the crowds through barriers. Whenever the mood struck him he whipped out a bullhorn to get off some Texas-twanged homilies. He had the White House bubble-top car equipped with a loudspeaker and a microphone so he could halt his motorcade at any vantage point to announce how happy he was "to see so many smilin' faces" in the throng that pressed about him.

Johnson's style was unmistakably his own. His big silver and blue jet, bearing the proud insignia "The United States of

America," with the presidential seal beneath the pilot's window, would land at an airport and taxi up to a point near the assembled crowd, held back by temporary barriers.

When the ramp was shoved up to the rear door of the plane, Johnson would emerge, tall, a shy smile on his face. Sometimes he squinted into the sun and the effect of humility was lost. The crowd would burst into a roar as he descended the steps to shake hands perfunctorily with fellow Democratic candidates and dignitaries. That over with, the President would swing around quickly and stride over toward the crowd which, at his first step, would strain to burst the barriers.

Sidling along the barriers with Secret Service men fore and aft and reporters and photographers falling over each other's feet, the President would go arm over arm down the line, touching as many hands as possible. Sometimes he would stop and invite a kiss from a child held in a parent's arms. A few times he had to compromise by kissing the child himself when his turned cheek was shyly rejected.

Once his motorcade began moving through crowded streets, the President gave the onlookers what accompanying newsmen dubbed the "fishtail flutter." It was a quickly undulating wave of the fingers of both outstretched hands. Whenever the street crowds swelled to large proportions, Johnson was out of his car in a whisk, surrounded by citizens eager to touch the President of the United States, if they were not lucky enough to shake his hands. Johnson always had his rewards for voters who pressed in close enough. They got a shiny, gold-colored LBJ pin to wear proudly in their lapels or on their dresses.

There was a personal exhilaration for the President in this contact with the man on the street. He felt he was keeping in touch with the average citizens, getting the feel of their communities and drawing inspiration from them. Back aboard his plane after being all but mauled by wellwishers, he seemed as refreshed as though he had dipped cool water from a spring he had feared might be running dry.

This would be a Lyndon Johnson tradition and the country

would see a great deal more of it before this man surrendered the stewardship which he was so happy to administer.

There were some frightening incidents. At Miami, Florida, several thousand whooping partisans were on hand to greet him when the President arrived at the Dupont Plaza Hotel to address a private meeting of the Florida "President's Club." It was made up of those who had contributed one thousand dollars or more toward the Democratic campaign fund. Police had roped off the motor entrance and a narrow driveway up which the Chief Executive was to walk to the hotel doorway.

Although most of those massed around the motor entrance were teen-agers, Johnson decided to shake hands. When he was ten feet from the doorway, a rope which had held the crowd back snapped and the President instantly was engulfed in a swirling, pushing mass of humanity. It was impossible for him to move.

"I want out of here," he commanded the equally beset Secret Service men. Valiantly they fought, pushed and shoved, moving Johnson inch by inch toward the doorway where a burly Florida State policeman had been forcefully turning back everyone who tried to enter. When the officer gave way, the President slipped through the doorway and the moment of near-panic was ended.

Anyone who had been in that crowd and who had wished to harm the President could easily have knifed him or shot him at close range. Because Kennedy had been killed at relatively long range a strange sort of security phobia seemed to have developed. Policemen walked the tops of buildings by which the presidential motorcade would pass. The structures had been searched and suspicious characters in the city detained, as they always should have been. In the Secret Service's "Queen Mary," the bulging old-style open Cadillac which had been converted for security purposes, there was now no attempt to hide the automatic weapons in the hands of sharpshooting agents. At every stop an agent with binoculars swept everything in sight.

Johnson assured worried associates—who had difficulty believing it—that the Secret Service had no qualms about his unannounced excursions into the crowds, was considerably more worried when he stood out as a target while addressing a throng from a microphone-festooned rostrum. The fear of the rifleman had taken over.

The fact that Lincoln, Garfield and McKinley had been killed at close range seemed to be ignored.

Asked why he persisted in inviting such incidents as that at Miami, the President's explanation was that he had to demonstrate "that I'm no royal highness." He was, in his own assessment, a plain man that the plain people could not help taking to their hearts as one of them. He felt he had to make himself as old shoe as most of them were. If this entailed an approach not often associated with the presidency, he was willing to risk it. He just didn't believe that the people, in Texas language, wanted a "stuck-up sort of a guy" for their Chief Executive.

Johnson had enormous turnouts almost everywhere he went in his relentless quest for universal approval from the populace. When he turned on his Chamber of Commerce speech and began shouting through the bullhorn, "What a wonderful state this is and what a glorious country we have," his listeners applauded more loudly than they might have if he had said "I'm going to wipe out all income taxes tomorrow." He was a slow-starting, soft-spoken salesman of tonic water who graduated as he went along into an evangelist for America the Beautiful, the all-wise, the all-secure, the all-progressive, greatest land on earth. Wasn't it good to be alive, wasn't it great to be an American and wasn't it a comfort to have him in the presidency?

Johnson was most expansive campaigning in New York and California. These were the states where he was credited with being politically weakest when he succeeded to the presidency. Now he knew that he was master of all he surveyed in the nation's two largest states. And it was sweet solace to him that two New Frontiersmen running for the Senate in those states wanted his political help desperately.

In mid-October, when he was campaigning in upper New York state, the President made the familiarly troublesome Bob Kennedy his political blood brother. The actual love exchanged between them at this point could have been contained in a thimble, but in the President's book, politics was politics.

In California, Pierre Salinger had entered the senatorial race with only an hour's notice that he was resigning as White House Press Secretary. Salinger had been confident that his close association with the late President Kennedy would be sufficient to send him to the Senate. This had been enough to win in the Democratic primary and to gain temporary appointment as a Senator. Johnson pumped for Salinger in campaigning in the state.

Both Kennedy and Salinger suffered from the "carpetbagger" issue since neither had resided in his state or could vote there when he had entered the Senate contest. In New York, Johnson's margin was so great that it helped pull Kennedy into office. In California the substantial Johnson margin was not enough and Salinger went down to defeat.

If Kennedy thus was restored as a potential rival of Johnson for the future, the brother of the dead President wasn't publicly buying the idea. He picked Mexico City and a student's question there to say "No, I'm not" going to seek the presidency in 1968.

But in this campaign utopia there remained some nagging doubts. Johnson did not seem to be able to kindle in his speeches the explosive charge that Kennedy invoked with a few crisp sentences accompanied by the characteristic finger-stabbing gesture. The good will Johnson worked up seemed hardly to rank with that generated by the Eisenhower grin. The President was in the middle bracket, too old to be a Kennedy who incited the uninhibited female jumpers and too young to equal the father image of Eisenhower.

The Johnson slogans in the campaign were pallid. "LBJ for the USA" stirred little excitement. Too many remembered that "All the Way With LBJ," hadn't really meant all the way in

1960. Only Goldwater's "In Your Heart You Know He's Right," ranked with such rabble-rousing classics as "Tippecanoe and Tyler Too," "He Kept Us Out of War" and "Back to Normalcy" in sounding the tintinnabulation of the political bells of the times. Too many felt, however, that even if Goldwater's heart was in the right place, his head was turned in the wrong direction.

Johnson would not concede that this was a major factor in his election victory. He speculated that some other Republican might have run better against him, but he felt that the manner in which he had administered the presidency in the little more than eleven months in which he had filled it had been the really deciding factor in his victory.

A vignette of the early days of the campaign indicated that this was not necessarily so.

The crowd that September morning was not an especially large one. It numbered several hundred persons as it fanned out from the rear platform of the Goldwater campaign train, which had stopped for a few brief moments at Athens, Ohio. High school and college students made up a large portion of the audience as the gray-haired, bronzed Senator appeared after an introduction by Representative Robert Taft, Jr., a candidate for the Senate.

The students came armed with home-lettered signs. During the "We want Barry" chant set up by the Republican presidential nominee's admirers, they waved and bobbed their signs. Most signs were hostile to the campaigning visitor. One said, "Don't Stop Here, We're Poor Enough." Another announced, "In Your Head You Know He's Wrong." Still another proclaimed, "Help Goldwater Stamp Out Peace." Far back in the crowd another placard, hoisted high by a teen-ager who jumped up and down, pumping his arms frantically for attention, said in amateurishly blocked letters: "Even Johnson Is Better Than Goldwater."

No one could know how many voters approved of—or even

heard of—a harsh indictment brought against both candidates by the Very Reverend Francis B. Sayre, Jr., Dean of Washington (Episcopal) Cathedral.

Dean Sayre avoided naming either nominee when he told his congregation on September 13, 1964, "This summer we beheld a pair of gatherings at the summit of political power, each of which was completely dominated by one man; the one a man of dangerous ignorance and devastating uncertainty, the other a man whose public house is splendid in its every appearance but whose private lack of ethic must inevitably introduce termites at the very foundation.

"The electorate of this mighty nation is left homeless, then, by such a pair of nominees. It knows not where to turn, it stares fascinated at the forces that have produced such a sterile choice—frustration and a federation of hostilities in the one party; and, in the other, behind a goodly façade, only cynical manipulation of power. . . ."

Whether this plague-on-both-your-houses attitude was shared by any substantial number of voters was difficult to determine. But it was not difficult for the average citizen to perceive as the campaign crawled along the low road that he was not being given the heralded choice between conservatism and liberalism.

Johnson went to great lengths to avoid being labeled a liberal. He was, he insisted, "President of all the people," with charity toward the right, center and left.

Goldwater's conservative doctrine got lost in a proliferation of positions on military and foreign policy matters. Where it surfaced it was largely negative in form, opposing medicare and anti-poverty programs without offering alternatives. When it was positive, it sometimes was not conservative at all—as with his proposal for a twenty-five per cent tax cut irrespective of budget balancing—or seemed backward-looking, as with his suggestion that TVA be sold.

At no point did the President or his Republican opponent

come to any serious discussion of major issues. Johnson talked in generalities of peace, prosperity and ending poverty. Goldwater tried out one attack after another, firing "soft on Communism" charges against the President, suggesting that morality had sunk to a low point in the White House and accusing his opponent of seeking "total power" over the lives of the people. He called Johnson "the biggest faker in the United States."

Johnson responded that the Republican nominee was dealing in "smears and scandal," was "impulsive and irresponsible" and was "a raving, ranting demagogue."

Even before it detoured into the morass of name-calling, the campaign veered off the main highway of significant concern with the problems facing the nation and what each candidate proposed to do about them.

Goldwater started it by proposing that NATO field commanders be given authority to use tactical nuclear weapons in an emergency. He refined this to say that the authority should rest only with the top NATO commander. He followed this up by proposing that NATO be given a stock of "small conventional nuclear weapons."

"Let me stress," he told the Veterans of Foreign Wars in Cleveland, Ohio, "that these small conventional nuclear weapons are no more powerful than the firepower you have faced on the battlefield." The administration hastened to explain that the smallest nuclear weapon available in Europe was ten times more powerful than any World War II blockbuster.

Johnson and his Cabinet members jumped on these proposals with glee. They were delighted that the Republican nominee had given them an excuse to enlarge upon the "trigger happy" and "irresponsible" charges his primary opponents had thrown at Goldwater.

Johnson told a news conference that "the control of nuclear weapons is one of the most solemn responsibilities of the President. . . .

"The man who is President can never get away from this responsibility and can never forget it," he said. "The American people rely on his good judgment. They want that authority vested in a civilian. They do not expect to abandon this duty to military men in the field, and I don't think that they have ever seriously considered that since the Founding Fathers drafted our Constitution.

"I believe that the final responsibility for all decisions on nuclear weapons must rest with the civilian head of this government, the President of the United States, and I think and reiterate that I believe that this is the way the American people want it."

There was a flap at the very opening of his formal campaign about how far Johnson got away from his responsibility or if he did at all, on a Labor Day trip to Detroit.

The President was supposed to be accompanied at all waking hours—and to have outside his door when he slept—an officer carrying top-secret codes by which the order to launch nuclear weapons could be given. On this trip to Detroit, the President elected to use a JetStar, the cost of which was considerably less than the $2,300 an hour the Democratic National Committee was billed when he traveled on political trips in *Air Force One*.

Army Major General Chester V. Clifton, who had the code "football" in his possession, and Rear Admiral George C. Burkley, the President's physician, were informed there was no room for them on the President's plane. It was the first time Johnson had traveled without their being at his side.

On the President's plane, in addition to the Chief Executive and his wife, were Democratic Senators Pat McNamara and Philip A. Hart of Michigan, Representative Neil Staebler, the Michigan Democratic nominee for Governor, and two House colleagues, Representatives James G. O'Hara and Harold M. Ryan. Also aboard were AFL-CIO officials Joseph D. Keenan and Jack Conway. Bringing up the rear were Secret Service agents Rufus Youngblood and Warren Taylor, as well as Richard N. Goodwin, a White House aide who had replaced Jack Valenti in order to confer with the president about the speech he was making in Detroit.

A second JetStar, on which Clifton and Burkley rode, encountered on the trip a pressurization breakdown and had to descend from 24,000 feet to 8,000 feet altitude. The White House announced later that no hazard was involved. The question remained whether Johnson could have acted in a nuclear emergency without having the code "football" at hand.

There was no satisfactory answer available because of national security regulations. There existed an electronics communications system by which some strategic nuclear weapons had been brought under the physical control of the President. But it did not extend to smaller tactical weapons and was not linked to any of the missiles and other weapons in the United States. Was the "football" needed to make it operative? National Security cloaked the answer.

There were some loopholes in the administration's position on presidential control of nuclear weapons but Goldwater was never able to exploit them to any appreciable advantage. As early as 1957 the Joint Committee on Atomic Energy in Congress had been provided information that the NATO supreme commander was being authorized to use nuclear weapons in any emergency in which the President was incapacitated or communications were destroyed. With respect to this, Goldwater said, "If I can be called 'trigger happy' for suggesting it, what can you call the President for having done it?"

Goldwater also fired charges that under the Johnson administration, "with its utter disregard for new weapons, our deliverable nuclear capacity may be cut down by ninety per cent in the next decade." This was based on his contention that "this administration, which inherited the mightiest arsenal for the defense of freedom ever created on earth, has so depleted it that we face the prospect of going into the decade of the 1970's without a single new manned bomber."

The Pentagon fired back with the declaration that Goldwater's statements were "without foundation," "contrary to the facts" and "totally false."

"The facts are that in 1970 we will have a capacity to deliver on target 2½ times as many warheads as we had in 1961 and a greater number than we have today," Assistant Secretary of Defense Arthur Sylvester said in a statement.

Johnson got directly into this argument with the assertion that United States military strength exceeded that of "any adversary or combination of adversaries." He said the U.S. had one thousand fully armed strategic missiles ready for retaliation, more than one thousand strategic bombers, had increased its combat divisions by forty-five per cent, had boosted airlift capacity seventy-five per cent and had increased the number of nuclear warheads in Europe by seventy-five per cent since 1960.

From there the President went on to announce in a "nonpolitical" speech in California that in two years the Democratic administration had developed an over-the-horizon radar warning system and two satellite killer systems. It turned out that the latter were, in McNamara's words, "a derivative" of the Nike-Zeus antimissile system which had been under development since 1957 and which had cost $2 billion.

The President also announced at a news conference that the United States secretly had built a fabulous new plane then designated the A-11, that could fly more than two thousand miles an hour—from New York to Chicago in less than thirty minutes—at altitudes up to seventy thousand feet. He said this "advanced experimental jet" was undergoing tests "to determine their capabilities as long-range interceptors."

As more facts came out, it was disclosed that the A-11 was designed as a successor to the U-2 spy plane, had no armament and little maneuverability and probably would have to be almost wholly redesigned if it were to become an interceptor.

The voters could be excused if they failed to penetrate the maze of contradictory statements on military matters and policy. Their natural inclination, though, was to string along with the current Commander-in-Chief and not with the Air Force Reserve Major General who was seeking to depose him at the ballot box.

As his own and public-opinion polls showed, Goldwater was not making any headway with his discussion of military affairs, his condemnation of Johnson's course in Vietnam, his suggestion that the Kennedy administration had timed the Cuban missile crisis to coincide with the 1962 campaign and his contention that Johnson might come up with a new international crisis at any moment.

The disheartening news in the polls contributed to the Alice in Wonderland effect of all the Republican nominee's comings and goings. He was finding, as the Queen said, that "it takes all of the running you can do, to keep in the same place. If you want to get somewhere else you must run at least twice as fast. . . ."

But Goldwater was not equipped by nature or aided by circumstances to attain the "twice as fast" speed that would have been necessary for him to pull up even with Johnson. Left to his own devices he probably would never have run for President. But he had, as he himself put it, "pooped around" too long in the conservative cause to withstand the demand from those of that viewpoint that he must seek the job.

Compared to Johnson's frenetic wooing of the voters, Goldwater's was a sedate performance. He was determined he wasn't going to wear himself out so he limited himself to an average of about four appearances a day. He liked people in small groups but he didn't care for crowds. He avoided handshaking as much as possible and vetoed plans of local Republicans to turn out street crowds for motorcades.

Once when he arrived at an airport late at night, tired from a day's activity, his plane was met by a turnout of about four hundred of the faithful.

"Who in the hell is responsible for this?" he demanded of his aides. They talked him out of his threat to brush by the crowd and speed off to the hotel. He finally made a few brief remarks and stalked off to his car.

The pattern of Goldwater meetings was symbolic of the election outcome. Nearly always the hall was packed by hard-core supporters, some of them bussed in from miles around. They cheered his every sentence as though they didn't care what he said and, in fact, didn't listen too closely.

When his audiences demonstrated as he arose to speak, the bronzed Republican nominee would stand motionless, ramrod straight, his jaw firm and his horn-rimmed glasses set down on his nose. There would be none of the familiar gestures by which candidates acknowledge the plaudits of the crowd. Finally, a little impatiently, he would stop the "We Want Barry" chant by saying: "You've got him."

Once in a while there was hostile heckling. Often there were insulting signs and on a couple of occasions eggs were thrown at him.

Goldwater chided Johnson constantly about the Billie Sol Estes and Bobby Baker investigations. A House committee had reported during the campaign that it found "no evidence" that Johnson or any member of Congress had tried to use political influence to help Billie Sol Estes build and maintain an agricultural empire in West Texas based on fraud.

The Senate Rules Committee had put the Baker case on ice until after the election. The Republicans could talk about it but could prove nothing.

The Republican nominee linked the Estes and Baker charges with the assertion that morality had declined in the White House. One of his favorite cracks, and one which never failed to bring the house down, was: "They've swept so much dirt under the rug at the White House that it can qualify for the soil bank."

All of this took on more significance when a thunderbolt struck the President's camp midway in the campaign with the disclosure that his closest aide for twenty-five years, Walter W. Jenkins, had been arrested twice on morals charges. Johnson was stunned and thrown off stride as he had been few times in his life.

In New York for an appearance at the Alfred E. Smith dinner, the President knew nothing of the arrest until a reporter sent through his press secretary a request for comment. Acting quickly to check this report, the President found it was true. For a few moments his sympathy for Jenkins was clouded with the despairing thought that this might provide the "break" for which Goldwater had been probing. He would not repudiate Jenkins nor could he defend his aide against the kind of charges that had resulted in two arrests, five years apart. He ordered an immediate FBI investigation of the whole affair.

The Secret Service was on hand, saying that it was time to go. "Where?" he asked dully. He was reminded that he had arranged to pay a visit to Jacqueline Kennedy before his appearance at the dinner. Did he have to go through with it at this time, he asked George Reedy. Yes, Reedy nodded, it had to be done.

The dazed Chief Executive walked out of the door, followed his guards to the limousine which waited below, got in and was whisked to Mrs. Kennedy's apartment. There he was gracious and attentive, saying the right things, doing what was expected while his mind was miles away.

It was small wonder that when he arrived back at the Al Smith dinner he seemed preoccupied and in such a hurry to get his speech over with that it fell flat.

The FBI reported that Jenkins had had "limited association with some individuals who are alleged to be, or who admittedly are, sex deviates." The FBI's public statement added that Director J. Edgar Hoover, who had sent a reassuring message with flowers to Jenkins' hospital room, "stated there was no information that Mr. Jenkins had ever engaged in improper acts with them."

The White House position was that Jenkins had been over-worked, was suffering from extreme fatigue, had eaten nothing and had had a couple of martinis before he was arrested in a YMCA washroom. The matter of who was responsible for load-ing Jenkins with so much work was not discussed.

The indicated political procedure was to let the matter die, since neither Goldwater or his associates could risk the reac-tion that might come from discussing in detail such a messy situation. But Johnson made one of those impulsive political mistakes that sometimes overtake even a master of the game.

The President said in San Diego that President Eisenhower's administration had had "the same type of problem" with an aide that he had encountered with Jenkins.

Eisenhower couldn't recall any such problem and, in fact, there was none. A young man who was proposed for a White House position had been investigated by the FBI, which gave an unfavorable report and he was never hired. In contrast, most of Johnson's assistants were not subjected to field investi-gations by the FBI until after the Jenkins case became public property. And some of them, like Jenkins, had been working for him for years.

Although the Jenkins case obviously was regarded by the President at the time as a matter of great moment, the voters seemed to react sympathetically. And a blunder in the Gold-water camp helped mitigate the effect of the "morality" issue.

Goldwater himself had to repudiate a film titled, "The Choice." It was designed to blame the Democratic administra-tion for everything from civil rights disorders to topless bath-ing suits for women. Some of its scenes were extremely realis-tic. When it was shown to him, the Republican nominee called the effort "nothing but a racist film." He added, "I publicly repudiate it."

Although the polls showed that the Republican nominee had been making some progress previously on the "morality" issue, the majority of the voters had made up their minds long before to give this man Lyndon Johnson a chance to prove in four years of elective office what he could do.

In this there was no inherent pledge of future allegiance to the LBJ flag. He had been the better of the choices they were presented with in 1964. He would have to earn his way through the labyrinth of presidential responsibilities before they would make up their minds in 1968 whether he was worthy of a second four-year term.

16 "The Great Society"

Lincoln signed the Emancipation proclamation. The Emancipation was proclamation and not a fact. It shall be my purpose and it is my duty to make it a fact."

Thus did Lyndon B. Johnson define one of his major objectives after twelve months in office and after his landslide victory for his first elective term in the presidency. It was a significant statement by a man who intended that his name should rank with Lincoln's in history. What Lincoln had begun, Johnson would complete.

The Urban League audience which heard these words responded by rising and breaking into thunderous applause. With Whitney Young, a Negro and the Executive Director of the League on his right hand, the President adjusted the microphones and leaned on the lectern which faced the packed ballroom. Clenching his left hand into a fist for emphasis, Johnson continued:

"And until every qualified person, regardless of the house where he worships . . . or the state where he resides . . . or color of his skin . . . or the way he spells his name . . . until he has the right—unquestioned and unrestrained—to go in and cast his ballot in every precinct in this country, I am not going to be satisfied."

Here was the determination of Lyndon B. Johnson, the activist President, to attain in his tenure in office the full assimilation of Negroes into American life that others felt it might take one hundred years to achieve. This would be a basic goal in bringing "The Great Society" into full being. It would be accomplished, if indeed it was, by employing the full range of the Johnson treatment, from subtlety to arm-twisting.

If international conditions would permit, Johnson would improve on Monroe's "era of good feelings" by trying to cope with, instead of ignoring, basic transformations in the American way of life. To achieve this he would follow the advice of Jefferson, who said it was the duty of the President "to endeavor, by all honorable means, to unite in himself the confidence of the whole people." More than anything else, Johnson wanted history to say that he had left the country considerably more united than he found it. He wanted also to have it recorded that during his time in office world freedom had been advanced and the danger of war had declined.

Those who looked only at the surface Lyndon Johnson might wonder if there was in this man the innate ability to translate his mammoth political victory into social progress and still hold the country united behind him. They had seen him use every resource of the executive department he commanded to solidify his political position. Tradition had been tossed casually out the back door when the President ordered his secretaries of State and Defense to mount the political firing line. He had used his Council of Economic Advisers to put out a series of rosy reports on the nation's prosperity just before the election. The Acting Attorney General was ordered to report on the administration's drive against crime to counter Goldwater's "crime in the streets" charges. So it went. It was almost literally true, as Goldwater contended after the election, that Johnson had used "the full muscle of the federal government" against him.

"It wasn't a case of the Republican party running against the

Democratic party," Goldwater said. "It was the Republican party running against the federal government."

Critics could not forget that Johnson was a man who set inordinate store on popular acclaim, who plunged into crowds and then exhibited to newsmen bandaged and bleeding hands as evidence that "they like me." Nor could they dismiss lightly his inability to countenance criticism, constructive or otherwise, or his penchant for bawling out fatigued staff members unmercifully when they made mistakes.

To many Johnson was often corny and at times uncouth. But those who saw only the surface failed to perceive the driving force within this man which would carry him to accomplishments history would have to take into account. Asked one day, "What makes Lyndon tick?" a long-time associate replied, "He likes to win and he likes to set records."

It was Johnson's conviction that unity of purpose was "the real voice of America." He spelled this out as early as May 30, 1964, when he told a University of Texas audience:

"It is one of the great tests of political leadership to make our people aware of this voice, aware that they share a fundamental unity of interest, purpose and belief.

"I am going to try to do this. And on the basis of this unity, I intend to try and achieve a broad national consensus which can end obstruction and paralysis, and can liberate the energies of the nation for the future. I want a happy nation, not a harassed people."

It was Johnson's ambition to be "President of all the people" as Eisenhower had been. But where Eisenhower had accomplished this in a passive manner, Johnson would approach his goals actively. On election night he said of his victory:

"It is a mandate for unity, for a government that serves no special interest, no business government, no labor government, no farm government, no one faction, no one group, but a government that is the servant of all of the people. It will be a government that provides equal opportunity for all and special privilege for none. It is a command to build on those principles and to move forward toward peace and a better life for all of our people.

"So from this night forward, this is to be our work, and in these pursuits I promise the best that is in me for as long as I am permitted to serve. I ask all those who supported me and all those that opposed me to forget our differences, because there are so many more things in America that unite us than can divide us, and these are times when our nation should forget our petty differences and stand united before all the world. . . ."

Johnson's ultimate implementation of his election victory would determine how far and how fast he would travel. It was always difficult to convince a President who had won by a landslide that the results were not necessarily attained because the people loved him for his great big, magnanimous, compassionate self. But Johnson was surprisingly realistic in assessing the factors which had led to his triumph.

He recognized that he had inherited a great measure of support from the fact that the country sympathetically wanted him to succeed in the presidency after Kennedy had been assassinated. He credited his success in getting the administration's legislative program moving in Congress with contributing to his general support. The President felt he had gained ground by decisive action in the Bay of Tonkin incident and with what he regarded as his prudent reaction to Communist China's detonation of a nuclear device and to the ouster of Khrushchev.

He was well aware that the election probably would have been much closer if he had been opposed by a "moderate" Republican rather than Goldwater. He felt that Goldwater had lost the election by his defense of extremism in his nomination acceptance speech. Turning Goldwater's phrase around, Johnson said in his Madison Square Garden speech at the close of the campaign that the creed of the American people was: "Extremism in the pursuit of the presidency is an unpardonable vice. Moderation in the affairs of the nation is the highest virtue."

In the election Johnson had achieved the kind of consensus he hoped he could keep in existence. It was, in many ways, the same type of coalition Roosevelt had put together under the Democratic banner in 1932 and had commanded, despite its abrasive internal disputes and its defections, in three subsequent presidential elections. Johnson began his elective term with the support of liberal, civil rights and union leaders on the left. Moderate Democrats and Republicans in the center had voted for him, although perhaps some of them had done so reluctantly. On the right, business groups and a fair share of southern Democrats had been with him. He had won a higher percentage of support from young people than any Democrat since Roosevelt. "Moderation" was the key word.

The resulting coalition would be difficult to maintain because of the conflicting interests represented in it. Johnson would have to be a spender for the liberals' sake and an economizer for the benefit of the business and conservative groups. He had learned from the late Speaker Sam Rayburn that it was politically wise always to provide "something for the folks." But while he was thus engaged, he would have to reckon with the six out of ten citizens the opinion polls said felt government was getting too big and preempting too many fields, but who voted for Johnson because they didn't want to shrink it to the size Goldwater advocated.

But Johnson was confident he could carry a substantial American majority along with him. He exhibited that confidence when he told the nation in his 1965 State-of-the-Union address that "we have achieved a unity of interest among our people unmatched in the history of freedom."

There was no question that Johnson's election victory had cut away some of the shackles that hobbled Kennedy in his efforts to become the kind of innovator successful Presidents usually proved themselves to be. There was sharp contrast, for example, in the depth and nature of the Democratic support available to the President in Congress.

While the largest individual segment of Democrats in the House of Representatives remained the predominantly conservative 101 members from the South, these were four fewer than Kennedy had to contend with in the Eighty-eighth Congress. Democrats in the more liberal East had increased from sixty-five to eighty-one, the largest gain of any area. In the Midwest the party count rose from forty-six to sixty-six and in the Far West from forty to forty-seven. The overall lineup in the Eighty-ninth Congress gave the Democrats 295 to the Republicans' 140 in the House, where the big battles would be fought over his legislative proposals. This contrasted with a 257–178 margin over the Republicans in the previous Congress.

The scope of the Democratic victory, on one hand, invited Johnson to strike out boldly to reconstruct the American way of life. But the consensus for moderation loomed as an amber signal of caution. The President recognized that if he could not keep the consensus intact he at least would have to devise means of carrying a majority of its elements forward with him. This would test his belief that the presidency was "an office of domestic persuasion more than domestic power."

Goldwater had contended during the presidential campaign that Johnson was hungry for power, that the President wanted to gain "total" control over the lives of Americans. There was no doubt that Johnson welcomed the power that came to him. But the record indicated he would be judicious in the use of it. He was well aware of the limiting factors of the courts and Congress and of the overriding restraint of public opinion. It is Johnson's view that a President can do a great many things he feels necessary but which aren't positively desired by the public. But he recognizes there are tolerance points beyond which any Chief Executive proceeds at his own political risk.

Eisenhower had expressed the opinion in 1962 that the presidency could become too powerful for the country's good. "I believe that the problem of the presidency is rarely an inadequacy of power," the former President said. "Ordinarily the problem is to use the already enormous power of the presidency judiciously, temperately and wisely."

Johnson agrees generally, however, with Kennedy's feeling that the issue of executive power is an overrated one. Kennedy had felt, as he told me, that the President "gets about as much authority as he needs to get the job done."

Kennedy noted that the Constitution had clothed the President with the broadest kind of authority as Commander-in-Chief and as chief national diplomat. But it had limited his power as Chief Magistrate to enforce the laws. In this field, Congress could decline to vote funds the President asked. The states had certain rights. The Chief Executive was under compulsion to preserve national unity and party support and this at times limited his actions. Private interests were always seesawing him. There were, Kennedy concluded, half throwing up his hands in an expressive gesture, almost unlimited checks and balances on what could be done in the domestic field.

In foreign affairs, Kennedy felt the President's power to act was almost limitless. With his advisers, of whom Johnson was one, he had made the war-risking decisions in the Cuban missile crisis strictly executive action. He had told selected members of Congress after the quarantine decision was made what he intended to do, but he did not consult them in advance and he ignored the belated objections of some of them.

Johnson would certainly be as strong in making foreign policy decisions and would be subject to the same type of retraints encountered by Kennedy in the domestic field. The difference, perhaps, might lie in Johnson's vaunted persuasiveness in removing some of these latter barriers.

As Johnson saw it, the heaviest burden of a President was to divine what was right and best for the country. As he told the Congress: "The greatest burden is not running the huge operations of government—or meeting daily troubles, large and small—or even working with the Congress. A President's hardest task is not to do what is right, but to know what is right."

It had been gratifying for Johnson that he had exceeded in the 1964 election the 60.8 per cent of the vote Roosevelt received in 1936. For if he wished to rank with Lincoln, Johnson also wanted history to say that in achievements he had surpassed FDR, whom he called "one of the giants of all times."

Nineteen years to the day after Roosevelt died, Johnson gathered about him at the White House thirty employees and former employees who had served the government during the Roosevelt years. He exhorted them to look into the future, as he said President Roosevelt would have done.

"In these days when so many stand for nothing and when so few can think of nothing except the past and the fault-finders are among us in many spots," he said, "let us look forward with our chin up and our chest out, as he did, to a better day not just for our own, but for human beings everywhere. He would have it that way."

The President went on to say that, in "pride and humility, I readily admit that my own course in life has been influenced by none such as this great man." One of his favorite quotations was FDR's statement: "Too many who prate about saving democracy are really only interested in saving things as they were. Democracy should concern itself with things as they should be."

On the first day he worked in his White House office Johnson had moved in a desk which had been used by Roosevelt. Relating this a year later, he said:

"Whenever I feel I've done a good day's work, whenever I feel I've really accomplished something, I look at that desk. And then I go back to work, because I know I've only begun."

But when the ambition to surpass Roosevelt was linked with the sweeping election victory Johnson had scored, there were some apparent hazards.

FDR had been politically intoxicated by his 1936 sweep at the polls and had decided he had been given a mandate to accomplish quickly all that he previously had believed might take years to attain. He had tried to pack the Supreme Court and to purge Southern Democratic dissidents. The result was a political catastrophe from which he was saved only by approaching war.

By 1939 Roosevelt had reversed his strategy and was moving much more cautiously toward the inevitable aiding of Britain than Henry L. Stimson and other advisers were advocating. FDR then was maneuvering to carry the consensus along with him, rather than charging forward with banners flying without the certainty that the people were following.

Johnson had read the smoke signals of those times and he would be cautious. But the President's associates insisted that this attitude could not be construed as indicating that he would accept a stalemate merely to preserve the consensus. One of them put it this way:

"A great deal has been said about this man's being a consummate politician. He is that. But what many people do not understand or won't recognize is that to him politics is a means and not an end. He wants to carve a place in history and he is aware that he cannot do that by maintaining a popular consensus at the cost of not attempting to promote programs that will raise dissent.

"In the 1950's we had eight years of consensus government. But it was government at a stand-still. Lyndon Johnson wants unity. But he will never become a mark-time President to preserve it."

Since he had come into office Johnson had been searching for the kind of descriptive phrase most Presidents found to label their administrations. Many of his predecessors had been content to borrow from men who went before them. FDR poached from the first Roosevelt's "Square Deal" in offering his "New Deal." Harry Truman made it "Fair Deal." Kennedy got away from the playing card analogy with "New Frontier." Johnson wanted something different and found it in the title of a book written in 1914 by Graham Wallas of the London School of Economics—"The Great Society."

In a speech at the University of Michigan on May 22, 1964, the President provided the outlines of a program he was to make the central theme of his administration.

"The Great Society," he said, "rests on abundance and liberty for all. It demands an end to poverty and racial injustice, to which we are totally committed in our time. But that is just the beginning."

As Johnson explained it, the program was one which would "pursue excellence" in three major categories—the cities, the countryside and education. As an indication of the magnitude of his proposed undertaking, he said that "in the next forty years we must rebuild the entire urban United States."

"Our society will never be great until our cities are great," he said. "Today the frontier of imagination and innovation is inside those cities and not beyond their borders." He added that the beauty of the American countryside was endangered.

"The water we drink, the food we eat, the very air that we breathe are threatened with pollution," he continued. "Our parks are overcrowded, our seashores overburdened. Green fields and dense forests are disappearing. Once man can no longer walk with beauty or wonder at nature his spirit will wither and his sustenance be wasted."

Johnson looked on education as the prime factor in moving toward "The Great Society."

"The Great Society is a place where every child can find knowledge to enrich his mind and to enlarge his talents," he said. "It is a place where leisure is a welcome chance to build and to reflect, not a feared cause of boredom and restlessness. It is a place where the city of man serves not only the needs of the body and the demands of commerce, but the desire for beauty and the hunger for community. It is a place where man can renew contact with nature."

If this depicted a Utopia hardly likely to be realized in the forseeable future, it nevertheless served as a dream one could wish might materialize.

Johnson was committed emotionally as well as logically to furthering the case of higher education. He said many times during the election campaign that a high school diploma no longer was enough. In one campaign speech he declared that "the answer to all of our national problems, the answer for all the problems of the world comes down, when you really analyze it, to one single word—education.

"Our society will never be great until every young mind is set free to scan the farthest reaches of thought and imagination," he said. "In education we must provide higher learning for all who qualify. But we must also encourage the excellence which inspires a talented student to enlarge the limits of his capacity."

The President's practical problem, however, lay in the difficulty of providing federal aid below the college level without running head-on into the controversy over help to parochial schools which always before had prevented congressional approval of such programs. There was also the issue of whether to deny federal aid to racially segregated schools.

He decided the objective would have to be reached by utilizing existing special aid funds, but the Johnson program was pointed toward providing 400,000 new public school classrooms and hiring 800,000 new teachers in a five-year period. There was also a provision for an increase in teachers' pay. As explained by Senator Hubert H. Humphrey, then the Vice President Elect, the program was aimed at concentrating teachers in urban slums and poor rural areas. It would, Humphrey said, "expand and enrich" colleges and provide aid for adult education.

"The appropriate federal role," Humphrey said, "is to help identify broad national goals in education and to assist our local authorities in reaching those goals. But it is essential to retain local control and direction of education."

For the country dwellers, Johnson had a program of expanded highway construction and a crash effort to find a cheap way to convert salt water into fresh water, thus freeing for irrigation and other purposes the flow of inland streams on which the sprawling cities drew heavily. The President also had a plan to recast the Department of Agriculture into an agency which would deal with rural social problems as well as the stabilization of agricultural commodities. Secretary of Agriculture Freeman envisioned his department as a clearing house for ideas and projects for rural towns and villages as well as the farms.

"Where we have been concerned only with agriculture as an industry—with the production, marketing and consumption of the produce of the land—we must be equally concerned with the non-farm rural economy," he said. "We must remember that farming, as such, can provide a decent income, under present conditions, for only one out of eight or ten of the families now living in rural America."

Johnson and his administration's officials had succeeded in delineating the problems that faced the country in more detail than his immediate predecessor. It remained to be seen whether the answers that were provided would be any more workable than those wrapped up in the projects which had been launched before. When he got his Cabinet together after the 1964 election, the President told its members that "The Great Society" would require substantial investments. But again he was the economizer, the ultimate budget-balancer.

"We cannot afford to waste a single dollar on outmoded programs which once may have been essential but which time and events have overtaken," he said. "Only if we are imaginative in reform will we be allowed to be imaginative in new programs."

"Reform"—the dollars squeezed out of the closing of defense bases, Veterans Administration hospitals and the obliteration of the out-moded military reserve system—would provide the necessary funds for social advances. But this hit too close to home for some politicians, many of whose constituents depended, directly or indirectly, on these bases, or who had come to regard their reserve pay as an inalienable right. It took what was inelegantly known as presidential "guts" for Johnson to stand foursquare behind McNamara in these ventures. It had to be said the President had the fortitude to back his convictions.

But there was no complacency in the White House about this course. There were jungle roads ahead, with snipers on all sides, for a President who was determined to enforce such "reforms" in order to have available the funds to finance social legislation without dipping further into the barrel of red ink that overflowed the federal budget. The President's dilemma was summarized by one of his closest advisers when he said:

"President Johnson wants to be an education President. He wants to be a natural resources President. He wants to rebuild the cities. He wants the good life for everyone. But he also wants to be an economy President. This will take some doing."

In the international sphere, where he was more supreme than almost any king or potentate in the world, Johnson faced tremendous challenges. Here it was necessary for him to prove that, as one of his associates said, "The Johnson treatment works as well in international relations as it does in domestic affairs." Only time and experience could establish the veracity of this statement on the part of a President who had been regarded, when he came into office, as proficient in the handling of domestic problems but as inexperienced and possibly deficient in coping with intricate world crises.

Johnson interpreted his election victory as a mandate to carry forward the basic policy of attempting to improve relations with Russia and attempting to reduce the risks of nuclear war. By the voters' verdict his hand was strengthened in dealing with the leaders of other nations. He no longer was a "temporary" President but one who was armed with a certificate of approval for his policies in the international field. Thus the President's primary concerns as he began his second year in office were with four foreign affairs problems.

He felt he must find some means—and none was readily available—for bringing to a successful close the war in Vietnam. In patience and persistence he must rebuild the shattered unity among U.S. allies in Europe. He must advance cautiously and warily in his contacts with what might be only a temporary government in Russia. He must seek to develop new U.S. initiatives to cope with Red China's explosion of a nuclear device. While he was embarked on these major objectives, he could not for a moment forget the problems posed in Latin-America by the Cuban Communists, the slumbering volcano of Cyprus or the Communist challenge in Africa.

Johnson had hoped he might begin grappling with his major problems immediately after the election. But he was forced to take time out to deal with a Congo crisis. There was involved the fate of 1,600 white foreigners held as hostages by Congolese rebels. Should the United States risk a threat to its image in Africa and in the United Nations by furnishing the planes to transport Belgian paratroopers to rescue them? Such a move might cost Johnson's government the key votes of African and Asian nations to block U.N. admission of the Chinese Communists as well as the votes needed to force a showdown with the Soviet bloc on the payment of U.N. dues.

There seemed never to be an easy or clear decision for the President to make. But Johnson, reportedly overruling some strong objections by his closest advisers, gave a firm answer. The United States would furnish the planes for what the free world regarded as a mission of mercy but which involved an action the African and Soviet bloc nations attacked as intervention in the Congo's internal affairs. It seemed that cannibalistic slaughter could be condoned by the Communists and their dupes as an "internal affair." But Americans could be proud that a President would respond to the humanitarian aspects of such a situation with a "Damn the torpedoes" defiance of the diplomatic repercussions.

Johnson's problem with U.S. allies was complicated by the intransigence of De Gaulle. The old policies which had made the nation's bitterest wartime enemies—Germany and Japan— its best post-war friends had run their course. What was needed now was an accommodation of the new spirit of self-reliance—as exemplified by De Gaulle—which had developed in the West. Kennedy had begun the talks which reached into this sphere. Johnson had not had much time to pursue this path. So when he met with Prime Minister Harold Wilson late in 1964, the President was cautiously prepared for any eventuality. Johnson had been told that Wilson was an unpredictable politician with no close associates who could be sounded out and who would have to be approached with the utmost delicacy. He was, in other words, a British De Gaulle.

As often happened in such situations, these two top-notch politicians hit it off rather well. When they got rid of their advisers and sat down to talk alone they developed an affinity that often seems to exist between men whose lives are devoted to advancing their political fortunes but who, having arrived at the top, are able to understand each other's viewpoint with a minimum of friction. The word in Washington was that Johnson and Wilson forged in their private conversations a closer alliance than had existed between Washington and London when the Tories ruled England.

At this point Johnson had embarked on a strategy which called for him to act as a sort of mediator between Britain and Germany, strengthening U.S. ties with each while waiting out De Gaulle's opposition to any European defense arrangement likely to be dominated by the United States and Britain. A close adviser to the President summed it up this way:

"The President is reviewing the facts of life with our British and German allies. He is pointing out to them the advantages of working together. He is suggesting that we three stand together and that we mitigate our differences. He is not discounting France's efforts to the contrary. But he is saying that we have more to gain in unity and the flexibility which would permit France to come fully into the alliance than we have in fighting among ourselves over such matters as the mixed-forces multilateral nuclear fleet."

The post-election deliberations over Vietnam were just as delicate in some ways. But the decisions were limited and far from spectacular. Essentially, Johnson decided to go along with the thus-far unsuccessful effort to get the dissident, religiously-divided population of South Vietnam behind the effort to wipe out the Communist Vietcong. The announced decision was to expand American economic and military aid, provided that Saigon stepped up its recruitment in the armed forces and the police. Linked with this would be an effort to enlist other Asian countries in helping provide economic and social backing for the Communist-pressed South Vietnamese. This seemed to represent temporizing on the part of a President who had been decisive in other areas. He obviously did not have at hand any promising solution to a war to which Eisenhower and Kennedy had committed the United States but which did not lend itself to any foreseeable successful conclusion or any graceful withdrawal.

As for Russia, at the end of 1964 the White House policy was to await developments. The "hot line" teletype between Washington and Moscow went unused except for line-testing exchanges of U.S. baseball and football scores with Moscow's contribution of soccer results. The line was open, but Johnson didn't really know to whom to address any significant message. Khrushchev was gone and who knew whether Alexei N. Kosygin or Leonid I. Brezhnev was the man to talk to?

The President and his advisers had only to look to modern Russian history to assume that a troika or dual government would not last long in Moscow. In time a single man had risen to the top and the feeling in the White House was that soon Russian history would repeat itself. The new Russian team gave assurance of the continuation of the coexistence policies. Soviet Foreign Minister Andrei Gromyko, who previously had conferred with Johnson, voiced the expected criticisms of United States policies in the U.N. But it was the considered judgment of Adlai E. Stevenson, head of the U.S. delegation, that "evidently the world objectives of the Soviet Union are unchanged." Stevenson added that he hoped "this harsh cold war talk is more propaganda than policy." Both Johnson and Stevenson knew for a relative certainty that it was.

Johnson had not been one of Stevenson's rooters when the latter was in the political arena. He had been irked by Stevenson's flamboyant and utterly futile injection of himself into the 1960 Democratic convention in Los Angeles, when Johnson and Kennedy were coming down to the wire in their quest for the Democratic presidential nomination. Stevenson had provided a great deal of diverting noise but not much else and Johnson hadn't enjoyed the diversion. Nevertheless, the President had come to lean heavily on Stevenson's analysis of the issues before the U.N.

Johnson was much more in sympathy with Stevenson's presentation of all the angles than Kennedy had been. Asked about the President's evaluation of his U.N. ambassador, a White House adviser put it this way:

"The President thinks Stevenson is the right man in the right place at the right time."

Perhaps the future course of relations with Russia lay in a presidential answer to the question of what was to be done to counter the newly arrived nuclear capacity of the Chinese Communists. Kennedy had spelled out this awesome problem when he said a few months before he died that the Chinese had called for war to advance the "final success" of Communism. He added, "When you introduce into this mix nuclear weapons . . . you have a more dangerous situation than we've faced since the end of the Second World War." Kennedy had said that "the struggle against nuclear spread is as much in the Soviet interest as in our own."

It was clear that Johnson subscribed to this view when Stevenson said, in discussing the Soviet attitude in a December, 1964, broadcast, that, "They, too, want to insure the world against the proliferation of nuclear weapons." This was more of a hope than a policy, however. Johnson had recognized the problem presented by the Chinese nuclear explosion when he had discussed this development and the dismissal of Khrushchev in the fall of 1964 in a telecast.

The President had demonstrated at that point he intended to make foreign policy without interference from any critics in Congress. Without any consultation with the men of the Senate who had been his colleagues, he announced:

"The nations which do not seek nuclear weapons can be sure that if they need our strong support against some threat of nuclear blackmail, they will have it."

Here was the strong President making foreign policy on his own. Perhaps this commitment would be embarrassing in the future. It was notice to India, Pakistan and Japan that the United States would not permit them to be cowed by China's nuclear ability. It was the type of policy to which a President committed his country and then might have to account in Congress for his action. But it was the kind of Presidential action which the members of the national legislature could not challenge successfully. Once a President put his prestige on any such line, Congress would be hard put to attempt to change his course.

Nevertheless the "threat of nuclear blackmail" by Red China hung over Johnson's better-than-all-worlds as heavily as Hitler's tactics had clouded Franklin Roosevelt's efforts to maintain peace. Johnson had some time, as FDR did not in 1939. It would take the Chinese Communists a few years to develop the delivery system for effective use of this device. But the time was short before Agamemnon again might confront the world.

This, then, was Johnson's almost insoluble long-range problem. He had, at the beginning of 1965, no clearly-defined policy to meet it. He remained wedded to the non-policy of opposing any diplomatic recognition of the seven hundred million Chinese who were being systematically indoctrinated with hatred of the Americans.

Finally, Johnson's decision would have to be made whether to temporize with the inevitable, or to meet it boldly by acting to neutralize the threat to world existence already being posed by Mao Tse-tung and his equally paranoid associates. Somehow this greatest populated of all nations must be admitted to the society of peoples, if only to promote the attendant responsibility of working to preserve the world instead of attempting to destroy it.

As he marched down the corridors of the years ahead of him it would be Lyndon Baines Johnson's destiny to preside over a peaceful reorganization of the world's power structure or over the dissolution of civilization. This was the rendezvous with history of the man from Texas.

Index

Acheson, Dean G., Secretary of State, 109, 111, 215

Actors Equity (labor union), 151

ADA. *See* Americans for Democratic Action

Adams, John, President, 164, 229

Adams, John Quincy, President, 16

AEC. *See* Atomic Energy Commission

AFL-CIO (labor union), 121, 268; Executive Council, 121–23

Agency for International Development, 180

Agriculture Department, 287

Air Force One (presidential plane), 3, 4, 5, 11, 66, 142–43, 268

Alabama, University of, 167

American Electric Power Company, 126

American Federation of Labor. *See* AFL-CIO

American Revolution, 164

American Society of Newspaper Editors, 152

American Telephone and Telegraph Company, 122–23

Americans for Constitutional Action, 49–50

Americans for Democratic Action (ADA), 225, 248, 250

Anderson, Clinton P., Senator, 91, 161

Anderson, George W., Admiral, 182

Anderson, Robert B., Secretary of the Treasury, 19, 105, 208

Andrews Air Force base (Washington, D.C.), 14

Anti-lynching bill (1937), 159

Anti-poll tax bills, 159

Anti-poverty program, Johnson's, 84–85, 95 ff, 128, 190–91

Appalachia bill, Johnson's, 191

Appropriations Committee: House, 60, 94, 180; Senate, 34; Subcommittee on Foreign Aid, 176, 180

Armed Services Committee, Senate, 34

Army Signal Corps, 154

Asian conflict, 117–18, 199–200. *See also* Vietnam conflict

Atomic Energy Commission (AEC), 48

Avery, Sewell, 46

Bailey, John M., 245

Baker, Lyndon Baines Johnson (son of Robert G.), 147

Baker, Robert G. (Bobby), 146–48, 226–27, 272

Ball, George W., Undersecretary of State, 179, 208

Barbara Anne (presidential yacht), 46

Barkley, Alben W., Vice President, 141

Barron, John (journalist), 78

Bartlett, Charles (columnist), 141, 239

Baudouin, King of Belgium, 18

ABOUT THE AUTHOR

Jack Bell, chief political writer for the Associated Press in Washington and chief of AP's Senate Staff, has been in the newspaper business all his life.

Born in Yates Center, Kansas, in 1904, he went to high school in Tulsa, Oklahoma, and college at the University of Missouri and the University of Oklahoma. He began working for the *Daily Oklahoman* at the age of twenty-one. Four years later he became its city editor.

In 1937 he joined the staff of the Associated Press in Washington, where he has covered every major political convention and presidential campaign since 1940 and White House news conferences since FDR's third term.

Among his notable newspaper achievements are his reporting on the Kennedy-Khrushchev Vienna Conference and a series on Senator Joseph McCarthy, for which he received the George Polk Award for outstanding wire service reporting.

Mr. Bell's previous books are *The Splendid Misery*, which deals with the presidency, and *Mr. Conservative: Barry Goldwater.*

Format by Sidney Feinberg
Set in Linotype Caledonia
Composed, printed and bound by American Book–Stratford Press, Inc.
HARPER & ROW, PUBLISHERS, INCORPORATED